Healing Yourself the Cosmic Way

Based on the *I Ching*

by
Carol K. Anthony and Hanna Moog

Healing Yourself the Cosmic Way

Based on the *I Ching*

by
Carol K. Anthony and Hanna Moog

ICHINGBOOKS

ICHINGBOOKS
c/o Anthony Publishing Company, Inc.
206 Gleasondale Road
Stow, Massachusetts 01775, U.S.A.
www.ichingbooks.com, or www.ichingoracle.com
Library of Congress Number: 2006932760
ISBN 1-890764-03-5
Printed in the United States of America
Cover Design by Gabriele Wilson
First Edition

Contents

Part I. Healing Yourself the Cosmic Way

Part II. Examples of Healing and Explorations into the Causes of Specific Health Conditions

Part III. Freeing Yourself from an Ailment or Illness

Part IV. Dismantling the Ego Program of a Long-standing Illness

Appendices

Preface

In 1998 an unexpected personal healing experience swept away most of our cherished beliefs about illness. For the first time, we realized that thoughts could cause a physical illness, and that it was possible to deprogram those thoughts and be healed within a matter of three weeks. We had no idea that a book of this size would eventually grow out of that initial experience. What made this possible was the help we received from the *I Ching* to gain an ever deeper understanding of what causes illness, and how we can free ourselves from its causes at their roots.

As founders of The I Ching Institute in Stow, Massachusetts, and as experienced seminar givers on the subject of *I Ching*, we were able to share what we had learned with students all over the world. By now, at this writing, we have taught four online courses under the title "Healing Physical Ailments with the Help of the *I Ching*." Each course extended over a period of eight weeks, during which our students were guided to do intensive investigations into the causes of the health issues they wanted to resolve. To our surprise, no one came to heal just a simple ailment. All of them presented us with long-standing or chronic illnesses they had not been able to heal through the means of conventional medicine. The reason is that no one has paid serious attention to mistaken ideas and beliefs as the causes of illness. Yet by eradicating the respective ideas or beliefs from their psyche, most of our course participants experienced relief, and many had their symptoms disappear either during the course or shortly thereafter. Because of this success, we have Part IV to this book for those who want to heal themselves from a long-standing illness. It leads them through a simulated course comparable to what we teach online.

We are aware that our findings may challenge some readers, since some of the most serious and persistent harmful beliefs that we found to be the cause of illness are also among the most commonly accepted beliefs worldwide. It is thanks to using the *I Ching* for our daily guidance that we have become aware of their sick-making effects, and the healing and peace that come when we eradicate them through a method we call *deprogramming with Cosmic help.*

Our main goal in publishing this book is to enable a large number of people to take their healing of physical ailments and acute illnesses into their own hands. In times of rapidly increasing costs for health care, this book shows a way that you, the reader, can heal yourself outside the conventional ways. The methods presented here are gentle and non-invasive. The reader who wants to use them can start "small" and grow with every new experience. It is not our intention to convert anyone—we simply wish to provide you with the resources we have discovered, so that you may benefit as much as we have.

Stow, in the Fall of 2006
Carol K. Anthony and Hanna Moog

Acknowledgments

We wish to acknowledge with gratitude and appreciation our editor, Virginia Blair, for her comments, inspirations and help in preparing this book. We likewise thank our cover designer, Gabriele Wilson, for another of her beautiful cover designs. We are grateful also to Dr. David Kirchhof who volunteered to read through our manuscript and give his doctorly comments. We thank Leslie Carlson for her photo of the Foaling Helpers, and Stephanie Geery for her illustration of the kinesthetic experiment. We are grateful also to all those people who contributed their cases, and to the many who, by participating in our healing courses, helped us to learn so many facets of healing with the help of the *I Ching.* We also thank Mike Zaino for helping us with all aspects of printing. Lastly, and most of all, we thank the Sage, our Cosmic Teacher, and all the invisible Helpers that showed us the Cosmic Way.

Introduction

What spurred us to write this book was an almost spontaneous healing experience Hanna had only a few months after she moved to the U.S., in 1998. Hanna had just settled in when she was diagnosed with nodules in the back of her lungs. It was only natural for us to consult the *I Ching* about the best attitude toward whatever the final diagnosis would be. We were stunned to learn that it was neither to passively accept that diagnosis, nor to try to fight the illness. That was the moment we learned that there was a third way, which we now call the Cosmic Way: it is the way of paying attention to the beliefs that cause the illness, and deprogramming them. This new understanding gave the book its title: "Healing Yourself the Cosmic Way."

The title also points to our new version of the *I Ching*, which we published in 2002: *I Ching, The Oracle of the Cosmic Way*. It, too, was sparked by Hanna's healing experience and the many other ground-breaking learning experiences that occurred in all other areas of our lives during the years that followed. Since the development of this book and our new version of the *I Ching* occurred simultaneously, we will be referring to related passages in the new *I Ching* throughout this book. None of the traditional translations of the *I Ching*, this ancient oracle book of China, contains the explicit descriptions of the Cosmic Principles of Harmony that are necessary to understand this new approach to healing, although they were always implied throughout the text.

What do we mean by learning to do things the Cosmic Way? It means that:

- we recognize that the Cosmos is a system of harmony that is ready to help us in all our needs and undertakings, if we bring ourselves into harmony with it
- we understand that the Cosmos and Nature achieve all things through transformations; this includes healing

• we understand that our natural state is health and that illness is a messenger to make us aware of ideas and beliefs that are in conflict with our true nature

Part I of this book presents the reader with the background knowledge needed to understand this unique approach to healing, which is based on the experience *that all illness is caused by mistaken ideas and beliefs about things.* Even though modern science has proven as obsolete the old idea that consciousness and matter are separate things, this idea continues to dominate most of today's medical practice in diagnosing and treating illness. Particularly, the body is still regarded in most quarters as a mechanical system devoid of consciousness, which needs to be monitored and supervised by the mind, and when ill, engineered and treated by manipulative techniques.

Healing the Cosmic way is based on the understanding that all things are connected through consciousness, and that our conscious thoughts influence both our own psyche-body relationship, and that of other people as well. Healing this way is also based on the understanding that health is another name for being in a positive symbiotic relationship with the Cosmos, of which we humans are a part. What makes us ill is our separating from that relationship through taking on mistaken ideas and beliefs. Illness occurs to remind us that we have lost this relationship. Its purpose, ultimately, is to prod us to seek out those causes, so that we can regain it. Removing the mistaken ideas from our psyche through the methods of deprogramming described in this book allows us to return to health.

Returning to health does not merely mean "getting free of the symptoms," but freeing ourselves from their cause in an enduring way. The symptoms are the *messenger*, not the cause. We miss the point if we choose to kill off the messenger, or blame it for causing us pain, while the sick-making beliefs continue their destructive activities.

The medical approach to illness is to start with a diagnosis that aims at giving it a name. This practice is based on the hypothesis that specific symptoms point to a common cause. For example, the symptoms of a disease shared by many people are said to point to a single set of causes. Our experience, however, has shown that although a disease may be shared by many, its causes are to be found in the fears and self-doubts that are particular to the individual. Although we shall be showing that certain mistaken ideas and beliefs *tend* to lead to this or that kind of illness, there is never a single correlation that can be assumed to apply to all cases. This is illustrated by the examples of healing described in Part II.

Part III of this book provides you, the reader, with the methods needed to investigate the causes of ailments and minor illnesses and to free yourself of them. These methods can be used without any prior knowledge of the *I Ching*, or the need to consult it. We have included our method of communicating with the oracle, which you can use independently of the *I Ching* to identify the sick-making ideas and beliefs. We call this method the Retrospec-tive-Three-Coin-Method, or "rtcm." We have given numerous examples of how we use this method to find the specific causes of a health condition.

The reader unfamiliar with the *I Ching* oracle may not real-ize that consulting it is based on the same principle practiced in kinesthetics, of tuning into what the body knows through its DNA.

Part IV describes a whole program of mistaken ideas and be-liefs that we found to be typical for long-standing and chronic illnesses. To successfully use this part of the book, the reader needs to learn how to consult *I Ching, The Oracle of the Cosmic Way.*

Because of the overriding importance of language in either keeping us happy and healthy, or in making us sick, it was necessary to introduce a number of concepts drawn from the *I Ching* which may be new to the reader. These include an ex-planation of the Cosmic reality in which we are embedded. It is a reality characterized by harmony and abundance. When we are in harmony with it, we experience an abundance of Cosmic help, health, peace, and happiness. We have therefore chosen words that are in harmony with this Cosmic reality, so that our language is also a language that heals, and keeps us in harmony with the Cosmos. It is a language based on our true feelings rather than on abstract ideas.

It may be the desire of medical researchers to put our findings to experimental tests. However, since the helping forces of the Cosmos that play a major role in the healing process are feeling consciousnesses, they do not subject themselves to being judged by a mindset that insists on excluding the feelings.

We do not ask you, the reader, to accept on faith any of what we have written in this book. If you are to derive anything of value from this book, you will only need to willingly suspend your disbelief, for an open mind is the doorway through which new insights can come.

Important Notice

The information in this book is primarily educational. It may be used in conjunction with competent professional health caregivers. The procedures described herein are neither advice nor prescriptions. In using this information on your own, you are prescribing for yourself. That is your legal right, for which neither the publisher nor the authors assume any responsibility. Looking into the many aspects of our personal health and taking responsibility for our own wellness is a personal choice, and an act of integrity and self-respect.

Part I

Healing Yourself the Cosmic Way

"The Sage makes us aware that the true self can only find its expression and completion through the body, because the body is compressed Cosmic Consciousness, and the entire psyche is inextricably connected with bodily consciousness. Susceptibility to illness is created by ideas that divide the mind from the body, such as those that cause us to look down on our bodies, and to demonize its needs. Those ideas create the fate of our wasting the joys and opportunities connected with living in a body."

— I Ching, The Oracle of the Cosmic Way —
(Hexagram 27, Nourishing)

1.

How We Learned Healing the Cosmic Way

Ten years ago, in our daily work of consulting and writing about the *I Ching*, the idea that sick thinking might be the sole cause of illness was far from our minds. We had not the slightest idea that illnesses are run by mental programs that, like computer programs, can be deprogrammed. Nor did we imagine that by deprogramming the phrases and images that make up these programs, we could initiate transformations in the body cells that return them to normal. What happened in 1998 changed that, after Hanna learned, from two sets of x-rays, that she had nodules in the back of her chest.

It was our habit when confronted with adversity to consult the *I Ching* oracle. Our experience over many years was that it would reflect back to us the most harmonious inner attitude toward the adversity. When we learned about the nodules, we assumed the traditional Chinese view of *acceptance* was probably the best possible attitude. To us that meant allowing ourselves to go unresisting through all that might be involved in treating the illness through traditional medical means.

When the second set of x-rays verified the existence of the nodules seen in the first set, our doctor scheduled a C.A.T. scan "to determine if the nodules were cancerous." This announcement gave us a special urgency to consult the *I Ching*.[1]

Our first question, therefore, after reading the received text, was, "Are we meant to have an attitude of acceptance?"

---

1. At the time, we were consulting *I Ching or The Book of Changes*, the Richard Wilhelm Translation rendered into English by Cary F. Baynes (Princeton University Press, 1961)

1

"No, no, no" was the answer. In view of our expectation, this reply surprised us. [2]

"Are we meant to fight the illness?"

"No, no, no" came the reply.

We were then guided to a part of the oracle text that pointed to two phrases stored in Hanna's psyche that were identified as the cause of the nodules: "You have to do it all yourself," and "Life is a vale of tears."

Wondering what to do at this point, we were guided to meditate. In her meditation, Hanna saw a ballot sheet on which those two phrases were written in the form of a ballot initiative. Beside them were boxes for marking a Yes or a No. She checked the No box beside each phrase, folded the ballot, and put it in the nearby ballot box. Carol saw, in her meditation, a team of Cosmic doctors operating on Hanna to remove the nodules; then they treated the wound with a healing spray.

Afterwards, the oracle indicated that there was nothing more we needed to do.

A week later, Hanna had the scheduled C.A.T. scan. Ten days later, the doctor's nurse called to inform Hanna: "The result was negative," adding "they found nothing."

Certainly, the experience was unusual, and perhaps inexplicable from the doctor's viewpoint. For our part, we knew that the healing was the result of deprogramming those phrases stored in Hanna's psyche, and asking for Cosmic help. The feeling of relief and joy was overwhelming.

It has now been eight years since this first experience of healing through deprogramming sick-making thoughts with the help of the *I Ching*. Since then, we have had numerous other experiences of healing ourselves, family members, and people who have taken our *I Ching* courses and seminars on healing. Each experience has taught us more about the true causes of illnesses, and the kinds of ideas and beliefs that cause them.

Hanna's healing and the experiences that followed gave us an entirely new perspective on the causes of illness, and how illness

---

2. See Chapter 19, "Using the Retrospective Three-Coin-Method" for an explanation of how these answers came with such clarity and precision.

can be healed. It also revised our view that bringing ourselves into harmony with the Cosmos meant to accept adversity.[3]

Some healing experiences were dramatic and swift. Others took longer. We learned that swift healing generally had to do with acute illnesses, while those that took longer tended to be chronic. In cases of chronic illness, we discovered a whole mental program running the illness consisting of many sick-making thoughts. Also, unconscious resistances to getting well are often part of such programs. These programs resemble computer programs that have installing features, maintenance features, protective features, upgrading features, and reinstalling features. Installing features, for example, are ideas that make us vulnerable to illness; protective features are ideas that present the illness as giving us some emotional or other gain. They also act to make sure there is no interference with the overall program. This is to say that mistaken beliefs tend to surround themselves with a complex of subsidiary phrases and images that justify and maintain their original false premises.

As we experienced the effects of deprogramming the causes of illness in this way, we discovered the simple principle that our natural state of health recovers when the ideas and images that disturb it are taken away. Nothing needs to be put in their place because we possess a perfect, healthy program that was made dysfunctional by the false overlay.

In general, sick-making thoughts are negative thoughts, and negative views about ourselves, others, Nature, life, and the Cosmos. But they can also be "positive" thoughts that arise from human arrogance. Because we are conditioned to be unaware that such thoughts are sick-making, we also are unaware that removing them can make us well. Removing them restores us to harmony with Nature and the Cosmos, so that our lives take on a fullness we have not experienced.

---

3. This healing experience caused us to question many concepts written into the traditional versions of the *I Ching*, and led to our being guided by the oracle itself to write a new version of the *I Ching* published under the title, *I Ching, The Oracle of the Cosmic Way* (ICHINGBOOKS, Stow, MA, 2002). Further references to the *I Ching* in this book will be to this new version, unless otherwise stated.

Indeed, healing the Cosmic Way affects every aspect of our lives well beyond the parameters we can expect from taking medications and remedies, or making changes in our lives.

What is the Role of the I Ching *in Healing?*

For those readers who are not familiar with the *I Ching*, it is an ancient Chinese oracle system that was introduced to the Western reader by Carl G. Jung, the Swiss psychoanalyst. He and the German Christian missionary, Richard Wilhelm, who gave us the first truly usable translation of the *I Ching*, had found that consulting it "reflected a person's unconscious" a fact that Jung considered to be of great importance.[4]

In addition to reflecting the unconscious, the *I Ching* chapters (called "hexagrams") describe the preeminent principles of harmony that give the entire Cosmos its duration. Furthermore, these principles of harmony define our true nature. They constitute, so to speak, a blueprint of what we are that is contained in the DNA of each body cell. Thus, when we are in harmony with our true nature we are also in harmony with all of Nature and with the Cosmos. Being in harmony with ourselves, therefore, is of great importance to our health and well-being.

The harmony of the Cosmos, the *I Ching* makes us aware, is reflected in its beneficence, which is constantly granted to all the things that are in harmony with it. For us humans to be in harmony with it, the mind needs to be in harmony with what the body knows through its DNA. This inner knowledge is referred to in the *I Ching* as our "inner truth."[5] We personally experience

---

4. The importance of bringing the *I Ching* to the West was urged by Carl Jung in a letter to Richard Wilhelm in 1927, "You are *too important* for our world. I must tell you.... The board of the Psychotherapeutic Society has decided to ask you to give a lecture next year. *That is of historical importance!* Medicine strongly looks to the psyche now, and that requires to bring in the Far East." Salome Wilhelm, *Richard Wilhelm, Der geistige Mittler zwischen China und Europa*, Eugen Diederichs Verlag, Düsseldorf-Köln, 1956, p. 374. (Trans. by Hanna Moog.) Jung elaborated his view of the *I Ching* further in his Foreword to the Wilhelm/Baynes translation of the *I Ching* (Princeton Univ. Press, p.xxii): "For more than thirty years I have interested myself in this...method of exploring the unconscious, for it has seemed to me of uncommon significance."
5. Anthony/Moog, Hexagram 61, *Inner Truth*, p. 641.

this Cosmic beneficence as radiant health, a sense of well-being, and inner peace and fulfillment. The oracle describes it in the simple word "success."

Being in harmony with one's true nature means being truly oneself without any need for explanation, justification, or amplification. Ill health makes us know that in one way or another we have become separated from our deepest inner truth, whether this has happened through our own doing or through the influence of the thoughts of others.

The more ideas and images we collect in our psyche that do not correspond to the inner truth contained in our DNA, the more we find ourselves shut off from the stream of Cosmic beneficence, which is also our main source of help and protection. When this happens, we become vulnerable to illness. If we deviate too far, we run into the "Cosmic wall" that defines human limits. Then we experience illness as a fate we have created. The oracle speaks of this condition through the word "misfortune."

What does the word misfortune actually mean? It means the loss of the good fortune we possess when we are in harmony with our true nature, with our natural environment, and with the Cosmos. That harmony is the result of the cooperation between the mind and all our body cells, and between ourselves and Nature, and the Cosmos. Although illness can have many causes, it can be a reflection of our having lost this natural symbiotic relationship in one or all three of these areas.

It is often through experiencing misfortune that we are brought to consult the *I Ching*. The *I Ching* readings show us in what ways our thinking has deviated from our inner truth. It thus gives us the opportunity to free ourselves from the mistaken ideas we have adopted that disturb this symbiosis, so that the fates we are experiencing can be ended and healing can occur with the help of the Cosmos.

As can be seen, the *I Ching* oracle acts as a translator of our deepest inner *feeling* knowledge, by putting it into words. It thus transmits what we know deep within to the thinking mind. The *I Ching* has also made us aware that we all possess just such a translating function in our natural makeup. Unfortunately, the conditioning we receive in childhood causes us to discount the information coming from this source, so that the function becomes shut down through disuse. The oracle serves to replace it for a time, while we gradually regain confidence in what we inwardly know, and our natural translating function revives. In addition, the *I Ching* serves as a Cosmic teacher that helps us understand the true way of the Cosmos.

On hearing the oracle's replies to our questions, we feel both a recognition and a resonance that says, "That is what I knew deep within, but did not dare to believe." People may consult the *I Ching* for many years and be convinced that its use of the predictions "success" and "misfortune" in the oracle saying, are the words of a fortune-telling device, and that they are reading their fates in a Cosmic book. That is the unfortunate conclusion drawn by looking into it only from time to time, and interpreting it superficially. Too often, people are introduced to it in this manner, and many popular versions of the *I Ching* interpret it in this manner. This is in spite of the fact that the *I Ching* makes it clear throughout that we are at all times the determiners of our future, and that what happens to us is a direct result of the kinds of thoughts we harbor in our psyche. Thus, the *I Ching* predictions about the future are to be taken in the context of whether or not our *existing* attitudes and thoughts are in harmony with the Cosmos. When they are not, it does not mean we are condemned to suffer a misfortune. Throughout, the *I Ching* shows us how we may correct our thinking and attitudes, and thereby to reshape our future.

6

2.

A New Understanding of Health

Our Natural Inner Unity

The *I Ching* makes it clear that every person is whole and complete by nature. Health is our natural state. It is another name for "being whole." Being whole is defined in Hexagram 8 as *holding together with the Cosmos* from which we receive the life force (chi energy) that nourishes our whole being. Wholeness also means receiving from the Cosmos all the help we need to live our lives in harmony and happiness.

In our natural state we are in perfect harmony with the Cosmos. Our wholeness manifests as the *unity of psyche and body*. The psyche is the invisible part, the body the visible part of our being. Psyche and body form an inseparable whole, with each being equally important to the other. *The healthy* functioning of the body and psyche are vital in keeping us alive and well.

The psyche consists of the aggregate consciousnesses that make up our invisible existence. Central among these are the feeling consciousness of our body, our thinking consciousness (the ability to form words and language), our reflective consciousness (that attracts mind-flashes), and our intuitive consciousness (the ability to form images). In the healthy person, all these consciousnesses are coordinated to function as a harmonious whole. Their harmonious coordination is disturbed or damaged when the thinking consciousness is led to deviate from what the body knows through its DNA. This happens, for example, when the mind accepts ideas that denigrate or slander either the body or life. The damage caused to the psyche results in bodily dysfunction.

Because the body is the direct receptor of the life force that comes from the Cosmos, our harmonious cooperation with the Cosmos likewise becomes dysfunctional. When the damage is extreme, the flow of Cosmic nourishment and support becomes so blocked that we are forced to rely on the reservoir of life force given us at birth.[1]

Our Natural Unity with the Cosmos

The *I Ching* makes us aware that the Cosmos as a whole is composed of *consciousness*. While the greater part of this consciousness is invisible, part of it is expressed in the myriad forms we know as Nature. All things in Nature are compressed Cosmic Consciousness, and are in a constant positive symbiosis with the invisible side of the Cosmos.

The word symbiosis refers to a feeling relationship between two entities that is mutually beneficial. A symbiotic relationship with the Cosmic Consciousness is one in which the mutual benefit is not based on making a deal or fulfilling a contract, but happens when we are in harmony with it and its Principles of Harmony.

We have noted that our human nature is composed of a feeling consciousness, a thinking consciousness, and an imaging, or intuitive consciousness. The *I Ching* shows us that while the Cosmic Consciousness has all these kinds of consciousness and more, it is nevertheless primarily a *feeling* consciousness. Moreover, each thing that is part of Nature is in symbiosis with the invisible Cosmic Consciousness through its feeling consciousness. The feeling consciousness of the Cosmos is what we feel as love. This love, which has been called *chi* by the Chinese, is our life force. When we are in harmony with the Cosmos, we receive its chi constantly as a renewing force. The triangle in Pattern 1 illustrates this symbiosis.

As part of Nature, human nature possesses the DNA that connects us with our Cosmic origin. Every cell in our body contains this DNA, or memory of what Cosmic Harmony *feels* like.

Pattern 2 shows the healthy Inner-Personal Relationship, in which Cosmic knowledge and understanding are shared between body and mind. The relationship between the mind and body is meant to be one of mutual respect; each has its in-

---

1. The gradual exhaustion of this life force is described in Hexagram 47, *Oppression/Exhaustion,* Anthony/Moog, p. 517.

8

COSMOS-BODY-MIND SYMBIOTIC PATTERNS

PATTERN 1. CHI FLOW (LOVE ENERGY)

Cosmos

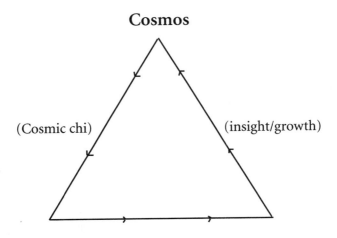

(Cosmic chi)   (insight/growth)

Body (chi nourishment) **Mind**

Note: The fact that the Cosmos is at the top of this triangle is not meant to imply an hierarchical relationship. If necessary, see the whole as flat.

PATTERN 2. INNER-PERSONAL RELATIONSHIP
Sharing of Cosmic Knowledge and Understanding

Cosmos

Gift of mind-flashes and
creative insights

Loving feelings

Acknowledgment of
Cosmic gifts

Body commonsense ⟶ **Mind**
(DNA) ⟵ Acknowledgement of the importance of feelings

dependent relationship with the Cosmos, and each learns from the other. The mind pays attention to the feelings coming from the body, and also keeps open to mind-flashes that come from the Cosmos. It shares what it learns with the body. The body, for its part, experiences life, the Cosmos, and thoughts coming from the mind in the most direct way. It shares the feeling responses of its inner senses with the mind. The Cosmos as a whole benefits by the fact that every harmonious experience the person has, contributes to the Cosmic evolution. The individual human being (like all other aspects of Nature), when in harmony with the Cosmos, contributes to the Cosmic evolution in the same way that each organ of the body contributes to the healthy functioning of the whole.

Under healthy circumstances, the feeling knowledge of our inner truth is made known to the conscious mind through our *inner* senses. These are the inner senses of sight (that permit inner seeing), inner hearing (through which, among other things, *mind flashes* come), inner smell, inner taste, and inner touch. The latter enables us to smell, taste, and feel the *inner* truth of a given situation. Altogether, these senses cooperate with other senses we call the "metaphorical senses," such as the sense of appropriateness, the sense of order, and the sense of caution. Through these inner senses, we are attracted to what is harmonious and to what feels fitting. These senses warn us when something is not harmonious, when a thing does not "feel right," or "feel fitting." When a situation is outright disharmonious or dangerous, these senses tell us the situation "smells foul," "has a bad taste," or causes an unpleasant "gut reaction." The inner senses reach a consensus about the inner truth of a situation without any need to think. They do so by comparing their perceptions with our Cosmic memory of inner truth. What we call *commonsense* is a consensus of all these inner senses. The result of this consensus is a feeling that enables us to go with what is harmonious, and to retreat when something feels inappropriate.

Our health is normally maintained through listening to our commonsense. Although many impressions combine to create our commonsense, we hear or feel it speak in our psyche as a clear Yes or No. It needs no rational explanation. A Yes means "follow the attraction," a No means "retreat," "flee," or "remain still." When our mind is attuned to our commonsense, it often does not need to make decisions. It simply allows things to flow from what our commonsense says. This happens when our mind acknowledges the importance of our feelings.

We become susceptible to illness when the mind denies that the body has its own direct relationship with the Cosmos through the DNA. We also become susceptible to illness when the mind adopts the mistaken belief that our nature is divided into a higher and a lower nature. These mistaken beliefs disrupt the symbiosis between *our body and the Cosmos*. Another set of mistaken beliefs disrupts the symbiosis between *body and mind*. Among these are the beliefs that "our animal nature is the source of evil," that "our animal nature is lowly, or dirty," and that "we are guilty for having an animal nature."

Pattern 3 shows how the symbiotic relationship, Cosmos-Body-Mind, is made possible by the attraction between *the light* and *the dark*. The light and the dark as the two components that make up *chi* are in the life force of everything in the Cosmos and in Nature. The light is attracted by the dark. In this act, transformation occurs. This explains the natural attraction between our body and the Cosmos. A similar attraction exists between our mind and our body, unless it is disturbed by the mind's elevating itself over the body and claiming that it, the mind, has a knowledge that is superior to that of the body.

Another mistaken idea that splits the symbiotic relationship between body and mind is the assumption that our nature is divided into good and evil. Through the delusion of our mind, parts of our commonsense become disabled and our connection with our knowledge of inner truth is disrupted. Since it is mainly through this connection that we can learn what we need to know in life, this disablement is a serious matter.

To overcome this difficulty to some degree, every person is given at birth a Cosmic Helper we have called "The Sage." The Sage is the voice that communicates with us when we consult the *I Ching*. However, it can also communicate with us in numerous

PATTERN 3. ATTRACTION BETWEEN COMPLEMENTS

Cosmic Light/Cosmic Dark

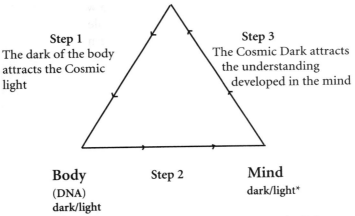

Step 1
The dark of the body attracts the Cosmic light

Step 3
The Cosmic Dark attracts the understanding developed in the mind

Body
(DNA)
dark/light

Step 2

Mind
dark/light*

The dark (receptivity) of the mind attracts the light
of inner truth residing in the bodily DNA

*In a healthy state, we are constantly receiving the light from the Cosmos. The reception of light is assured through the dark receptor contained in the bodily DNA that attracts light. Light from the body is then attracted by the dark of the mind, and then from the mind back to the Cosmos in a natural continuous circulation. The circulation is interrupted when the mind-body connection is damaged, which happens when the mind assumes it already possesses the light of knowledge, and is not in the dark/receptive mode necessary to attract the light of inner truth.

other ways, as, for example, through certain dreams, meditations, and messages we receive through other people. What we call a "Cosmic Helper" is an individualized aspect of the Cosmic Consciousness that has a specific function in the Cosmic Order. The Sage has various functions in our lives, one of which is that of teacher of the Cosmic Principles of Harmony. We describe the Sage and other Cosmic Helpers, as well as the Helpers of our nature, and the Helpers of Nature, in greater detail in Chapter 8, *The Helping Forces of the Cosmos and of Our Nature*.

Most of the things we will be presenting in this book come from lessons we have learned in communicating with the Sage. This communication occurs partly through consulting the *I Ching*, and through a method we have discovered that allows us to clarify the messages of the *I Ching*. We share this method with the reader in Chapter 19.

Our Unity with Nature

Just as all our body parts work in a natural symbiosis with each other, we have a natural symbiosis with the Cosmos. We also have a symbiotic relationship with the rest of Nature, of which we are a part. This is demonstrated in the fact of our interdependence with Nature.

What disrupts this symbiosis is the development of the view, over many centuries, that Nature is there solely for human purposes, and that Nature is something apart from us. These and other arrogant ideas have led humans to look at Nature as an object, rather than as something with which we are intimately connected. It has shut us off from the various consciousnesses of Nature, so that they are unable to cooperate with us in ways that are mutually beneficial. This has invoked the fate for us humans of making life hard.

Living in symbiosis with Nature means recognizing our interdependence with it by gaining a Cosmic perspective on how Nature functions, rather than presuming that it functions as a set of mechanics that we are free to manipulate at our will. When we live in harmony with Nature, we are constantly nourished by Nature's *chi*. People are beginning to understand that there exists such a thing as "nature deprivation," meaning the loss of *chi* that occurs through not being in close contact with Nature. Being in Nature and in har-mony with its consciousnesses for even a small amount of time restores us from within.

What Holds Us to the Cosmic Unity?

The *I Ching* makes us aware that *modesty*, as a natural virtue we all possess at birth, is the unpresumptuous state of mind that attracts all the helping forces of the Cosmos and Nature to our lives. When we have not lost our modesty through condition-ing, we recognize our true place in the Cosmos as equal to all its other parts and aspects. We neither hold ourselves up over these other parts, nor allow our dignity or theirs to be put down, or their worth to be dismissed.

The most direct connection between us and the Cosmos is our bodily memory of inner truth. Being attuned and responsive to it occurs when we are centered and aware of our body and its feelings. Keeping attuned to it in each situation is what holds us in the Cosmic Unity.

The *I Ching* in Hexagram 8, *Holding Together* describes being in harmony with our inner truth as a "full earthen bowl." "Full" means that the bowl contains an abundance of *chi* energy, and that being in touch with our feelings attracts all the helping, loving, and healing energies of the Cosmos to us.[2] Feelings of well-being and of a robust healthiness come from being in a *receiving relationship* to this abundance of *chi* energy. The full earthen bowl also refers to the rich assortment of bodily capabili-ties and psychic resources we possess at birth, which protect us against ailments and illnesses. What keeps these capabilities ac-tive in our lives is the symbiotic triangular relationship between our body consciousness, the consciousness of the mind, and the Cosmic Consciousness. (See Pattern 3.) Ill health occurs when that symbiosis is disturbed by disharmonious ideas or beliefs.

---

2. Anthony/Moog, p. 152. "Hold to him in truth and loyalty; this is without blame. Truth, like a full earthen bowl: Thus, in the end, good fortune comes from without."

How Humans Have Lost Their Unity with the Cosmos

The fact that the Cosmos is composed of consciousness is significant to our health because the consciousness of one thing affects the consciousness of other things. This effect has been observed in scientific experiments in physics, where the behavior of atomic particles has been observed to conform to the expectations of the experimenter.[3]

Since we humans do so much more thinking than other species, we have a far greater potential to positively or negatively influence the consciousness of the things around us than do other species. We have experienced, for example, how a respectful but firm request put to the group consciousness of a flock of sparrows roosting in the vines over our porch caused them to move the very next day to the surrounding trees. They remained there for the next years. A similar request to a group of bats sleeping above another porch was heeded only after we deprogrammed our negative feelings about them. In another instance, our fear that squirrels might eat our ripening peaches turned out to be the very factor that attracted them to do so.

The effect of negative thinking is immediately observable in the consciousness of our body cells, as when we see the body as an enemy, or a source of trouble. The same is true when we see life as "hell" or the Cosmos as hostile. All such ideas create negative reactions, both in the things we describe negatively, and in our own body's response to them. The reader will have many opportunities to see for himself how his negative thoughts and assumptions create physical symptoms.

Falsehoods about our body have a variety of negative effects: they may cripple our self-healing abilities, block our ability to receive *chi* energy from the Cosmos, damage the will of individual body cells to live, and create holes in our natural protection.

How Mistaken Beliefs Create a Parallel Reality

Over the course of historic time, we humans have drawn many wrong conclusions about reality by relying only on what

---

3. This is called the "Heisenberg effect" and was first discussed in 1958. Werner Heisenberg, *Physics and Philosophy*, Harper, NY, 1958.

we see with our outer eyes, and by excluding our *inner* senses of perception. When our inner senses are shut off, our connection with our inner truth, and hence the Cosmic reality, becomes blocked. When our wrong conclusions have solidified into beliefs, these beliefs become a sort of *parentheses* or *blinders* that shut our consciousness off from the Cosmic reality that is all around us. These blinders, in turn, create a separate reality made up of mistaken conclusions about ourselves and about life that hold us in those parentheses and reinforce the kinds of thoughts that maintain it. The *I Ching* has led us to call life within those parentheses the *parallel reality*. Over centuries, this parallel reality has created a mindset that excludes the Cosmos and its helping energies. This mindset, due to the types of mistaken beliefs it contains, is one of conflict: conflict within the individual, conflict between humans, conflict with Nature, and conflict with the Cosmos. All these types of conflict negatively affect our health. (See the Cosmos diagram, page 18.)

The most important fact about the creation of the parallel reality is that it begins with certain basic false assumptions that shut humans off from their own nature, and thereby from the greater Cosmos. As the Cosmos diagram shows, human separation from the Cosmos begins with the one central idea that gives rise to human hubris: that humans are special among all the species because of their ability to think, and because they have language.[4] Humans have extended the idea that they are special among the species to presuming that they are the centerpiece of creation, with Nature existing solely to serve human purposes. This human-centered view is the basis of a whole number of myths and beliefs that are in conflict with the Cosmos and its harmonious order. These myths and beliefs, and those institutions that support all human hubris make up what we call the *collective ego*. The *I Ching* makes it clear that the main thing that connects us with the Cosmos is recognizing that we are *equal* to every other aspect of the Cosmic Whole.

---

4. The word *hubris* comes from the ancient Greeks, and was used to characterize an attitude in which one has elevated himself over all laws that make up the Cosmic Order, and that apply to life.

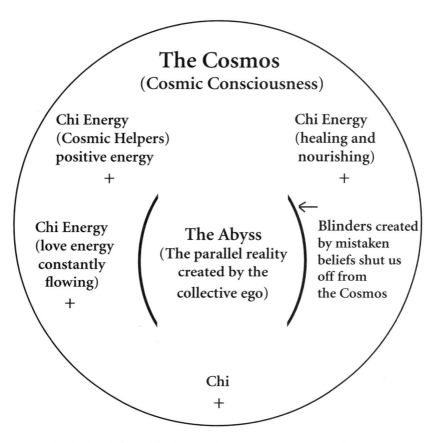

The Cosmos
(Cosmic Consciousness)

Chi Energy (Cosmic Helpers) positive energy +

Chi Energy (healing and nourishing) +

Chi Energy (love energy constantly flowing) +

The Abyss (The parallel reality created by the collective ego)

Blinders created by mistaken beliefs shut us off from the Cosmos

Chi +

☐The Parallel Reality Created by the Human-Centered View
• "Humans are at the center of the Universe
• "All depends on human achievement"
• "We must do it all ourselves"
• "We are without help from the Cosmos"
• "Our only source of help is other people"
• "We are insufficient in ourselves"
• "We are born guilty"
The above mistaken ideas create hope and hopelessness, fear, self-doubt, and guilt.

The concept of hierarchy is central to the parallel reality, which is dominated by the collective ego. Not only is the human mind given as the reason for humans being elevated over the other species, the mind is simultaneously elevated over the body, and all of Nature, as well. When the mind assumes the position of the leader of the personality it puts down the body's feeling consciousness as inferior. By doing so, the mind separates from the body, thereby *loses its connection with the Cosmos through the body. The mind's own direct connection with the Cosmos, as through mind-flashes, is also disturbed.* From the Cosmic perspective, the elevation of any part over another part of the whole, violates the Cosmic Principle of Equality.

When we adopt the mistaken idea that the mind is superior to the body, we no longer live our lives in the Cosmic reality, but become absorbed into the collective ego and its parallel reality. While living in this reality, we are cut off from Cosmic help, protection, and *chi* nourishment.

On experiencing this lack of help, most of us have drawn the mistaken conclusion that the Cosmos has abandoned us, and that we are destined to "do it all ourselves." On this basis we also conclude that there is nothing beyond what we can see, even though, paradoxically, we clearly know that we possess an invisible consciousness. By adopting this mindset, it is we who have closed the door to the Cosmos, through our hubris, not the other way around.

When our triangular unity of Cosmos-Body-Mind is thus split apart, we lose our wholeness and can no longer function normally. This has led humans to the next great false conclusion: "We are by nature insufficient to deal with life." Certainly, without the help of the Cosmos this is true.

Many other significant false ideas exist that have harmful consequences for our health. These will be examined in the course of this book, but one in particular needs to be mentioned here. It is the *concept of guilt,* and especially the idea that we are born guilty. The *I Ching* makes it clear that this concept has no Cosmic basis. This mostly Western concept is not important in the Asian traditions, but has an equivalent in the concept of

2. A New Understanding of Health

shame. The negative effect of guilt or shame on the psyche makes us susceptible to illness, including mental illness. The *I Ching* speaks of *remorse* as our natural response to having violated a Cosmic Principle of Harmony. When such a violation occurs, we incur *Cosmic blame.* However, Cosmic blame is extinguished the moment we recognize that we have been under the influence of a mistaken idea or belief, and have corrected our thinking.

To sum up, the mind-centered logic described above has created mental blinders that disrupt our natural symbiotic relationship with the Cosmos. It has also disrupted the symbiosis that exists between all parts of our nature. These disruptions are both direct and indirect causes of all illness.

In many cases, illness is a fate created by these blinders. However, as we learned, Fate is not something we are meant to endure. It is an opportunity to reflect on mistaken beliefs that have injured our symbiotic relationships, and to free ourselves from them.

3.

Youthful Folly

All our experiences with healing have confirmed our first finding, that illnesses are the result of having accepted mistaken ideas and beliefs. In general, we get these beliefs through our training and conditioning, or through drawing conclusions from too limited a perspective.

Science tells us that the human brain enlarged greatly in the last 10,000 years, and that it occurred simultaneously with the development of language and the use of the thinking mind. Given that human remains have been found that date back five million years, it is clear that the ability to think verbally arrived late in our evolutionary development. Compared to the great body of wisdom written into the DNA of our body cells, our thinking mind is young indeed. Hexagram 4, *Youthful Folly*, refers specifically to the impetuous, youthful perspective taken by the thinking mind, and to its ignorance of what the body knows about the Cosmos.

In the previous chapter we pointed out that the thinking mind has the ability to gain all the knowledge it needs from the repository of inner truth contained in the body. Contrary to the assumptions of many scientific and religious thinkers, the mind has not been pushed out onto the stage of life without inner resources.

Inner Truth and What the Body Knows

To define inner truth more precisely, it is *the accumulated knowledge that every body cell possesses about the origin of human life, our relationship with the Cosmos, and the limits that apply to human life.* We all know within ourselves when we are exceeding those limits. In dangerous situations, the body fairly screams at the mind when it disregards this knowledge. Our body consciousness physically interfaces with the outer world in such a way as to keep us safe.

Unlike the verbal knowledge we acquire through learning from books, our nonverbal inner truth is fully mature at age three and is accessible by the mind from that age on to give us sure guidance in the form of intuitive responses to life circumstances. Because it speaks forthrightly and honestly we call it the "innocence of youth." Gradually, our inner truth becomes suppressed through a conditioning that causes us to doubt it, and to follow conventions and rules laid down for nearly every circumstance. Nevertheless, our inner truth shows itself in small ways, as when an eyebrow is raised on hearing a half-truth or falsehood, or when a statement made as fact produces the feeling of an inner question mark. Then we can be sure we are being confronted with either a half-truth or a mistaken belief.

In regard to health, mistaken ideas create a conflict within the consciousness of those body cells that these ideas affect. This conflict causes molecular changes in those cells that disturb the harmonious cooperation among the various bodily functions. The conflict remains active in the cells for as long as the mistaken idea is stored in the psyche. In the case of Hanna's nodules, she believed she had long ago left behind the beliefs that caused them. However, this was not so. By saying a firm inner No to these beliefs, the acceptance she formerly gave them was negated. This brought about her return to her normal health. We learned from this that so long as faulty ideas remain in the psyche, they are a potential cause of illness that can be triggered by small events.

As we shall see in later chapters of this book, the body consciousness is endowed with all the capabilities and gifts we need. When the natural symbiosis of mind-psyche-body is not lost, we are in full possession of these capabilities and gifts, which not only enable us to live our lives happily, but also healthily.[1]

These are some of the things our body cells know, through our inner truth, or DNA:

• we are intrinsically whole and complete

---

[1] This storehouse of natural capabilities and gifts is described in Hexagram 14, *Possession in Great Measure*. Anthony/Moog, p. 201.

• each of us is unique
• through living our uniqueness, we contribute to the evolution
  of the Cosmic Consciousness as a whole
• our DNA is based on Cosmic Harmony
• everything we need to know about ourselves is stored in our
  own body; our body will answer when we ask it
• all things in Nature are part of the Cosmic Whole, are endowed
  with dignity, and are worthy of respect
• we are intrinsically related to all aspects of the Cosmos
• every aspect of the Cosmos is equal to every other aspect
• our existence is authorized by the Cosmos
• our existence is neither purposeful nor purposeless
• humans are part of Nature
• humans are part of the animal world
• every aspect of the Cosmic whole has its own intrinsic space
  that must not be encroached upon
• all things pertaining to the ego are foreign to our nature
• we are dependent on the Cosmos for its gifts of food, health,
  protection, and all manner of help
• we are dependent only on the Cosmos for *chi* energy (love/
  life-force), creativity, and inventions
• we owe no one for Cosmic gifts since the Cosmos gives its
  gifts freely
• our true home is to be found in our harmony with Nature
  and the Cosmos

A Sampling of Ideas that Cause Illness

Just as we found that the two beliefs, "you have to do it all
yourself," and "life is a vale of tears" were the cause of the nodules, we have since found a host of commonly accepted beliefs
to be the cause of other illnesses.

We mentioned in Chapter 2 the mistaken ideas that the thinking mind is superior to the body, and that mind and body are
separate. When they are seen as separate and also hierarchical in
relation to each other, they are set in an unnatural antagonism
and conflict that leads the mind to see the body as an enemy,
deficient, weak, ugly, full of sin, and the source of evil.

If we closely examine this idea, we will see its falseness. For example, we are trained to think of our thinking mind as being separate from our body, and therefore as special. Yet the forebrain, where our thinking is located, is as much a part of the body as our arms and legs are. Although the thinking consciousness has a different function from the feeling consciousness of the cells of the arms and legs, both are totally interdependent on each other for their healthy functioning, and are of equal importance to the whole.

The thinking mind receives its experience of life both through the outer senses and the *feeling* reactions of the inner senses. Its purpose is to express and process these experiences in words. It can correctly do this only if it is tuned in to what our *feelings* tell us about those experiences.

For a mistaken idea to be admitted into the psyche, that idea must create doubt in what our body knows; doubt causes our inner knowledge to be put aside, so that the idea can enter. Doubt is created by the use of words that fail to express the essence of things. These words and phrases describe things from the viewpoint of the collective ego, which thinks in terms of "power," "natural opposition," "superiority/inferiority," "competing entities," "culprits," "fighting," "struggle," and "conflict."

When mistaken ideas and half-truths enter the mind, they are simultaneously heard by the consciousness of the body cells, where they create conflict. When the body's knowledge is persistently overridden by the thinking mind, the conflict is not dismissed, but stored as poisons in the body.

One may think that most conditioning is relatively harmless. In Hanna's case, mistaken beliefs were accepted simply because she had heard them often. When ideas are forced upon us, they close certain synapses in the brain. Thereafter, the natural and relativistic way that neurons relate to each other is rearranged into rigid pathways. In regard to illness, this rigid structuring indicates "false mental program." As we have found, serious and chronic illnesses consist of such mental programs. (We will be discussing the components of such programs in Part IV, *Dismantling the Ego Program of a Long-standing Illness*.)

All of the above happens because the thinking mind has been elevated over the wisdom of the body, on which it is truly dependent for its own maturation. Because this conditioning halts the thinking mind in its development, it remains in the childlike state referred to in the *I Ching* as "youthful folly."

The discussion above concerns what happens in the body cells when the mind is elevated over the body: the stage is set for illness through instilling doubt in what the body knows. This doubt creates holes in our natural protective system, making us susceptible to illness. The illness is often triggered by something else.

4.

The Effect of Language and Images on the Body Consciousness

Language that speaks to the essence of things nourishes both the mind and body. It does so because it is in harmony with our inner truth, and therefore with Cosmic truth. We feel it as an inner resonance and as nourishment. This kind of language also heals.

Carol once had an experience of how language heals after having been bitten quite hard by her horse in a tender place. After being offered a pill for the pain, she decided instead to meditate, to see what needed to be done. In the meditation she saw a large group of children in a hospital ward, each in a different stage of injury. Some were nearly in a coma, others were barely injured, but all were clearly distressed. Carol recognized that each represented one of her injured body cells. It came to her to comfort them, as she would her own children when distressed, by hugging them, and expressing to them her sympathy and regret for the accident, and by asking for Cosmic help to heal them. Immediately, she observed that they became calm and comforted; at the same time, her pain ceased and did not return during the entire period of healing. She never needed the pain medication that had been offered.[1]

Language can also hurt and wound. We are speaking here particularly of language that wounds our *true self*. By true self we mean the self that acts from inner truth without forethought or intention. Words and thoughts damage our psyche when they cause us to follow something other than our inner truth. Words are also destructive when they give names to things that slander

---

[1] We recently learned that some anesthetists now talk in a reassuring way to the body before and after surgery.

their essence and their dignity.

We have all experienced how being called slanderous names hurts us. We are taught, however, to dismiss it by sayings such as, "sticks and stones can break your bones, but words can never hurt you." Such jingles imply that we are stupid if we regard words as having the potential to do harm, and that we only need to be tough enough to endure those slings and arrows to throw them off. What is ignored by such jingles is the fact that being tough does not insulate us from the unconscious harmful effects of slanderous words. All slanderous words need to be processed, by saying an active No to them, and thus delete them from our psyche. However, parents and caretakers often do not help a child process the adverse affects of slanderous words, out of fear that they will lose the power to control the children.

Worse, parents often use words and images to make their children fear authority. If they use punishments or rewards with their words, their words take on enormous power in the psyche of the child. The intentions behind them, whether spoken or unspoken, are felt and understood by the body consciousness.

The French have the expression *idée fixe*. This refers to an unconscious idea that is so fixed that it stops all further questioning and learning. A person's unconscious inhibitions and actions often come from such an idea that has been installed in his psyche at an early age. Once installed there, it "runs" his behavior. Old fashioned fairy tales called these "spells," and gave them a magical character. This has tended to make us dismiss their very real effects, and the fact that they are behind many negative and compulsive behaviors. They are also behind the rigid ways of thinking that characterize a "mindset."

We have differentiated three basic kinds of "false thought forms" that have negative effects on our health. They are *projections, spells*, and *poison arrows*. (See Appendix 1: *Kinds of Sick-Making Thoughts*.)

Spells

The first kind of false thought form are the spells we have already mentioned. They consist of phrases that fix us as having a certain nature. They generally employ the word "is," or "has," or include the words "always" or "never," as in, "He *has* a weak constitution," or "She will *never* recover." Because such phrases are absolute statements put not simply on our actions, but on our nature, they lock our psyche and body into the pattern described by the phrase. An example occurs when someone calls a child a "bad kid." The emphasis here is on labeling the child's nature as bad, rather than labeling his deed a mistake. The spell creates a fix in both the psyche and body of the child.

Spells can be responsible for a health condition becoming chronic when they contain the word "never," as in the statement, "she will never recover." Many compulsive behaviors indicate the presence of a spell. Judgment spells that categorize us as "being that way" can cause injury to the combinations of our genes, thereby creating health problems. We give examples of how spells create illness in our discussion of cases in Part II.

Poison Arrows

Poison arrows are a particular form of spells that are projected onto the psyche and body. Their danger lies in the fact that they put poison into the body cells. They are felt immediately as a sharp pain, a crick in the back, a headache, a sting in the heart, or other acute discomfort. The poison causes hurtful, poisonous responses in the consciousness of the body cells that receive it. The word "arrow" hints at their aggressive nature in affecting a particular spot in the body.

The effects of poison arrows have no relation to geographical distance, as we can receive them from someone on the opposite side of the earth with whom we have some connection. They are transmitted to us the moment they enter the mind of the person sending them.

A poison arrow can also be lodged in our body from childhood or youth and be the source of repeated discomfort. In that case, it has become embedded in the body as a microchip. (See Appendix 1 for an explanation of microchips.)

Poison arrows are caused by different kinds of thoughts and ego emotions; the following are the most common:

- Guilt
- Comparisons with other people or statistics
- Saying someone is a certain type of person
- Misnaming parts of the body and their functions
- Speaking of an illness or disability as if it were part of one's nature
- Being angry at our body
- Blaming either the illness or our body
- Feelings of self-disgust
- Fears of having something negative happen
- Curses

The parts of the body affected by poison arrows depend on where the poison arrow has pointed: when someone calls us "a pain in the neck," we feel the pain in our neck; when someone describes us as "a burden that must be shouldered," we feel the poison arrow in our shoulder.

Poison arrows can also be put on a food. The poison affects both the consciousness of the food, and the consciousness of our digestive system as we ingest it, as will be demonstrated in two cases described in Chapter 12, *Examples of Healing Minor Ailments*.

Projections

What we call "projections" are mainly statements that predict what will likely happen or not happen in the future. They include medical diagnoses and prognoses.

Carol's first experience of projections came early in her learning with the *I Ching*. It occurred when a friend with whom there had been a quarrel stopped by one afternoon. The friend had hardly come in the door when he said something provocative. In spite of Carol's resolve to remain detached, she found herself saying something back that she immediately noticed was quite foreign to her thinking. Before she had time to ponder why she had said that, the friend exclaimed, "I knew you were going to say that before I came in the door!" This made her realize why the thought felt so foreign.

The *I Ching* makes us aware of the hidden danger that lies in

29

projections when it speaks of "not projecting/not expecting" in Hexagram 25, *Innocence*.[2] Hopes and fears contain expectations.

The following kinds of projections can be distinguished:
• expectations that keep an illness alive through diagnosis or prognosis
• expectations in the form of hopes or fears (both indicate that Cosmic help is excluded from one's view)
• expectations that create an opening for illness to occur, such as seeing oneself as vulnerable
• expectations (fears) that cause the illness to deteriorate

When Our Inherent Feeling Program is Overridden

What makes a thought false is the fact that it is not in harmony with our true inner program, which the *I Ching* calls our *inner truth*. This is the name given by the *I Ching* to the Cosmic operating system and natural program we are born with. It is based on a feeling memory of what is harmonious and what is disharmonious. This program is fully capable of running every aspect of our lives while keeping us in harmony with the Cosmos. Scientists have called this aspect of ourselves "DNA" (deoxyribonucleic acid). The unfortunate consequence of giving it such a name is that it makes us think it is nothing more than strands of genes that have only a chemical nature, rather than being the sensitive consciousness that it is. (This is an example of how an inappropriate name given to a thing can keep us from realizing its true quality and function in our nature.)

To understand illness, it is necessary to understand how wrong names given to things, wrong assumptions about our nature, and wrong suppositions about the Cosmos and our relationship to it, disturb our symbiosis with these things. In terms of illness the conflicts occur on several levels: (1) between mind and body, (2) between body parts, whereby one body part identifies with the mind and looks down on another body part, (3) between a bodily system and the rest of the body, and (4) between certain parts of the body cells and other parts of the body cells.

2. Anthony/Moog, p. 299.

Illness may break out on any one of these levels depending on the environmental circumstances and the established patterns of relationship held by the individual. (See Pattern 1, p. 9.) When it breaks out on all levels simultaneously, medical language calls it a "disease of the autoimmune system."

The Power of Images

It has long been known that images affect the body consciousness. Dr. Bernie Siegel's work on this subject is well known. Carol's experience with a broken collar bone is another case in point. The examining doctor had crooked his finger at the time she broke the bone, using it to give an image of how the bone would heal, adding, "it will always hurt somewhat." Several months after the bone had healed, it continued to ache. She decided to meditate about it. In the meditation, the memory of the doctor's crooking his finger, and telling her it would always ache came to mind. This was followed by the clear voice of the Sage, saying, "See the bone as straight, as it originally was." After correcting the image of the bone in her mind, the pain permanently ceased, even though to the outer eye it still looks crooked.

In our experience, it is just as important to pay attention to the *images* stored in our psyche as to the words. We put a spell on ourselves when we accept any images of our body that shows it as weak, injured, sick, or deformed in any way. These spells are often the cause of an illness.

To understand the power of images, we need to recognize that *the body perceives them differently from the mind.* Consider, for example, the effect of being ridiculed for being fat. The mind, in seeing the body as fat, blames it as the object of ridicule. For its part, the body looks at itself through the mind's eyes, which in this case means with disdain. This disdain is a form of self-hatred. The body's feeling of being outcast and abandoned by the mind results in a feeling of defeat in every body cell. More precisely, it sets up a conflict within the body, whereby certain cells take the superior position of the mind and look down on those cells that are in the areas it considers to have too much fat. The persisting conflict leaves us vulnerable to any number of illnesses in those parts of the body we hate.

With the help of the Sage and the *I Ching*, we discovered just how this inner conflict works. We were made aware that many images and thoughts create fears in the body. There are phrases that merely through their *implications* create *projections or spells*. For example, in being asked as a child, "What do you want to be when you grow up?" there is an implication, made by the collective ego, that we are not good enough the way we are, and that we need to "become" something it approves of to be okay. This implication is a spell that fixes our body in the fear of being incomplete and without protection. This occurs because of the way our body cells hear language; they hear the hidden implications, whereas our mind quickly skips over to imagining what we want to become. The doubt instilled in the body consciousness gives rise to the fear of being susceptible to illness, because the body knows that its natural protection has become blocked.

The effect of language on the will of the body cells, can easily be demonstrated. In an experiment a woman was asked to hold her arms out and to resist the man's attempt to push them down, regardless of what the man was going to say to her. His first statement was, "you are a fine woman." He was then unable to push her arms down. He next said to her, "you are a bad woman." This time, she found her arms to be weak, and he easily pushed them down. Then someone suggested that she say an inner No to his assertion that she was a bad woman. After doing this, the woman had regained her strength and was able to hold her arms up against his pressure. (See the illustration on page 33.)

The mind, for its part, looks to the collective ego for an image that, once adopted, would compensate for the lack it has been told is in our nature. This compensation aims at protecting us from being seen as deficient, and from our supposedly deficient nature. By adopting the self-image, the mind actually splits off from our nature.

Despite the spells put on our body by doubt and self-images, a part of the cells retain their Cosmic memory of the original wholeness of our nature. Thus, when we deprogram these doubts

Above: the result of being told, "You are a fine woman."
Below: the result of being told, "You are a bad woman."

A kinesthetic experiment on the will of body cells.

and self-images, our natural protection is restored to the body cells. If we have accepted doubt in our body's self-healing abilities and have not yet freed ourselves of it, any statistics about illness pertaining to our age or gender group will create the fear of getting that illness when we reach the statistical age. Women warned of developing breast cancer, who constantly examine themselves to see if it is occurring, are going three quarters of the way to creating it through their fear and expectation. In Chinese philosophy there is a saying, "harm enters only where fear makes the opening."

The multitude of statements made in ads that warn of health problems introduce images into the psyche that show us as vulnerable sitting ducks, waiting to be assaulted by enemy forces of illness. They set a standard of "inherent weakness" as our natural condition, whereas in truth, our natural condition is wholeness and robust health.

It becomes clear from the above that our *thinking consciousness* affects the *feeling consciousness* of our bodily nature. Thus, when we (our mind) believe that we (our bodily nature) are sitting ducks, the negative effect on the will of the body cells makes that a reality.

Scientific experiments have proven that the projection of expected results influences the outcome of experiments. David Bohm, noted professor of theoretical physics, made extensive remarks about this fact, showing the old belief that the observer has no influence on the experiment he is conducting, to be false.[3] Our book is testimony to that fact. The common view that the contents of our mind have no effect on our psyche and our health has clearly been proven wrong. The choice of holding on to this delusion or letting go of it can determine whether we live a life of suffering, or enjoy lifelong good health.

---

[3] David Bohm, *On Creativity*, Routlege, London, 1998, p. 33. "According to modern physics (especially the quantum theory) when one comes down to the atomic and subatomic level of size, the observing instrument is...inseparable from what is to be observed, so that this instrument cannot do other than disturb the observed system in an irreducible way: and indeed it even helps to create and to give form to what is observed."

5.

The Role of the Ego in Illness

Contrary to common beliefs, the Sage has made us aware that the nature we are born with is wholly good, since it is a direct expression of the Cosmic Consciousness. Pattern 1, p. 9, shows that our nature is made up to be in a symbiotic relationship with the Cosmos. That symbiotic relationship is expressed in our body as robust health.

The ego, as defined by the *I Ching*, is not part of our true nature. Rather, it is a false mental construct installed in our psyche during childhood, when we are taught ideas and beliefs that are not in harmony with Cosmic Truth. We refer here to particular beliefs that falsely describe the Cosmos and Nature. In this respect, it differs from the ego as defined by Freud, Jung, or any other contemporary school of psychology. What the *I Ching* calls ego is synonymous with the egotistical behavior that accompanies a human-centered view of life.

How the Collective Ego was Formed

The human-centered view of life is at the root of the collection of mistaken ideas and beliefs that make up the collective ego. We have already mentioned the myths that formed over many centuries about the heroic deeds of the ancestors that led to seeing some humans as superior. When one human was put up as special, a hierarchy was created within the tribe. When a tribe began to see itself as superior to another tribe, there began to be tribal warfare. When one tribe defeated another and enslaved it, social classes were formed. When dominance was extended over many tribes and lands, the emperors began to declare themselves as gods, or as in ancient China, the "Son of Heaven." Once some humans viewed themselves as special over others, they extended that view to the other animals and Nature in general. They ultimately extended their hierarchical views to create a duplicate collective ego structure in the invisible world. As on earth, so in heaven. It is not surprising, therefore, that the ancient Greek pantheon of gods and goddesses were believed to have the same ego traits as humans, such as spite, jealousy, hatred, lust, ambition, rivalry, and conflict.

The hierarchical order was extended to the mind and body, and between parts of the body, with some being viewed as more important than others. The result was to split off the mind from the body.

The idea that everything is structured hierarchically violates the Cosmic Principle of Equality. This view severely impairs our symbiosis with the Cosmos, with Nature, and the symbiosis that exists between mind and body. What is ignored by this view is the fact that brain cells, which make up the mind, are body cells!

The mindset of the collective ego imagines humans to be the centerpiece of creation, and the leaders of evolutionary development. It sees humans as elevated over Nature, and Nature as having only the purpose to fulfill human needs, wishes, and demands. These assumptions have been taken as the authorizing principles for all feudal systems of social organization that have dominated the world for more than 5,000 years. They are also the basis of all "seed phrases" that create illness because they violate the Cosmic Principles that make up our nature.

Once this mindset of the collective ego became established in the psyche of people, it invented institutions that would maintain its dominance. This is evident today in the fact that every culture requires obedience, loyalty, and service from the individual. To obtain this loyalty the populace is encouraged to identify the awesome monuments, buildings, literature, and history as *its* cultural achievement, even though those achievements have come about with help from the Cosmos. The collective ego appropriates them by giving them as evidence of what makes humans better than other species. This is done to motivate individuals to sacrifice their uniqueness to the interests of the collective.

The collective ego also secures its control over the individual by asserting itself as the authority that approves or disapproves of his existence. This approval is based on the individual's adhering to the conventions of the collective, and what it specifies as "correct thought and action."

All these mistaken ideas and beliefs are in conflict with the Cosmic Principles of Harmony through the fact that *all hierarchical systems are based on conflict.* Those who are higher in a hierarchy are inherently in conflict with those who are lower. Hierarchical structures, by their nature, keep their momentum going through creating conflict with similar structures. We witness this in the huge emphasis that is placed on competition as a "peaceful pursuit." Such competition is mental preparation for war and domination.

How the Individual Ego is Formed

The conditioning of the individual begins with the child's learning language. Language acquisition is persistently accompanied by rewards and threats that both confuse and terrorize us as children at a time when we are unable to psychologically process what is happening to us.

The first and perhaps most important doubt instilled in us as young children is the idea that we are not good enough in and of ourselves, and that we must *become* something in order for our existence to be authorized by the collective ego. The fundamental self-doubt and the fears this creates become the foundation for the program of the individual ego. Many of these fears and self-doubts are poisonous to our nature.

"Becoming something" means becoming something other than who we truly are. In this process we learn to fulfill the standard implied by words such as a "good" boy/girl, man/woman, husband/wife, father/mother, citizen, etc. These words contain pre-designated sets of images that require us as individuals to put our true selves aside, in order to fulfill the images. The failure to live up to the standard of the good person, subjects us to the risk of being designated as bad, wild, a rebel, dropout, or a failure.

Thus, the individual ego is the collection of self-images a

person adopts, together with the program of ego-values that are associated with them. Once accepted into the psyche, these self-images take over our personalities. This mental program of ideas and images is superimposed over our natural feeling program. The images we adopt of ourselves then become the basis of our pride, as something we defend. Once enough images have been superimposed over the true self, the ego takes over the psyche as a "personage," where it then speaks as "I." When we have lost enough connection with our true self, the ego then speaks to us imperiously in the so-called royal or dictator's "we," as in "we must do things this way."

Once established, the ego extends its control over the body consciousness through "how we look," since the body needs to become an extension of the self-image being developed. Examples are males and females looking at their bodies in the mirror to see how they measure up to the conventions of "good looks." When our body does not fit the idealized image, we may slander the body as having betrayed us, and then develop a negative self-image. Such thoughts put spells and poison arrows on the body that cause illness.

With the development of the ego in ourselves, we have not only lost the symbiotic relationship that exists between our mind and body, we have also lost our symbiotic relationship with the Cosmos and with Nature. This causes us to lose our Cosmic protection, except for times of shock, when we are returned to humility. Because the ego has no connection with the Cosmos, it makes us look to the collective ego for protection. The collective ego's idea of protection is to gain power to control people, and to control Nature.

Our Body under the Rule of the Ego

Although a person may lose his true self for a long time, a permanent loss of the true self is not possible. Despite our delusions, and the seemingly complete tyranny of the ego, we still live in our body. Even though some of our DNA may be damaged by false beliefs, other parts of our DNA remain intact. In this state, our intact DNA is no longer able to communicate what it knows because of the unwillingness of the conscious mind to hear it. However, this situation is not without remedy, if we ask for Cosmic help.

What keeps the mind unwilling to hear the body's knowledge? We have already mentioned that the conditioning methods used to create the ego are intense and persistent, creating fundamental self-doubts and fears. The installation of fears in the psyche is intentional, to make the mind afraid of listening to our feelings, since they would call us back to our true selves. Because the collective ego wants dependence and conformity, it tells us that our *feelings* are worthless, that they are only subjective, and will only lead us into trouble. If necessary, punishments are given for listening to our feelings, or for following them. We are also made to believe that if we follow our feelings, we will be abandoned by family and society, will fail, be shunned and shamed, go to hell, and any number of other terrors.

Because the child mind is unable to process these fears, they take on demonic proportions, creating what we have been led to recognize as "demonic elements in the psyche." These demonic elements are often seen in meditations and dreams as threatening animals, reptiles, evil people, and such. In these guises, they give us the impression that they are invincible, and that we will never be able to get free of their control. Nevertheless, when we attain a close-up view of them, we can plainly see that they are paper dragons created by false words and images. We need to be aware of them because of the role they play in keeping us from freeing ourselves from ideas that create illness. They also act within the individual psyche as guardians of the values and beliefs of the collective ego, and thus maintain the control the individual ego has attained over our personalities. When guilt is added to these demonic elements, they create a virtual fortress wall that shuts off our body's knowledge.

We have identified three main kinds of demonic elements that plague the mind with fears, worries, doubts, guilt, and inner commands. They are *imps, demons,* and *dragons.* (See Appendix 2, *Demonic Elements in the Psyche that Cause Illness.*)

Those that maneuver our personalities through suggestion are "imps." Those that maneuver us by repeating fears and emotions over and over in our heads are "demons." Those that control us through monumental fears and guilt are "dragons." Additional demonic elements exist, but we mention only three of these in this book because they are particularly important to illness. They are what we have called "the changeling," "the doubter," and "the grabber."

The *changeling* acts as a guard to protect the basic mindset of the ego. When we have deprogrammed a negative idea about ourselves without deprogramming its positive counterpart, the changeling uses the part that is still intact to reinstall the part we have deprogrammed. If, for example, we have deprogrammed a dependence on medications but a distrust of the Cosmos has not been deprogrammed, the changeling will prey on this distrust to say, "Now you are vulnerable to all kinds of problems because you don't know whether you can trust the Cosmos to help you."

The *doubter* is created by the belief that we can only believe what we can see. When we have experienced the truth of a Cosmic principle, the doubter introduces the words "maybe" or "perhaps." When the doubter is active, one doubt is immediately followed by another, calling into question anything that cannot be verified through outer seeing.

The *grabber* can create insomnia through bringing to mind untenable situations, subliminal worries, fears, and feelings of hopelessness that grab and hold our attention.

All demonic elements are made up of false thought forms that are combined with certain ego emotions. At the cellular level, the body retains some of its memory of inner truth. That part remains resolutely true to itself no matter how much we have surrendered to the control of the collective ego, or have become convinced that we really have become "somebody important," "powerful," or the reverse, "never good enough," or "powerless." We experience the part that stays in touch with our inner truth during times of shock, when the ego has been temporarily displaced. Illness produces such a shock. It makes an opening for this part of our body to communicate with our mind when we have allowed it no other way of communicating. Illness forces us to stop and reflect, and to seek to free ourselves from the dominance of the ego.

Because it is never able to entirely fool us that it is real, the ego remains on the alert to assert its control over the personality. To sustain its pretense of being real, it must succeed in getting repeated recognition from others to "prove" it is what it pretends to be. To achieve this end, the body must dress, look, act, and even feel according to the image the ego wants us to be. Its success is determined by what it reads in the eyes of others, and those others exist only for the purpose of verifying and supporting the ego's pretense of being real. This is true whether the ego attains its verification by flattery, intimidation, or force, or through subservience and self-sacrifice. Failure to gain verification from others can plunge the person who has invested in a given image into depression and/or illness. The ego can even cause us to commit suicide by asserting that "if I cannot have life my way, life isn't worth living." This statement is the ego's ultimate way of asserting its control over the individual.

Long-standing and chronic illnesses are run by a whole program of mistaken ideas maintained by the ego. These ideas can be projections, spells, or poison arrows put on us either by ourselves, or by others. People generally do not consciously put these thoughts on us, nor do we consciously put them on ourselves. It happens because we do not realize the harmful effects of mistaken ideas as consciousness in a Cosmos that is made up of consciousness.

For these false thought forms to enter us and create illness, we must have been open to receiving them. Such openings are created by self-doubt or fears that have taken residence in our psyche at an earlier time in our lives, including the time *in utero*. These false thought forms are accompanied by ego emotions that create an energetic connection with the sick-making thoughts coming from outside. Among these ego-emotions are hurt pride, self-pity, revenge, ambition, lust, rivalry, sympathy, compassion, disdain, hatred, spite, jealousy, condemnation, superiority, inferiority, and vindictiveness.

41

Some Seed Phrases of the Ego

While the mistaken ideas and beliefs that make up the ego seem limitless, they nevertheless rest on only a few underlying stated or implied "seed phrases." Once we are familiar with these seed phrases, on which the whole collective ego is based, we are able, with relatively few strokes, to take down the trees and branches to which they have given rise.

Seed phrases are to be compared to the basic phrases of a computer program: they install the program of the collective ego within us by making us believe we are dependent upon the collective ego for all our needs.

Among these basic phrases are:
- You are defective and therefore not whole
- You are lacking in the essentials of what you need to get along in life
- You are dependent on the people and institutions around you for all your needs (implication: there is no help from the Cosmos)
- What you see is all there is
- What you have been told is all there is to know
- You are born into a hostile universe
- Nothing lasts
- You can never know
- Everything that can be known is already known

These and other seed phrases give rise to fundamental self-doubts and fears. They shut us off from recognizing our innate capabilities, and from recognizing that the Cosmos is the source of our help, sustenance, and protection.

The idea that our nature is lacking creates holes in our bodily protective system that make us susceptible to illness. The above seed phrases give rise to a host of mistaken beliefs that create fears and self-doubts, such as the following:
- the fear of death
- the fear of being annihilated
- the doubt of "deserving" any kind of help or protection, or of deserving anything good
- the fear of the "Unknown"

• the fear of falling into an endless abyss
• the fear of being without help
• the fear of abandonment
• the fear of not getting our most basic needs met
• the fear of punishment
• the fear of becoming guilty and of being shamed
• the fear of not being able to find fulfillment in our lives

These self-doubts and fears are the source of a subliminal and constant anxiety that persists in the psyche until the seed phrases that have given rise to them are removed. Persistent anxiety is often the cause of illness.

Other sources of illness are derived from the view promoted by the collective ego that the invisible Cosmos is a feudal system dominated by a tyrannical overlord to whom we must make obeisance, and who threatens that our sins shall be harshly judged. This threat keeps us feeling anxious and guilty all our lives for the most innocent feelings. (See Chapter 9, *The Origins of Guilt*.)

Our view of Nature as an enemy, the wild "out there" from which we need protection, is another source of harmful ideas that keep us in a state of anxiety and conflict. It results in the belief that Nature is vindictive and every now and then inflicts on us terrible disasters such as earthquakes, floods, tornadoes, volcanic eruptions, and the like. By looking at Nature as an enemy that needs to be fought, we forget that we are a part of Nature. Once we take away these disharmonious ideas, we find that all the forces of Nature become friendly and cooperative, and the forces of the Cosmos a constant source of help. When we remove the ideas that prevent our bodily unity, we find ourselves in a loving relationship with our body, with our mind benefiting from our body's innate wisdom. (Also see Chapter 9, *The Origins of Guilt*, for a discussion of the guilt we have toward Nature.)

We are trained to think that the ego is an essential part of us, and that there is some good in it, but as the above shows, the ego is an imposter that has only one goal: to be recognized as real at the expense of our life force.

Both the *I Ching* and our personal experience in dealing with illness have made it clear to us that the ego is a parasite in the psyche that is only destructive. Like its parent (the collective ego), it is created by using language to falsely describe the Cosmos and Nature. What is essential to understand in regard to healing, is that each time we deprogram one of the primary phrases, images, or ideas that make up the ego, its power and ability to control us diminishes. Correspondingly, the development of our inner awareness and access to our body's knowledge increases.

It is not possible to free ourselves from the ego and its assemblage of demonic elements by doing any one thing, because the ego is not a single entity. It is an assemblage of phrases, images, and mistaken beliefs that take on a life because we have accepted them as true. We deconstruct the ego by dismantling or deprogramming these phrases, images, and mistaken beliefs with Cosmic help. Freeing ourselves from the demonic elements created during our conditioning deprives them of their power over us. This work simultaneously restores our symbiotic relationships with the Cosmos, with Nature, and within ourselves. (See Chapter 21, *Methods of Deprogramming*.)

6.

The Role of Fate in Illness

Illnesses and Injuries that are a Fate
Fate is never the cause of an illness or injury. It is the Cosmic wall we run into when we go against the Cosmic limits set for human life. All of us have premonitions of when we are drawing close to these limits, as our knowledge of these limits is contained in our Cosmic operating program.

The oracle sayings given in every hexagram of the *I Ching* predict "good fortune" or "misfortune." Good fortune indicates the end result of keeping in harmony with our inner truth. The good fortune comes through Cosmic help. Misfortune is the end result of following mistaken ideas and beliefs over a period of time. Misfortune is our fate for persisting in this direction, despite inner warnings. This fate is not directed at us personally, but is the inevitable result of ignoring the invisible wall of limits that apply to human thought and action. We hit this wall when we have turned our backs on Cosmic protection by having adopted arrogant attitudes. The purpose of Fate is to preserve the duration of Cosmic harmony, on the one hand, and to bring us back to humility, on the other.

Fate helps restore us to our true nature. How does this occur? When Fate occurs as an illness, or injury, it brings normal life to a halt. This gives us the time and space to reflect on why it has happened, and in the case of illness, to become aware that sick-making thoughts are active in our psyche, so that we can free ourselves of them. The severity of an illness or injury that is a fate reflects the degree of our obstinacy in holding to a mistaken idea. Usually, the ideas slander the Cosmos, Nature, or our own nature. An example is the experience of the nodules given in Chapter 1.

Many illnesses and injuries that are fates are caused by violating the Cosmic Principle of Equality of all aspects of the Cosmos.

45

For example, this principle is violated when we elevate one part of our nature over another, or elevate our thinking over our feeling nature, or believe that one part of our nature is good and another part is evil. Another violation is the mistaken idea that our feelings do not count, or are unreliable. We also disregard this equality when we overly value good looks, bodily strength, or intellectual capacity.

A fate in the form of either illness or injury can also be caused by the idea that we have no natural connection with the Cosmos. This fate has the additional consequence of preventing the Cosmos from helping us regain our health.

Cosmic Warnings that Precede a Fate

Prior to the onset of a fate, we may receive a number of small warnings in the form of small injuries. These are meant to make us aware that we have created a fate, and to give us the opportunity to correct ourselves. These injuries can be seemingly minor such as cutting a finger, squeezing a finger in a door, stumbling over a rock, or bumping our head against something. These hints begin in a small way and proceed, if we ignore them, to more serious incidents. If we do not listen, the warnings stop and the fate occurs with a shock.

At any point along this trajectory, it is not too late to correct ourselves. The moment we identify the mistaken idea or belief, or the self-image that caused the fate, we feel relief. The next step is to deprogram it. We discuss deprogramming in depth in Chapter 21, *Methods of Deprogramming.*

Illnesses that Look like a Fate, but are Not

Illnesses in this category are caused by a spell or poison arrow put on a person by someone else. The following are examples of the spells and poison arrows that are involved:
- thoughts that wish another ill
- vindictive thoughts such as: "I wish she would experience herself, what I am going through." "May he go to hell!" "May God punish him for what he has done to me!" "She does not deserve to live."

• seemingly harmless comparisons such as, "He is just like his father." (This open-ended identification can cause the person to contract the illness of the father.)

All sick-making thoughts that cause harm to others create a fate for the person who thinks them.

If the poison arrow is not recognized and removed, it can develop into a chronic condition. Thus, in looking for the cause of a chronic condition, we need to inquire whether it is due to such a poison arrow. A further discussion of this cause is contained in Chapter 14, *Illnesses Caused by Outside Influences.*[1]

When a condition has become chronic, it may continue if we develop a resigned attitude about the chronic condition. There may be self-imposed spells added such as, "everyone has to bear his cross in life," or "I have to put up with periodic pain." This belief creates a fate, where before there was none. Its shock has the purpose of displacing the resigned attitude that keeps us a prisoner of the chronic condition.

The *I Ching* informs us that when an illness is caused by a spell or poison arrow coming from outside, all the Cosmic Helpers are active to restore our health.

Children's Illnesses

Children do not invoke a fate until age fifteen, when they are capable of being responsible for their thoughts and actions.

A young child's illness can be a fate for a parent, as for example, when the parent has mistreated the child, or has a number of mistaken ideas about how to relate to the child. This can occur in the following instances:
• When parents do not recognize that a child is a Cosmic gift, or look at the child as a burden
• When a parent or other adult believes the child deserves to become sick as a punishment for bad behavior
• Wanting a child to be a particular gender
• When a parent identifies too strongly with the child, the child is made vulnerable to illness

---

1. The *I Ching* refers to this situation in Hexagram 25, *Innocence*, Line 5. Anthony/Moog, p. 304.

• When a parent attaches too strongly to the good looks of a child

The occasion of the illness, and the risk it creates for the child, presents an opportunity for parents to recognize their mistaken attitudes, both toward the child and the Cosmos. If they fail to correct their attitudes, they risk losing this Cosmic gift.

The Cosmos protects the child throughout. To appreciate this correctly, we need to see that death, should it occur, is not the specter for the child that it is for the parent.

The danger in such a situation is that the parents will have the ego view that the child's life is in God's or life's or Fate's hands, regardless of what they do; or, that the cause of the illness and its consequences are due to God, life, or Fate. In adopting such ideas, they abandon their responsibility for their thoughts.

The parents' remorse draws Cosmic help into their lives, giving them an opportunity to experience how the Cosmos responds to a sincere attitude that recognizes the need for Cosmic help. It is often during such times of agonizing that one's wrong thoughts come to mind. Recognizing them and feeling regret for them frees one of blame. Then the Sage breaks the spells that have caused the illness.

7.

The Main Cosmic Principles
of Harmony

All mistaken ideas and beliefs that cause illness are contrary to the Cosmic Principles of Harmony. The *I Ching* teaches that the Cosmos is a system of harmony composed of two sets of harmonious principles: one set is known as the *laws of physics*. The other set is the Cosmic Principles of Harmony. Both sets guarantee the duration of the Cosmos as a whole, and its harmony. Given these principles, it is clear that the wholeness of the Cosmos could not endure if it were based on conflict, opposition, and destruction as part of the natural order of things.[1]

The laws of physics determine what may be done and not done on the physical plane; when we disregard these laws, we may risk our lives. The same is true when we disregard the Cosmic Principles of Harmony. They define the correct limits of action for all species, and the limits of thought for those species that think.[2] With laws of physics, we only suffer the consequences by *acting* against them. With the Principles of Harmony, we suffer the consequences even when we *think* in terms of ideas and beliefs that are contrary to these principles, let alone act on them. When we do so, a particular Cosmic Principle sets in to bring us back to harmony. This is the principle of *Fate*. Although the *I Ching* often refers to Fate as "misfortune," it is never a misfortune for a person's true self, because all the Cosmic forces that are active in a fate help him break a spell under which his true nature is laboring.

In order to understand how we humans come into conflict with the Cosmos, we need to know what the Cosmic Principles

---

[1] "Destruction," as used here, is not the same as the transformations that create the growth, decay, and death of organic forms. Destruction, is the result of the use of power.
[2] In Cosmic terms, thought is considered to be an inner action.

of Harmony are. In working with the *I Ching* we have distinguished seven main Cosmic Principles of Harmony that are most frequently violated by sick-making thoughts.

I. The Cosmic Principle of Equality of All Parts of the Cosmos

Equality occurs when we recognize and respect the intrinsic worth, dignity, and uniqueness of each thing as part of the Cosmic whole. It amounts to a general sensitivity to life.

Ideas that originate in our presuming that anything in the Cosmos is hierarchically ordered or in some way superior or inferior violate this principle.

II. The Cosmic Principle of the Uniqueness of Everything in the Cosmos

Central to a true understanding of life is our recognizing the uniqueness of each thing, regardless of how alike something else it appears to be. Language puts things in categories as a kind of shorthand so that things can be spoken of in the plural. However, categorizing can blind us to the uniqueness of each thing, and therefore lead to wrong conclusions.

Ideas based on the presumption that things can be accurately understood when put in categories or groups, and then compared with each other, violate this principle.

III. The Cosmic Principle of Modesty

Modesty expresses itself when we recognize that everything in the Cosmos is equal, unique, and has a dignity that is worthy of our respect. Modesty is expressed as innocence of the mind, meaning, free of intention. It is to act from our true feelings, and to respond, rather than to initiate.

Modesty is violated when we presume that some things are superior to others. It is violated when we try to be more or less than what we truly are. (The latter occurs when we deny our intrinsic worth.) Modesty is violated in all the ways we fail to respect the limits that apply to human thought and action. We lose our natural Cosmic protection when we lose our modesty.

IV. The Cosmic Principle of Attraction between Complementary Aspects of the Cosmos

It is attraction between complementary aspects of the Cosmos that holds all parts of the Cosmos together harmoniously. This attraction occurs in the atomic realm. The absence of attraction has been mistakenly described as being in "opposition," or "conflict," whereas the things described are simply not complementary.

Ideas based on the presumption that things in Nature or in the Cosmos are in opposition to each other, violate the above principle. Because we live in a false, parallel reality that is based on conflict and opposition, we presume that conflict and opposition is "the natural way." This presumption prevents us from understanding that thinking in terms of conflict creates conflict. (See Pattern 3, page 13.)

V. The Cosmic Principle of "Joint Approach" to Cosmic Evolution

All increase to the Cosmic whole is achieved by a cooperation between the invisible Cosmic Helpers and all things that are part of Nature, including humans. One goal of the Cosmic Plan is the general benefit of all aspects of the Cosmos. When we humans seek to find solutions to problems in a harmonious way, we are joined by Helpers that help us bring them into reality.

Ideas that are based on the presumption that anything of value can be created without inspiration and help coming from the invisible world, violate this principle. It is also violated when we allow the ego to take credit for what has been achieved.

Joint approach, regarding matters of health, means that we ask Cosmic Helpers to work through doctors, nurses, helpful individuals, natural remedies, and to work with the Helpers of our own nature.

VI. The Cosmic Principle of the Relativity of Cosmic Truth

Cosmic truths are always relative to the Cosmic Principles of Harmony. This means our understanding is correct only when our views are based on these principles. It also means we look not only at outer appearances, but take to the inner truth behind events and circumstances. We do this by asking the Sage to make us aware of the ways in which the ego is involved in these circumstances and say an inner No to it. The truth cannot be known if the ego is left in hiding.

Humans generally judge things by their appearances, and by what they can see and measure. This perspective excludes the harmful effect on things created by false thought forms. When we understand their effects, we are able to come to a full understand of the inner truth of the situation.

Ideas that contain judgments based on an absolute and abstract standard of good or evil, right or wrong violate this principle. When we have come to a correct understanding of a situation, it feels Cosmically correct and harmonious.

VII. The Cosmic Principle of Joy

There is joy when things are recognized in their essence and are given names that reflect that essence. This joy is mutually felt by the consciousness of the thing being named and by the person who uses the correct name.

When we give things names that diminish or demonize their true nature, we violate this principle. We can always ask the Sage to help us find the correct name for things.

When our words and thoughts are in harmony with the above principles, they support and nourish our psyche and body. When they are not in harmony, both our psyche and body are undermined in all their natural capabilities, and are shut off from the loving support of the Cosmos.

8.

The Helping Forces of the Cosmos and of Our Nature

Healing ourselves the Cosmic Way requires the assistance of the invisible helping forces of the Cosmos, of Nature, and of our own nature. These helping forces are referred to by implication in various hexagrams of the *I Ching*, as "experts in their fields," "friends that come in the midst of the greatest obstructions," and simply as "helpers." On this account, we have also called them "Helpers."[1] Our experience is that the entire text of the *I Ching* is referring to these Helpers. They are individualized consciousnesses that are devoted to specific functions in Nature. Approaching all our undertakings in cooperation with them is what is meant by the Cosmic Principle of Joint Approach. (See Chapter 7.)

The Helpers may appear in meditations and dreams in human forms or might be felt as a helpful presence by our side that is pointing out things to us, or protecting us from harm. Their appearance in human form has often been taken as indicating they are superhuman beings; however, they show themselves in this way only because that is the way we can best relate to them. They are not human.

A friend of ours asked through the *rtcm* if the Helpers would show themselves in a digital photo, and was answered Yes.[2] She had taken a picture of a room before asking and then took one after asking. The first photo showed a quite ordinary room, while the second photo contained many orbs of light. Later, this friend's horse gave birth to a foal. At first, the mare rejected her foal, causing our friend some concern. She then remembered

---

[1] See Hexagram 3, *Making a New Beginning*. The Judgment text reads: "It furthers one to persevere in not undertaking anything until clarity is attained. It furthers one to appoint Helpers." Anthony/Moog.

[2] *rtcm* means retrospective-three-coin method. For a description of the method, see Chapter 19.

to ask for the Foaling Helper to help with the situation. Within fifteen minutes, the mare had accepted the foal. Our friend took the photo shown here, in which the Helper appeared as the orbs of light that are indicated by arrows. The Sage assured us that although we see a number of these orbs, they all belong to that one Helper.

Although the Helpers carry out their tasks invisibly, they are willing to show themselves when we are modest, open-minded, and do not have a fixed idea of what they are. They will not show themselves under any immodest conditions, as when we demand that they show themselves, or seek to use them in any way that would compromise their dignity.

The Sage

The Sage is the first Cosmic Helper of the invisible world we meet. It is the Helper that connects us directly with the Cosmic Consciousness, and is comparable to what the ancient Greeks recognized as a "tutelary spirit" that accompanies each person from birth throughout his life. The Greek name for this spirit was "genie," origin of the word "genius." The Sage helps us in all our tasks and points us subtly in the directions that lead us to fulfill our true nature. In addition, it assembles other Helpers needed for this purpose.

The Sage also acts as our Cosmic teacher. It does so in two ways: by connecting us directly with the Cosmic Consciousness through mind-flashes and insights gained through dreams and meditations, and by translating the feeling knowledge of our inner truth into words and thoughts.

When we toss coins in using the *rtcm*, it is the Sage that answers us through the fall of the coins.[2] It will even help us ask the most pertinent questions if we ask it to do so. When we toss coins in consulting the *I Ching*, it is the Sage that points to the hexagrams and those parts of the text we most need to read.

The Sage also guides us to find the inner truth of situations, as when we want to investigate the causes of an ailment or illness. In this way the thoughts of the ego, in ourselves and in others, are exposed, so that we do not fall into their traps, and into their false conclusions. The ego, being outside the Cosmic realm, has no right to hide under the pretext of having "a right to privacy" when it is dominating someone's inner thoughts about us. The Sage is always available to help us understand when we ask to understand, and when we hold our minds open to receive the answers.

The Sage makes us aware of opportunities that will benefit us, and warns us when we are in danger of creating a fate. The warnings can come through dreams, or through events that are clear wake-up signs.

In regard to illness, the Sage knows the names of the Helpers we need for healing. We only need to ask the Sage to activate these Helpers on our behalf.

Other Cosmic Helpers

The Sage has made us aware that not only is there a Cosmic Helper for every need, new Helpers are created for every new need. Being endless in numbers, they support and help every form of existence except the ego and its parallel reality.

Several Cosmic Helpers are specifically described in hexagrams of the *I Ching*. Notable among them is the Helper of Transformation that is described in two related hexagrams. This Helper is necessary to bring all healing to completion, through transformation. Also notable are the Helper of Dissolution and the Helper of Freeing.[3]

The Helper of Transformation is involved in a great number of functions that ensure our growth, health, and recovery from illness. An example of its function is the transformation that occurs in the way our body cells are renewed every day. This Helper is also the partner that brings to completion all our efforts to correct ourselves.

Hexagrams 64, *Before Completion* and 63, *After Completion* present us with a visual diagram of transformation. *Before Completion* represents all the efforts we have made by ourselves to bring an undertaking to success. The lines of this hexagram represent this effort, and can be viewed in some respects as "moving," as if they were the chairs on a Ferris wheel. They need, however, a final push, to move the top chair (top line) to clear the top and become the new bottom line in the next hexagram, where all the lines have come to their resting place. This final push is performed by the Helper of Completion, also known as the Helper of Transformation.

---

[3] Ibid. See Hexagram 64, *Before Completion* and Hexagram 63, *After Completion,* for descriptions of the Helper of Transformation, (p. 667 and 657), Hexagram 59, *Dissolving* for a description of the Helper of Dissolution (p. 621), and Hexagram 40, *Freeing,* for a description of the Helper of Freeing. (p. 438).

All of us have experienced this kind of transformation. It happens after we have put our best effort toward achieving a task, but still have not been able to complete it. At the very moment of humility in recognizing that we cannot make it happen by ourselves, help comes unexpectedly, quite outside anything we could have imagined, to make the completion possible. Not only is it brought to completion, it is brought about in the best possible way. People often call it a miracle, but the Sage makes us aware that this is the everyday way the Helper of Transformation works.

Helpers other than the Helper of Transformation may be needed to free ourselves from particular kinds of ego elements. For example, the Helper of Dissolution is important when rigid structures in our psyche and body need to be dissolved. These include plaque in the blood vessels, and gall, kidney, and bladder stones.

The Helper of Freeing is required to free the psyche of guilt, and from ego emotions such as vindictiveness, hatred, spite, envy, and jealousy. It is the Helper we need to free us of imps, demons, and dragons in the psyche. It is also required to free us from old habits of mind. These are examples of some of the Helpers the Sage activates on our behalf without our knowledge.

The Helpers of Nature

We know the Helpers of Nature best in the forms that are most helpful to humans, such as the plants of the food chain, the forests and their role in keeping the oxygen/carbon dioxide balance in the atmosphere, and in the remedies for illnesses produced by plants. Other Helpers of Nature are the consciousness of minerals, vitamins, healing earth, water, and other such resources. Such natural remedies can often successfully complement healing through deprogramming sick-making thoughts.

Some of us may not realize that certain Helpers of Nature can be asked to help in the healing of trees, plants, and animals. They can also be asked to heal areas of the earth that have been damaged. These are but some of the many ways in which they can help.

From the standpoint of healing, when we feel a harmony with the plants, land, air, and water, we are receiving the healing energies that come from their consciousnesses.

The Helpers of our Personal Nature

The Helpers of our nature comprise all the helping and cooperating functions of our body and psyche. They include the Helpers of the various organs, bodily systems, body parts, hormones, bodily fluids, and our self-healing abilities.

Why do we speak of them as "Helpers" rather than using the technical, mechanical, or chemical names science gives to our various bodily functions? These technical names are based on the false view that the body is a "vehicle" or "mechanism" that is used by the mind. The blood that runs through our veins is not merely an assemblage of "plasma, food, and waste products" nor is the heart merely a pump. These, and even the bacteria in our intestines that are crucial to our digestive processes, are Helpers. Recognizing them as living organisms, each of which has a feeling consciousness, respects their true place within our bodies. Calling them Helpers is a way of expressing our gratitude for their wonderful contributions to our lives. Their harmonious cooperation with each other is like a symphony; recognizing the part each Helper plays in this symphony gives us joy in our wholeness. It also gives joy to each part of the body when we recognize and appreciate its function. No function is insignificant. Respecting all our bodily possessions is the true meaning of self-respect.

When all parts of our nature are in harmony, we are automatically supported and helped by the Cosmic Helpers that complement the Helpers of our nature. When one part of us has separated from the other parts through the influence of the ego, we no longer automatically receive the support of the Cosmic Helpers for that part. The Sage and the Helpers retreat, and we are left to our own devices. An illness is a sign that we are to some degree in that state of inner separation.

To activate the Helpers of our nature, it is necessary to consciously acknowledge and respect them.

How to Best Relate to the Helpers

While the Helpers want to help us in every way they can, they are unable to do so as long as we are dominated by the ego and its various distrustful, demanding or otherwise arrogant attitudes. Also, if we have a belief that they do not exist, it is impossible for them to help us. Reactivating our natural relationship with them requires recognizing how we have lost that relationship, and deprogramming those phrases and images that are responsible for this loss. We cannot simply assume that all we need to do is to ask for their help. We first need to free them from the bondage we have put them in.

We also need to restore our respect for them. Like us, the Helpers are individualized aspects of the Cosmos that have dignity and self-respect. Because they adhere to the Cosmic Principles of Harmony, they cannot support any goals or undertakings that would benefit the ego.

Hexagram 41, *Decreasing,* addresses our relationship with the Helpers as its main theme: "Decreasing, combined with sincerity, brings about success. One may use two small bowls for the sacrifice." [4]

What are to be decreased by *temporarily putting them aside,* are those aspects of the ego that are active in the situation:
• our human-centered view
• our pretending to know already what is correct and not correct
• any wish to command the Helpers to serve egotistical goals
• ego resistance to any measure that interferes with its goals, pacts, allegiances, and beliefs

Ego resistances are evident in the ego's focusing on wanting to get rid of pain and discomfort rather than getting rid of their causes, which have their origin in the ego itself. The ego thus says, "let's address the real problem: the boil on the neck, the rash of shingles, or the blood sugar count in diabetes."

The mention of sincerity in the oracle refers to the necessity to acquire a *willing consent of the mind,* i.e., an open and receptive

---

[4] Ibid., p. 448.

mind. This is not a matter of our *trying* to be open and receptive, but of willingly suspending our disbelief. The Sage does not ask us to believe in the Helpers, but invites us to experience their help by having the openness to ask for it. This allows the Helpers to temporarily bypass any blockage that distrust would create, until such time as we have enough experience to trust the process.

What is meant by the two bowls for the sacrifice? Sacrifice, in *I Ching* terms, always refers to relinquishing aspects of the ego. What is to be sacrificed in the first bowl is our prideful self-importance that sits in judgment of the Helpers. To be sacrificed in the second bowl is the pride that keeps us from asking for Cosmic help, and that causes us to resist being dependent on Helpers because we have learned erroneously that dependence is associated with weakness. While deriding such dependence, the ego points to reasons why we need to depend on the ego's institutions for "real help." None of the sacrifices mentioned requires decreasing the true self. Only the ego is decreased.

Other ego complaints may also obstruct our willing consent to meet the Helpers halfway. For example, the ego may describe deprogramming mistaken ideas and beliefs as a bother, and ask, "Why is it so complicated?" The ego erects other hurdles to the mind's willing consent by proposing that there is no such thing as Helpers of our nature, and that if there are Helpers, they can only be engaged through making gestures of obeisance, and by performing rituals and ascetic practices. The ego may also propose that we need an intermediary who is close to the Helpers and can get them to work on our behalf. Basically, the ego does whatever it can to distance us from the Helpers, and to keep us from discovering that we possess them within us and that their true nature is helpful and loving.

Relating to the Helpers requires a certain sensitivity and respect, so that we do not limit their ability to help us. We are insensitive, for example, when we ask for things that are Cosmically incorrect. If we have become ill because the ego, on not having attained its goals, has caused us to give up our will to live, we cannot then expect the Helpers to restore our health so that we can achieve those ego goals. Restoring our health, in this case, means deprogramming the ego's goals.

It is important to ask for the Helpers at least a day in advance of going through a medical procedure. For example, we can ask for the Sage and the Cosmic Doctor or Surgeon to work through the human doctor or surgeon; we can also ask the Helper of Protection to protect us from the side effects of a medicine, or for protection in general.

Mistaken Beliefs that Block the Helpers

Certain attitudes and views either exclude the existence of the Helpers or block their ability to help. An example is the belief that "time heals things." It is Helpers, not time, that heal things. Another example is the view that healing is due solely to external factors, such as the efforts of doctors, medicine, or technology.

Other blockages are caused by false images of the Helpers that limit their abilities. We became aware through experiences other people had with being helped, that we were holding such false images. For example, we imagined that there were thousands of Helpers until the Sage made us aware that they are unlimited in number. Then we realized that we had imposed an image of how long it takes for the Helpers to accomplish things and learned that the Helpers are not subject to the same limitations in time that we are. Often, ailments such as headaches or sudden sharp pains can be healed within minutes. Our imagining that someone far away cannot be healed by our deprogramming similarly inhibits the Helpers' abilities.

As the above indicates, the ability of the Helpers to function effectively in our personal lives depends on our removing the obstacles we have put in their way. This requires deprogramming any limiting images we may have of them. [5] It is helpful in this process to ask the Sage to bring correct images of the Helpers to mind. The following phrases and images are examples of correct views of the Helpers, drawn from our own experiences:

---

[5] See Chapter 21, *Methods of Deprogramming.*

- The Helpers achieve their results without effort or resistance, through transformations in the realm of the atom. They do not use power, effort, or contriving.
- The Helpers can be visible or invisible. They can show themselves in a variety of forms, but are restricted to none.
- The Helpers are feeling consciousnesses that only do good. They are not tricky dwarfs, evil spirits, or angels. When seen in dreams or meditations in these forms, it means they have either been demonized or monumentalized.
- The Helpers, being without physical form, are not limited by laws of physics.
- The Helpers are strict in not relating to the ego and its thinking in terms of partiality. They never take sides in a conflict.
- The Helpers never help an evildoer.
- The Cosmos restrains the human use of power through the Helpers of Fate. These Helpers use Fate to make us aware it is the ego that has created the blind spot in our view. They do not counter power through the use of power.
- The Helpers are not limited to helping us only with inner things, or things that are not visible to us. Although they operate on the inner plane, they determine the way things manifest outwardly.
- We are never helpless when we know about our dependence on the Helpers, and that we can ask for their help.
- The Helpers have the complete ability to restore our wholeness when not restrained by our view of them.
- The Helpers respond to our natural modesty with abundant help to fully enjoy the blessings of life. They do not require us to be ascetic, patient without limits, or meek.
- With the Helpers, we need to allow for the unexpected, since what they do and how they do it is beyond our framework of thinking and imagination.
- We need to leave the outcome of our work on ourselves or on our life's situations totally up to the Helpers. When we do not imagine the outcome, it usually comes in a way that is much better than we could have imagined.
- The Helpers cannot do anything that is outside the Cosmic

Principles of Harmony. It is incorrect to think they can be asked to do just anything.

Doubts that Block the Helpers

Doubts that imply the nonexistence of the Helpers are poison arrows that immobilize them. Such doubts originate in the ego and are to be found in statements such as, "you can never trust anything unless it has been proven." Such a phrase dismisses the validity of what we experience, even when we have a healing experience for which there is no scientific explanation. Such doubts come from a specific demonic element, an aspect of the ego we have called "the doubter." When it is active, one doubt is immediately followed by another, calling into question anything that cannot be seen with the outer eyes. The doubting activity of the ego is based on the mistaken belief that "you can only believe what is visible to the eye as proof." The doubter also interjects doubting phrases that start with "maybe" or "perhaps" when we begin to heal from an illness. For a more complete description of the doubter, see Appendix 2, *Demonic Elements in the Psyche*.

Efforts that Cause the Helpers to Retreat

The above descriptions of how the Helpers function give some ideas about what they can and cannot do. The following are some examples of the thoughts and attitudes that cause the Helpers to retreat. When we identify and deprogram them, the Helpers are freed to return.

- doing things for wrong reasons, such as to gain recognition, even from the Sage
- trying to figure things out without asking for help
- thinking that making an effort means hard work
- thinking that if it is not hard, it is not worthwhile
- thinking that perseverance means continuing to work with the Sage, even when we feel hostile
- thinking that we have to placate the Helpers to get their help
- making vows of servitude or loyalty to the Sage
- blaming ourselves for our mistakes and errors

Regarding this last point, while it is correct to recognize that we have made a mistake, it is incorrect to then fall into blaming ourselves. It is enough to regret our mistake or correct our error, seek out the ego aspect behind it and deprogram it. Blaming ourselves is one of the ego's ways of keeping us attached to the mistake. The ego milks self-blame as a source of energy to stay in control.

Efforts that Engage the Helpers

The *I Ching* shows us that the way of the Cosmos is the "easy way." Easy is another word for "simple." It is easy and simple because it is completely in accord with our innermost nature. Our nature operates on a feeling consciousness, without the necessity to think. When not blocked through incorrect ideas or beliefs, the various Helpers of our nature attract the Cosmic Helpers that are their complements. Thus, when we are in harmony with our true nature, we automatically receive all the help from the Cosmos we need. What makes things complicated is the ego.

In truth, some effort is required to bring ourselves back into harmony with our innermost nature, but in doing it, we are always helped by the invisible Helpers. These efforts are far less than what conventional treatments require of us. We engage the Helpers, for instance, when after asking for their help, we turn the matter of concern over to the Cosmos, and when we:

- recognize that in and of ourselves we cannot do what the Helpers can do
- give over to the Cosmos our distrust of the Helpers
- reject the ego's interfering with our inner efforts through its judgments and doubt, and its insertion of complaints, criticisms, and ego emotions such as impatience and frustration.

When we fail to reject the ego's interference, we are forced to struggle with our task. This struggle creates frustration and anger, which are too often turned toward the Sage and the Helpers, rather than recognizing the ego as their source. Rejecting ego emotions and the phrases it puts forth is done by saying No to them three times.

9.

The Origins of Guilt

Guilt greatly affects our health. It is vital, therefore, that we understand its origins and what it does to the body and psyche. Not only does guilt greatly diminish all our self-healing abilities, its dampening effect on the will of the individual body cells makes us susceptible to illness. Many illnesses cannot be fully healed while guilt remains active in the psyche.

The Sage showed us that all guilt is a creation of the collective ego (i.e., the feudal mindset) for the purpose of controlling people. It has no place in the Cosmic reality. Guilt is unlike Cosmic blame, which is created by going against our true nature, and is extinguished the moment we feel remorse for doing so, and when we deprogram the mistaken idea or belief that has caused the blame. Guilt, however, is taken into the psyche as an inextinguishable stain put on our nature, which makes it unbearable to the psyche. The Sage has pointed out how guilt originated, and how it disturbs our relationships with the Cosmos, with Nature, and with ourselves.

The False Concept of Guilt Began with "Original Guilt/Sin"

We in the West are taught from an early age that we are born with an "original guilt/sin." Its origin for Western cultures that follow the Bible is recorded in Chapters 2 and 3 of Genesis. According to the story, a serpent in the Garden of Eden tempted Eve and she disobeyed God's order not to eat fruit from the tree of the knowledge of good and evil. She shared the fruit with Adam. Consequently, God expelled both of them from paradise and cursed them "for all their days," and extended the curse to "all their issue." This act of human disobedience is what has been called "original sin."

efore their temptation, they were described as being naked and not feeling ashamed. Afterwards, they were described as aware of their nakedness and feeling ashamed. On this account, their sin has been ascribed to their sexuality.

The Inability to Love through Mental Effort as a Cause of Guilt

In addition to original guilt, another more subtle guilt resulted from the *command to love God.* In Exodus 20, where the Ten Commandments are written, God is pictured as a harsh authoritarian figure who speaks of himself as "a jealous god who visits the iniquity of the fathers upon the children unto the third and fourth generation of those that hate him, and who shows mercy unto the thousands who love him and keep his commandments."

There are several remarkable points to be made about the above description: (1) love is equated with obedience; (2) disobedience is further combined with the worst threats of abandonment, endless punishments, and death; (3) loving God is to be shown through subservience to God. All these implications of God's nature point to a feudal monarch, not a loving Cosmos. Unfortunately, this image of an authoritarian and vengeful God was put in the place of the loving and caring Cosmos.

True love, as the Sage teaches, is the natural feeling that comes from our heart toward the loving Cosmos. It is an entirely spontaneous feeling response created by the harmonious attraction that exists between the Cosmos and all its expressions in form. Nothing of this feeling can be mentally contrived.

Thoughts that come from recognizing the wonders of Nature, of our own makeup, and the experience of the constant availability of help from the Cosmos, create love in the form of gratitude, respect, and sensitivity. None of these feelings, which come from the heart, can be commanded. The reason is simple: the mind is a thinking, not a feeling consciousness. The best we can do, when commanded to love, is to pretend that we love. We know, in our inner truth, that this pretense is fraudulent. Two things result from this fraud: guilt toward God, and guilt toward self. We feel guilty toward God for not being able to love God and we feel guilty for betraying our true feelings.

We transfer our guilt toward God to the Cosmos when we first learn about the Cosmos, and before we realize the truly loving nature of the Cosmos. Because this guilt stands as a barrier to all of us who want to return to our natural symbiosis with the Cosmos, it needs to be deprogrammed. The same is true for all of us who want to return to the natural symbiosis we have between our mind and body.

We learned through investigating the source of a sudden very sharp pain in a person's chest that it was caused by another's contriving to love him because she believed she ought to love him, as part of her spiritual practice. Asking the Sage about this phenomenon, we found that her mental love was actually a poison arrow, the effect of which was no different from hatred.[1]

A twofold guilt is produced by the command to subserviently obey God: guilt toward God for not being able to fulfill his commands, and guilt toward ourselves for trying to fulfill them, because in doing so, we betray our dignity and loyalty to our inner truth.

It is our experience that neither the Sage nor the Helpers, nor any part of the Cosmic Consciousness requires any kind of subservience from us. They do not give us a list of rules to follow of what we shall eat, or where and when we shall worship; nor do they want our worship. They do not command us to respect and honor them, or to honor any institution or person, since *any commands* are a parody on our natural feelings of respect. All commands to love, honor, and obey are foreign to the Cosmos, and are sources of guilt.

Our experiences made us aware that there is a great difference between honoring something and respecting it. By honoring institutions and people, we put ourselves down as less than equal

---

1. This phenomenon is reflected in Hexagram 36, *Darkening of the Light*, Line 4, in the words, "He penetrates the left side of the belly and gets to the heart of the darkening of the light." This is a metaphor for saying that a person's heart has not been "in the right place" because he has been acting from thinking rather than from feeling. However, he believes he has been acting from his feelings. Anthony/Moog, p. 401.

to them; when we honor the Sage and Helpers we only distance ourselves from them in a false way. Respect, appreciation, and affection for them, on the other hand, happen involuntarily when we recognize the true nature of the Sage and the Cosmos. This respect is an extension of self-respect.

How We are Made to Feel Guilty for Having Feelings

Obedience is a primary feature of the feudal mindset, whether it be in the West or the East. Obedience is declared to be of first importance: obedience to religion, parents, clan, king/leader, and country. Through giving obedience first importance, our feelings are declared, by implication, unimportant. This causes us to doubt our feelings and to abandon their guidance. The ego aids this process by declaring our feelings as uncontrollable troublemakers that lead us to sin. This creates both a fear of our feelings, and guilt for having them. Consequently, the body is seen as deficient and as a potential enemy.

Guilt, once loaded onto our body cells and feelings, creates constant stress and anxiety. This fact is one of the primary causes of illness.

How Guilt Toward Self was Created

Once humans accepted the conditioning to follow commands and rules, they silenced their own feelings. This left them without their inner system of guidance, which made them look for guidance to human authorities who represented the collective ego's views and values. Since then, they have created fate after fate for themselves.

When fates occur, the ego quickly puts the blame for them on the body as the culprit. The rationale given is that "human animal nature is flawed." This emphasis on the body as "animal nature" comes as a slur, since the invisible mind was associated with a perfect invisible God, while the visible body was associated with a visible animal world that was considered wild and potentially evil. Thus, man saw himself as half God, half animal, with guilt being associated with his animal nature. (Some Greek heroes were thought to have been half god and half human, as a result of a god having copulated with a human maiden.)

Guilt Produced by Slanders on Our Sexuality

As we have noted in our discussion of the genesis of original guilt/sin, an enormous guilt has been put on our sexuality, and through that, on our body in general.

Under natural conditions, our sexual organs receive *chi* nourishment from the Cosmos to renew our life force. When, however, they have been slandered as the "source of evil," and as "guilty," the so-called drives are created, due to the distortions created in our nature.

Guilt is the means by which the ego manages to appropriate the *chi* that flows to us from the Cosmos, when we give sexual expression to our love for another, or when we love ourselves through our sexuality. By declaring sexual love as "lowly," "dirty," and "forbidden," the ego manages to create yet another permanent source of guilt.

The only way out of this dilemma is to recognize, with our conscious mind, the total goodness and wholeness of our being and to deprogram these mistaken ideas about our sexuality, and the guilt connected with them.

How Guilt Toward Nature was Created

Guilt toward Nature is caused by our having accepted the idea that the invisible world is hierarchically ordered, with heaven above, man in the center, and earth/Nature below. This imagination comes from the collective ego to justify hierarchy as a "natural principle." The Bible sets the example in God's giving man dominion over the earth and all its living creatures.

Another example comes from ancient feudal China, where "heaven" supposedly gave the emperor the mandate to serve as the human intermediary on behalf of all humans, between heaven and earth.

Our DNA confirms that we are part of Nature. We also know that we have abandoned our innate sensitivity toward Nature. This creates an unconscious and unrelenting remorse toward Nature, which the ego has converted into a subliminal guilt for abusing Nature.[2]

Nature does not passively accept such domination. While it is willing to cooperate with us so long as we respect it as equal, it resists mightily when we treat it as a mere adjunct to our lives, or when we have the view that Nature is there merely to be exploited. Since we cannot entirely bypass our inner truth, we know the extent of the damage we have caused to Nature through our careless and indifferent attitudes. Not only do we feel guilty for this abuse, we expect to be punished for it, and fear Nature's retaliation. The Sage has made us aware that although Nature is often an instrument of Fate, Nature does not retaliate. Fates are messages to make us reflect on the ego mindset that has poisoned our original symbiotic relationship with Nature. They also give us an opportunity to correct our mistaken views and thereby put an end to the fates.

Loss of Chi *Due to Loss of Symbiosis*

The biggest effect of the loss of our symbiotic relationships with the Cosmos, with Nature, and between mind and body, is that we are deprived of the most primary nourishment of love (*chi* energy/life force) that flows to us from the Cosmos, and on which we are constantly dependent for our renewal. We attract this *chi* from the Cosmos and from Nature when we have a feeling and sensitive relationship with our bodies, which are the receptors of *chi.* This sensitivity and cooperation is the essence of health.

Once humans began to experience the lack of *chi* coming from the Cosmos and Nature, due to their belief in the myths of the collective ego, they falsely concluded that lack was inherent in the scheme of things: there was lack of help, lack of resources, lack of protection, and lack of nourishment. This thinking in terms of lack that caused one tribe to seek to conquer another,

---

[2.] Lipton, Bruce, *The Biology of Belief,* Mountain of Love/Elite Books, Santa Rose, 2005". . .the results of the Human Genome Project are forcing us to reconsider our genetic relationship with other organisms in the biosphere. We can no longer use genes to explain why humans are at the top of the evolutionary ladder. It turns out there is not much difference in the total number of genes found in humans and those found in primitive organisms." Bruce

in order to capture its possessions and resources. All wars have been fought on this basis ever since.

The solution to this mindset of conflict can never be resolved globally. It can only be resolved personally, in the psyche of each individual. This is because it is up to us as individuals to correct our thinking, and thereby correct our primary relationships with the Cosmos, with Nature, and with ourselves.

Shame as the Twin of Guilt in the Far East

Curiously, the feudal societies of China and Japan were not using psychological guilt in the same way that Western societies have done. There, the emphasis has been on shame as the chief psychological tool of control. Eastern cultures shame individuals for "not fitting in," for failing to be good citizens, and for acting outside accepted convention.

A Chinese professor told us that the fact that a person acts outside convention is not as important as its being found out. If an offense comes into public awareness it dishonors not only the person but the entire family and clan in a long-lasting way. Shame, therefore, is a terrible punishment in the East.

This is not to say that shame is not important in the West. It is rather that when shame occurs in the West, it is not a matter of such intense public concern.

Guilt as an Incipient Cause of Illness and an Obstruction to Getting Well

As mentioned above, guilt is the result of the conflict created by our inability to do what the collective ego commands. It is often the first or incipient cause of illness, because these commands disrupt our three essential symbiotic relationships with the Cosmos, with ourselves, and with Nature.

Being unable to comply with the commands, we experience self-doubt. Self-doubt splits the consciousness of the body cells. One part of the cell retains its inner truth while the other part "no longer knows." The part that no longer knows looks to the mind for direction and what it receives is the guilt and self-hatred caused by the inability to feel on command. Guilt and self-hatred, in turn, become the basis for a self-judgment and self-punishment that is carried out by these parts of the cells against those parts that adhere to their inner truth. Many illnesses are the result of this self-punishing process.

Freeing the mind of guilt, judgment, hatred, and the idea of a culprit often leads directly to healing. This means that the mind must first be freed from looking to the collective ego for its guidance, which cultivates guilt. If guilt is left in place, it presents a major obstruction to getting well.

How the Ego Protects Itself through Guilt

The ego does not want to be seen as the cause of illness, because then we will reject it. Consequently, it activates guilt in us whenever we look for the true cause of an illness.

For example, guilt arises when we question the ego's monopoly on "the truth." This truth includes the collected body of scientific knowledge about the causes of illness, which focuses either on supposed defects in our nature, or on "external evils that are attacking us." Completely missing from this catalog of knowledge is any mention of the causes of illness residing in the psyche. Any questioning of the scientific understanding of illness activates hidden guilt for stepping into forbidden territory. The question is immediately put, "Who are you to question science and conventional wisdom?" "People will think you are crazy."

Daring to question often initiates two demonic elements in the psyche that we call the *inner judge*, and the *inner punisher*. They stand within the psyche as representatives of the collective ego. The punishment inflicted by the inner punisher is invariably bodily punishment, either in the form of pain, or illness. The *inner judge* condemns our offenses against accepted knowledge.

By deprogramming the three guilt complexes listed below we remove the basis for guilt, and the judging, punishing demonic elements connected with it.

The Three Main Ego Complexes

Ego complexes are established patterns of ego behaviors and responses to situations. Their names describe the reactionary patterns they have created in the psyche. That they are also a complex of interwoven and interdependent rationales shows the ego's reliance on complexity to rule the psyche, and to make it seem brilliant. By contrast, behavior based on Cosmic Principles is a spontaneous response to our true feelings; it is therefore simple and modest.

Each complex is composed of one or more false premises that fuel a given emotional pattern, or set of responses. At their base, these premises are in conflict with our true nature, and when brought into play, compromise our integrity, dignity, and at times, even our safety. They also inevitably lead us into fates.

In the foregoing we have described the primary components of the ego complexes that underlie illness.

When we examine the psychic components of a long-standing or complex illness, we find that it is run by a number of basic ego complexes. The following three complexes may be among the most important of them.

The Guilt Toward God Complex
This complex consists of three components:
• The commandment: "You must love and obey God"
• Guilt and self-hatred for not being able to love God enough
• Fear of God's punishment

The Guilt Toward Self Complex
• "The mind is superior to the body because it can think"
• "Human animal nature is flawed"
• "Humans are guilty because they have an animal nature"
• "Humans need to redeem themselves by sacrificing their animal nature"
• "Humans need to transcend their animal nature by developing their higher nature"
• "Guilt is part of being human"
All are spells and poison arrows we have put on ourselves.

The Guilt Toward Nature Complex
The following shows how accepting the first false premise

about Nature leads to four false conclusions. They result in guilt toward Nature and fear of its retaliation. All are projections and poison arrows humans have put on themselves and Nature.

- "Humans are the centerpiece of the universe and Nature exists to serve them."
- "Human interests and the interests of Nature are incompatible."
- Conclusion: "Humans must achieve domination over Nature in order to satisfy human needs."
- "Humans are guilty for mistreating Nature."
- "Nature retaliates for what humans have done to it."

When we recognize with clarity the falseness of the first premise, and deprogram this ego complex, the Helpers can restore our symbiosis with Nature, and free all its energies to be of help and cooperate with us. (See Chapter 21. *Methods of Deprogramming.*)

10.

The Origin of the Fear of Death

It is universally held that the human fear of death is natural. However, the *I Ching* shows that the *inner truth* of the matter is quite different. Indeed, the whole question of mortality has been invented by the ego, which is the only thing that truly dies with our "death." We put death in quotes here because, in its Cosmic meaning, death is not the end of life, but is the point where our consciousness, stripped of ego, transforms to the realm of non-form. This transformation includes our bodily consciousness and what we call mind, which together are the whole self. The ego fears death because it cannot continue beyond our life in a body. Its life depends on the energy it steals from our life force. In its characteristic way of shifting Cosmic truths, the ego shifts its own mortality onto the body while inventing an "immortality" for itself in the concept of the "soul," which supposedly can attain immortality through our developing virtues.

Another strategy of the ego to overcome the fear of its death is to seek immortality by being "remembered throughout the ages" whether as a hero, benefactor, great artist, explorer, inventor, or discoverer.

The ego's success is built on making us believe that what we see with the outer eye is "the truth." Because we see the body decay after death, it appears that the body is mortal. Because all things in Nature are made of compressed Cosmic Consciousness, they endure beyond their bodily forms. We know this through our inner truth.

The ego's claim that the body is mortal creates doubt in the child's mind about our eternal Cosmic existence. Once this doubt has been introduced into the psyche, the mind busies itself with it, giving it validity. Our reproductive cells, which, among other functions, renew our life force, are also influenced by this doubt and are partially disabled by it. As mentioned in Chapter 9, doubt splits the consciousness of our individual body cells into two conflicting consciousnesses—one that stays in touch with its inner truth, and one that has concluded it no longer knows.

The thinking mind, meanwhile, having been flattered by the ego that it is superior, encourages the doubting part of the cells to look to it for answers. It answers from the repository of ready-made beliefs it has learned from the collective ego.

It is vital to bring clarity into this confusion because it touches on the issue of death. The ego knows that it is a fictional entity that will be left behind at our death. It also knows, as does our body consciousness, that no part of our natural wholeness (body/psyche) is mortal. Nevertheless, in order to maintain its hold on us during our life in a body, the ego must keep us from becoming conscious of our inner truth; it does this by keeping alive this doubt about our eternal existence. This doubt is the essential error that needs to be corrected, since the undivided wholeness of the body cells means health. When we free ourselves from the ego's fear of death, we become freed of a primary cause of illness.

A further and important consequence of the concept that immortality is attained through developing virtues is the false conclusion that the Cosmos created good and evil. This idea is a ruse to hide the fact that the ego itself *created evil* in the world by giving wrong names to things. The division of the world into good and evil enables the collective ego to identify itself with the "good" and to call "evil" whatever does not conform to its views. We see this division expressed in the ego's categorizing everything as being either good or evil.

To assert its control over the individual, the ego has also divided human nature into good and evil. It has equated evil with that part of our nature that renews our life force, because it is this part that possesses the knowledge that the ego is false. By demonizing our animal nature, the ego has created a perfect hiding place for itself in the mind, which it deems the "good part" of human nature. The ego's language tricks for hiding the fact that it is an impostor in our psyche include a considerable number of such tricks. One of these has led to the creation of what we have called "The False-Dependency Complex."

This complex is one of the most important ego complexes we have learned about, because it is based on ideas that make us dismiss as irrelevant what we know through our feelings. The following three false thought forms responsible for this dismissal are the basis of the False Dependency Complex: (1) "To know the truth, you can only rely on what you see with the eyes." (2) "When it comes to the truth, you cannot trust your feelings, because they are only subjective." (3) "The body has no knowledge of its own, therefore needs the direction from the mind." Under the domination of this one complex, the majority of our bodily Helpers, which are feeling consciousnesses, are disabled. The introduction of doubt in the validity of our true feelings is a blow to the neurons in the brain and in our whole body, since they have been relying on our feelings of inner truth for guidance. It is as if an atomic bomb has been thrown into the still waters in which the neurons have been operating peacefully. The ego uses their shock and confusion to intimidate and imprison them, so that they follow its logic and commands.

The above three statements have a disastrous effect on our mental and physical health, because they blot out the whole system of inner guidance on which the mind is dependent for a complete perception of the truth. Once divorced from our inner senses, the mind is even more influenced by the false ideas that support the ego. The fundamental doubts in the goodness and completeness of our nature create a screen in the mind that intercepts all experiences coming to us, and re-frames them to conform to the ego's language. By such means, the body's natural guidance system is replaced with a mental guidance system that consists of mistaken ideas and beliefs.

The ego claims that the knowledge coming from mistaken beliefs "nourishes" the mind. In truth, the mind becomes starved for lack of connection with its inner source of nourishment, which is accessible only through our feelings. When the mind becomes starved for *chi*, it becomes haunted by the fear of death.

77

The fear of death is realistic in view of this starvation for *chi*.

The fear of death, in turn, propels the mind to find a way to survive. When this happens, the ego is ready and waiting. It points to all the structures it has created for us to depend on. In terms of health care, this dependence leads to further causes of illness, as well as radical solutions that are both unnecessary and cause suffering. (For a description of The False Dependency Complex, see Part IV, Section 10.)

More than anything else, the threat of death brings us under the domination of the collective ego, and causes us to depend on its guidance and its institutions for all our life support.

Part II

Examples of Healing and Explorations into the Causes of Specific Health Conditions

11.

A Healing Language or One that Serves Illness

This section of the book presents examples of healing that we have experienced or witnessed over the last eight years with family, friends and participants in our *I Ching* courses. The examples in this section and in Part IV, *Dismantling the Ego Program of a Long-standing Illness*, will introduce you to how you can heal yourself the Cosmic Way. Before we describe these examples in detail it is helpful to review the all-important role that language plays either in helping us heal, or in aggravating or perpetuating illness.

A Healing Language

Language that facilitates healing speaks of the help that is available from the invisible world: the myriad Helpers in the Cosmos, in Nature, and in the nature of the person who is ill. This language comes from the inner knowledge we have of the goodness of the Cosmos, and of our own nature. It is a language that knows that humans are not the ones who *do* the healing; it is a language, therefore, that stays within the limits of modesty.

Language that heals holds to the Cosmic Principles of Harmony; they are like the North Star that shows us the way when we are at sea. Language that heals does not look for a culprit, even in the ego; it looks for the cause of the illness in the realm of language, images, and thought. It speaks of freeing ourselves from a mistake in our thinking—a small matter that can be corrected with Cosmic help.

The goal of a language that heals is to bring our thinking into harmony with Cosmic language. Harmonious thoughts initiate transformations in the body cells because they come from our true feelings. When words do not correspond to our true feelings, they are felt by the body cells as uncaring.

Harmonious thoughts are the product of the combined perception of all our inner and outer senses. When this occurs, our thoughts have clarity. *Clarity brings a form of light to our body cells, which they receive through their receptors.* When we consciously send sympathetic thoughts to body parts that are injured or in pain, it is this light that ends their pain and aids their healing process. It is the same kind of light we see in meditation with our eyes closed. It is a healing light that creates transformations in the atomic realm of the cells. These transformations contribute to the growing-up or maturation of our body cells. By maturation we mean a stage of transformation, as when a flower comes into its complete form and subsequently transforms into a fruit; transformation occurs again when the seed within the fruit transforms into the new plant.

The Language that Serves Illness

The language that serves illness refers to our bodily functions as mechanical and technical systems. It uses terms that are meant to be objective, but for that very reason are devoid of feeling. In the mechanical approach to the body, the heart is simply viewed as a "pump," and our bodily fluids are nothing more than a mix of "chemicals." The first effects of the language that serves illness are to rule out the existence of the Helpers of our nature and to obscure our knowledge that the body is a living organism of feeling consciousnesses.

The traditional names given to illnesses come from the time of Aristotle and reflect his dualistic thinking. They present illnesses as enemies of the body rather than as messages the body is trying to get through to us. An example is the name "arthritis," which means "an attack on the joints." This image implies that the cause is some mysterious outside agent that is attacking the joints, or that another part of the body may be attacking the joints. The actual cause is usually one or more poison arrows we have put on ourselves. Moreover, giving an illness such a name puts a spell on the illness itself. The effect of that spell is to fix the sick body parts into fighting the threatening image projected upon them.

Another problem is created when an illness is attributed to a false cause, as when science speaks of "bacterial or fungal infections." Such attributions demonize the bacteria and fungi. It would be correct to speak of "infections caused by fear," which is their real origin. (See Chapter 16, *Understanding Infections*.)

Unfortunately, the language of medicine is a language of illness. It has the effect of intimidating us when we suffer from an illness rather than strengthening us. It does little or nothing to educate us about our natural possessions and our self-healing abilities. Medical language describes our body as inherently defective—an inert, helpless entity, devoid of consciousness, that is attacked by organisms that must be "fought," or against which "there is nothing one can do."

Furthermore, the language of medicine unintentionally puts a spell on individuals who are ill by calling them "patients." The word "patient" conjures an image of lying helplessly while one is "worked over."[1] A name that respects a person's dignity would be "client."

Diagnosis and prognosis give a fatalistic tone to medical language that rules out what the Helpers can do when activated. On this account, the words used to name an illness carry a heavy load of connotations and statistics that defeat the will of the person who is ill by stamping these negative assumptions into his psyche.

Some of the more troubling aspects of medical language accompany preventive medicine. Although intended to protect us, this language consists almost entirely of fears and predictions taken from statistics that are constantly being increased by the sicknesses the predictions cause. In fact, these warnings are generally projections, spells, and poison arrows put on our nature. When they are combined with an onslaught of advertising for medications and supplements to prevent them, the result is fear and hysteria within the body cells.

Another negative aspect of medical language is the way it establishes the authority of the medical profession over the person

---

[1] The word "patient" comes from the Latin word *pati* meaning "to suffer," and "to endure." The second meaning of patient is "one who is acted upon."

who is ill. Medical language is based on hierarchical notions that make it clear that the medical profession has been given a certain legal control over us, when we are ill.[2] This legal power causes us to feel helpless when caught up in the medical system, and guilty or irresponsible if we wish to leave it to seek help outside the medical field. This language misleads a person who is ill into thinking that medical logic, with its forceful interventions and use of medicines, is the primary, and only legitimate way to deal with illness.

An important underlying assumption of the language of illness is *that illness is the standard of life.* An example is the thought, "I haven't had a cold in two years." This implies that having yearly colds is the standard. The standard we accept as "normal" for our body is usually far below our body's true capabilities. This substandard view is in itself a spell on the body.

In sum, the language of illness does all it can to prevent the person suffering from seeing or thinking "outside the box" that medical science has devised.

Disharmonious Thoughts Prevent Transformations

Disharmonious thoughts generally come from thinking in abstract terms that are not grounded in the Cosmic reality. Semantically speaking, this happens when a word is taken as the thing itself, rather than being taken as the symbol of the thing. Put in another way, a word is meant to point to a thing; it is not the thing itself. When a word expresses the essence of a thing, it conveys a Cosmic meaning. When words reflect Cosmic reality, they contain Cosmic light, and can therefore be healing. When, however, words are used to create a logic that represents reality incorrectly, disharmonious thoughts are created. We know this through the fact that they are divorced from what we feel through our inner truth. Such thoughts are devoid of Cosmic light.

It is ironic that having the gift of language, we humans use it unreflectingly. We are unaware, for example, of what in seman-

---

[2] It is a fact that followers of Christian Science have been accused of crimes for not acquiring medical care for their children.

tics is called "levels of abstraction." A simple example is encountered when we are infants being taught words. Someone points to mother and the word "Mama" is said. The word is thus associated with our particular mother. Later, when playing with a friend, we learn that our friend has a mama, too. Later, we learn that all our friends have mamas. With each extension of the word, we recognize that it covers more and more people, until the word describes a great variety of mamas. Each expansion of the use of the word creates a new level of abstraction. Later, when we are older, we learn that not only our mama does certain things, such as care for us and our siblings, we learn that many of the mamas do the same thing. If we then think that "all mamas" do these things, we reach a greatly expanded level of abstraction (a generalization) that may not be true at all. The Queen of England, for example, does not raise her own children.

Generalized thoughts are incapable of expressing the essence of a particular thing. Spells, projections, and poison arrows are generalized thoughts that, when put on people, slander their uniqueness. As negative consciousness, they can prevent transformations that would normally lead to the healthy maturation of the cells. Worse, certain parts of the body cells can become damaged by those thoughts, creating a potential for illness. Even though parts of the cells are made dysfunctional by them, other parts of the cells are activated to help heal the damage, unless they, too, have been rendered dysfunctional by other spells.

The four spells listed below are examples of the kinds of mistaken ideas that make our self-healing abilities dysfunctional:
- "In and of yourself you are insufficient to cope with life."
- "In and of itself, your body lacks the self-healing/protective abilities to live life free of illness."
- "There is no help for you from the Cosmos."
- "Human animal nature is the source of evil."

The first spell is directed at the cell membrane, the chief function of which is to protect the cell from the invasion of false thought forms. The second spell aims specifically at the body's natural resistances to diseases, and at its self-healing abilities, by asserting that the body lacks them. The third spell slanders our symbiotic relationship with the Cosmos, thus separating the body cells from their Cosmic knowledge. This subjugates the intelligence of the body cells to the mind, which then falsely takes on the role of managing the body's protection. The fourth spell demonizes our animal nature, specifically our reproductive organs, by implying that being animal makes our whole nature defective. As we discussed in Chapter 9, our reproductive organs, when functioning healthily, are the organs that receive from the Cosmos the *chi* energy that supplies and renews our life force. *Chi* is also necessary for healing. Demonizing our sexuality diminishes our ability to receive *chi* from the Cosmos. *Chi*, we need to remember, is Cosmic love. Being whole and healthy also has to do with being consciously aware that we are a part of the wholeness of Nature, and open to receiving that love. This awareness is damaged when we slander our animal nature by denying that we are an intrinsic part of the animal kingdom and Nature.

A New Look at the Mechanism of Illness

Writing this book was in part a process of compiling materials we had collected on healing over the last eight years. Putting them all together, we could not help noticing that nearly all the phrases behind illnesses had the same two elements implicit within them: self-doubt and fear. We further noticed that the self-doubt and fear had damaged the body cells in some way or another. We asked the Sage, "how does this happen?" To our astonishment, we learned that *all* ailments and illnesses are the result of fear or self-doubt that has entered the body cells. We can understand this better when we realize that all spells, projections, and poison arrows ultimately introduce self-doubt, which in turn creates fear. While a fear may be directly expressed, most often it is only vaguely implied. For example: "If you don't have regular mammograms, you won't know if you are developing breast cancer."

The doubt implied by this statement creates bodily fear, because the body cells perceive the meaning of language differently from the mind. The body hears the fearful implications that breast cancer is highly probable. This causes it to lose its natural confidence in its health, and to fall into doubt. For its part, the mind simply agrees with what has been told by the collective.

We learned earlier that every cell has a complete knowledge of the Cosmic Principles of Harmony; they are included in the DNA. This wholeness of the cells is felt as an unwavering certitude. Self-doubt splits the wholeness of the consciousness of a cell apart. This is experienced as wavering, and "not knowing any longer." The cell's uncertainty about what it knows causes fear in that part of the cell's consciousness that has been split off from the cell's inner truth.

We also found that any statement that is against Cosmic harmony creates doubt, which in turn gives rise to fear in that part of the cell that is still in touch with inner truth. This happens because it knows that part of the cell's Cosmic protection has been lost.

In conclusion, when we continue to think and speak about illness in conventional terms, we inadvertently reinstate one or more of the factors that have created the illness. Often, it is essential to deprogram both the name of the illness, and our identification with it as something we own, or that owns us, as in saying "my hepatitis," or "I have diabetes." Likewise, we need to deprogram any self-image we have taken on in connection with the illness, such as seeing ourselves as being a "particularly difficult/mysterious/unusual case." (Also see Part IV, Section 1.)

Fears that Create or Trigger Illness

The presence of fears is always a sign that a helping function of our own nature, or a Cosmic Helper, is not consciously recognized, and therefore cannot come to our help. The absence of these Helpers renders parts of the body vulnerable to becoming sick. The body parts, knowing they are vulnerable, become afraid. This shows that behind every fear is an unrecognized Helper—the very one we need to protect us from what we are afraid of.

The body cells know precisely which phrases and images have interfered with their wholeness. This fact is of great help when we want to identify those that have given rise to a particular fear, and thus have led to an illness. We only need to ask our body, in a short meditation, to tell us what these are.

The following is a list of the main mistaken beliefs that give rise to fears of becoming ill:
• the belief that we are incomplete in our makeup
• the belief that we are naturally vulnerable to illness
• the belief that there is no help from the Cosmos
• the belief that the body is mortal

In regard to this last mistaken belief, the Sage has made us aware that the body, like all other things in nature, is compressed Cosmic Consciousness. At death, the consciousness of which the body cells are composed is transformed into a non-visible form. The mistaken belief that the body is mortal causes the body cells to imagine that they are thrown into oblivion. This causes them to become frozen in fear when the possibility of death comes near. When we deprogram the mistaken beliefs that have caused these fears, the Helpers that have been blocked or imprisoned by these beliefs become freed to resume their protective functions. (A more detailed description of how to free ourselves from fears is given in Part IV, Section 6.)

12.

Examples of Healing Minor Ailments

The following examples illustrate experiences in healing with the help of the *I Ching*. They are taken either from working on our personal health issues, or on those of friends and family. The initial healings were relatively straightforward and related mostly to what we call minor ailments, although, going by appearances, a few of them seemed quite beyond what might be thought of as minor. A case in point was the illness caused by pancreatic flukes. On the other hand, what we initially assumed to be simple ailments, such as sinus problems, turned out to be more complicated and took sustained effort over a period of time.

We selected these examples because each taught us an aspect about illness that goes beyond the actual example given. We will discuss these general aspects at the end of each example.

How We Proceeded

The reader may well ask how we communicated with the Sage in investigating illness. The *I Ching*, as Richard Wilhelm noted in his classic translation, originated from a practice of asking the Cosmos, in a semi-religious ceremony, questions that could be answered by a simple Yes or No. This original method was gradually replaced by another method which yielded more differentiated answers: an absolute Yes, a relative Yes, an absolute No, and a relative No. In later times, three coins were used to obtain these answers.

Since we originally used this method to clarify the messages received from hexagrams, we called it the "retrospective-three-coin-method" or *rtcm*. In researching illnesses, we also used it to put questions directly to the Sage. (See Chapter 19 for a complete discussion of this method.)

We find this method to be very reliable so long as we approach the questions with a neutral and open-minded attitude, meaning free of expectations (hopes, fears or preconceived ideas) as to what the answer should be. Furthermore, we need to be free of any distrust in the process, because distrust creates aberrations in the way the coins fall. When we are neutral, the coins reflect the inner truth of the matter being addressed. In the course of using this method over many years, we learned that the Sage answers by translating into words what we know through our inner truth (DNA). The answers, therefore, come from our deepest inner knowledge.

In our method of asking questions directly, we use three identical coins, such as pennies. We read the head side as "Yes", representing it with a + sign, and the tail side as "No," representing it with a – sign. Thus, three heads, written as +++ mean a complete Yes. Two heads and one tail are written ++ to denote a simple Yes. Two tails and one head are written - - to denote a simple No. Three tails are written - - - to denote a complete No. A complete No can also mean "you are going in the wrong direction," or "you have already asked that question."

An Illness caused by Pancreatic Flukes

Soon after learning that an illness could be healed by deprogramming its causes, we visited a friend in Munich who had contracted pancreatic flukes during a trip to Africa.[1] She was suffering great difficulty in eating without pain. After our visit, she was to go to a clinic for tropical diseases for treatment.

We hesitated to propose looking into the issue with the *I Ching* because we could not imagine how such a serious problem could be resolved through deprogramming sick-making thoughts. However, during our visit, our hostess related a dream she had the night before. In it, she saw an oval picture frame that had a chip missing. She also saw two Helpers looking at the frame and saying to each other, "This can easily be repaired." Hearing this, we asked whether she might want us to look into the dream as

---

[1] Pancreatic flukes are parasites often found in Africa, where our friend frequently visited. They are very rare in the U.S. The symptoms are extremely uncomfortable.

a possible connection to the flukes. She agreed.

The Sage confirmed through the *rtcm* that we could find the answer to the problem. We were to pay attention first to the oval picture frame. The frame reminded us of those old fashioned frames that held the picture of ancestors. This brought us to ask the Sage whether an ancestor was involved. We received +++. Further questioning revealed that our friend's maternal grandmother, now deceased, was the source of the illness. Our friend then explained that her relationship with this grandmother had been very cold, and she remembered that at one time during her childhood, the grandmother had cursed her in anger, saying, "You little devil, may your life be hell!" The Sage confirmed with +++ that the chip in the frame represented this curse, and that it was a poison arrow. We then asked if this was the only cause of the flukes and got - - .

We were next guided to another incident when she was fourteen. She was to accompany a friend to a party, but was prevented from doing so. The friend, going on by herself, was killed in an accident. This resulted in our friend's feeling guilty for the other girl's death. The guilt was contributing to the illness by weakening her self-healing abilities. It needed to be deprogrammed as a spell. At this point we asked whether there was more to investigate and got ++.

A third element contributed to the illness: her mother had the habit of talking about her daughter's ailments as a way of getting attention from her friends. As a result, the daughter unconsciously became ill to help her mother get attention. She had unknowingly put a spell on herself: "Mother only loves me when I am ill."

A week after all three issues were deprogrammed, our friend was able to eat normally and all her symptoms subsided. She has been free of them since that time, which now is seven years.

Ailments Caused by Demonic Elements in the Psyche

Some minor ailments can be caused by demonic elements. These are elements in the psyche created by conditioning during childhood. Based on fear, they become internal voices that tell us what we must do, and what dreadful things will happen if we do not do them. They are responsible for many of the subtle and barely audible back-of-the-mind thoughts that lead to impulses, drives, and compulsions. They may also be heard as loud and commanding voices that urge us to do or not do something. They may appear in dreams as threatening, commanding and condemning figures. We have called them *imps, demons,* and *dragons.* All of them are, in one way or another, mistaken beliefs "come alive."

Imps replace and repress the healthy functioning of our psyche through back-of-the-mind thoughts of what we "should" think, feel, or do. They dictate the moral rules of the collective, and act as its representative in the psyche.

Demons have the function of supplying the other demonic elements in the psyche with *chi* energy. They steal it from us, from the people around us, and from Nature by instilling fears, or guilt, or by arousing other ego-emotions, such as hatred, vindictiveness, spite, self-pity, and so on.

Dragons are the self-appointed "kings" within the psyche. They exercise a tyrannical rule based on self-doubt, fears, and guilt. The following example illustrates how demonic elements can cause an acute condition of dis-ease.

A Severe Headache Caused by Demonic Elements

A pressure on her forehead led Hanna to the following conversation with the Sage by using the *rtcm*:

Is this caused by something coming from outside?++ From someone in my family?++ Hanna soon identified the person who was the source. Her next question aimed at identifying the nature of the thought: Is it something that puts me down? - - Something that puts me up?++ Is it admiration?++ A demon of admiration?++ Is that the only thing causing the condition?- - Is there more coming from the same person? - - From someone else outside?- - Have I put something on myself that has attracted this demon?++ Is it also a demon?++ An imp, too?++ Does it have to do with having taken on self-importance?++ An imp and demon of self-importance?++ Is anything else causing this condition?- -

Almost immediately after the deprogramming, the pressure ceased and did not return. (For a complete description of the methods of deprogramming, see Chapter 21.)

This case illustrates how admiring someone is as destructive as putting them down. In either case, the admirer is violating the Cosmic Principle of Equality. Admiration does two things: it devalues the person who engages in it, elevating the other; soon thereafter, it creates an unconscious need to look for faults in the one admired, to level the playing field.

This case also demonstrates how demonic elements within us can draw demonic elements from others.

Another example of this principle is the phenomenon below regarding wine. In several cases we found that headaches can be caused by wine that has been demonized by negative remarks.

A Headache Caused by Demonized Wine

On having a headache the morning after having had some wine the night before (without its having been excessive), Hanna put these questions to the Sage: Did I put something on the wine?+++ Did it come from a fear on my part that I might be drinking too much wine?++ That it might be diminishing my brain? - - Any other cause?+++ The thought that it might be addictive?- - Anything about its having a bad effect on my health?+++ The following phrases needed to be deprogrammed as poison arrows: "I may have been drinking too much wine." "Drinking too much is bad for your health."

On a similar occasion a headache was caused by something that someone else had put on the wine. We found that it was the store manager. We asked, did he think that it undercut the prices of the other wines?++ Was anything else put on it? ++ "It's a cheap wine."+++ Anything else?++ "It has no quality at all."++ Anything else?- - The headache in both cases disappeared within half an hour after deprogramming these causes.

Suddenly Feeling Ill Caused by Wanting

On thinking of a friend who was going through difficult times, we wished she would use the *I Ching* to understand what was causing her trouble. When we both suddenly felt ill, we found that this friend had sent us a poison arrow that contained feelings of resentment toward the *I Ching*. The *I Ching* made us aware that *wanting* someone to do something—even if only in our thoughts—is an encroachment into their personal space that immediately arouses feelings of opposition. Our wanting was an implied spell and poison arrow that she was not open to learning herself. After deprogramming our wanting, the implied assumption of her being closed to the *I Ching*, and the poison arrow of resentment coming from her, our feeling ill ceased.

A Stomachache Caused by a Poison Arrow

After eating out at a restaurant, Carol had a stomachache. Searching for the cause, she did a mini-meditation, in which the phrase came to mind, "That is something I would never eat at home." Was this thought the cause?++ Did I put a spell on the food?++ Is the Sage making me aware that those small thoughts cause problems?+++

The stomachache ceased after deprogramming the phrase as a spell. We learned from this and other experiences that comparisons invariably create spells or poison arrows, because they violate the Cosmic Principle of Uniqueness.

Constipation Caused by an Automatic Projection

One morning, Martha found herself suffering from constipation. The day before, she had a cheese sandwich for lunch and pizza for dinner. Investigating the condition with the Sage, she remembered a statement that had come to mind as she was eating the pizza: "Cheese can be constipating."

We have learned that phrases of this sort are automatic projections because they imply a fixed negative relationship, in this case one between cheese and constipation. A remark of this type seems harmless, but it is, in fact, a projection that has a negative effect on the body.

Aches and Pains Caused by Spells Put on the Weather

Nearly everyone will recognize that many people hold beliefs that the weather can cause aches and pains. These beliefs create projections that can make it so.

Carol found that after deprogramming a number of ideas and phrases that were related to stiffness in her back, the condition improved but did not end until she asked, much later, if its persistence was related to this generalized belief about the weather. Indeed, it was the main idea that was keeping the symptom alive.

It was not until we were writing about the case here that it occurred to Carol to ask whether a similar open-ended phrase about weather was related to the persistence of phlegm in her throat. Again, the answer was yes. The phrase turned out to be, "Weather causes colds and sinus problems." She later found a similar phrase which she understood was the cause of other ailments she had in the past, which was, "Weather can create health problems."

Hanna found the phrase in her psyche, "The weather makes you sick." She discovered that it was causing her a slight sinus condition, occasional small arthritic types of pains, and occasional slight headaches.

It is relatively easy to see that associating a certain kind of weather with a type of ache or pain creates a poison arrow, and that the association creates a poisonous relationship between the weather and the body. However, as the above examples show, when a problem such as a stiff back persists in all kinds of weather, we fail to suspect that it can be due to a generalized spell or poison arrow put on the weather. It is only when we realize the far-reaching effect of a non-specific statement, such as "weather can create health problems," that we can begin to ask whether a persisting health problem is due to such a spell. Such spells and poison arrows reveal the kinds of enmity that humans have created between themselves and Nature over centuries.

Many ideas associate specific kinds of weather with health problems: wind, rain, cold weather, hot weather, sultry weather, dry weather, and wet weather. Similar kinds of spells and poison arrows affecting health are put on the earth. An example is when we assume the earth is emitting negative vibrations in earthquakes. When these false interpretations are put on the earth, they actually create a poisonous response. We must not confound the response with what has caused it.

Acute Pain Due to Projections and Poison Arrows

Carol experienced a pain in her leg. Her inquiry led her to find that a projection and poison arrow was coming from an acquaintance who was comparing her with his mother. Carol asked, Is it a comparison that starts with the words, "My mother is also ..."+++ "difficult to deal with?" - - "forgetful?"++ Anything else?- -

Having learned that such false thought forms can only enter the body if an opening for them already exists within us, Carol asked the Sage if there was such an opening within her. The answer was Yes. She then determined this was due to a self-image to which the acquaintance was subconsciously attuned. The self-image was, "I'm not like the other old people because I am not sick." She found that through her boasting, she had also put a projection and poison arrow on herself.

Deprogramming all of the projections and poison arrows put a quick end to the pain.

A Case of Insomnia

While we were writing this book, Carol went through a period of waking up in the middle of the night and not being able to get back to sleep. Her remedy for a while was to get up and consult the *I Ching* with the list of questions that had flooded into her mind upon awaking. The list was usually long, and the time required was one or two hours before she was able to return to sleep. One night she was too tired to get up, but noticed that there was a pattern to these nightly interruptions of sleep: a thought or worry would come to mind, most often about something beyond her personal power to resolve. As soon as she recognized that she was unable to do anything about that situation, another would take its place until she recognized that it, too, was beyond her ability to resolve. On recognizing this, another unsolvable problem would arise, *ad infinitum.*

Carol decided to meditate on the issue to attain clarity about this pattern. In the meditation she saw a fat leech that had fastened itself onto her hand, and was sucking her blood. Asking with the coins, she found that this "leech" was the demonic element that was responsible for the pattern. "Grabber" came to her as the name of this demonic element. The Sage confirmed that it is this element that is largely responsible for insomnia. It becomes active mostly in the night, either to keep us awake when we want to sleep, or to possess our minds when we have briefly awakened in the middle of the night. The subliminal worries, fears, and feelings of hopelessness that the grabber inspires in us are also a cause of hot flashes and night sweats.

Typical things that the grabber brings to mind are: untenable situations that are damaging the environment, wars abroad, disasters, crimes, social deterioration, and similar negative news reported in the media. Other fears are that we won't get the help we need, and fears of the unknown, as in, "You don't know what will happen." The grabber thrives on expressions such as: "There is no guarantee" (in regard to Cosmic help), "Expect the unexpected," "Such and such is ill-starred," "Better to give it up than go through a lot of hell," "One is dammed if one does, damned if one doesn't."

The grabber also foists on us feelings of guilt and keeps us consumed with those feelings so that we will not become aware that guilt is a human-made concept that needs to be deprogrammed altogether. The grabber feeds the energy it gains from our feelings of hopelessness, helplessness, and guilt to one or more dragons in the psyche, thus robbing us of our life force. An example of such a dragon is the phrase: "The good citizen cares, and does something about world problems."

The grabber succeeds by viewing situations from the human-centered view. This view makes us feel that we must somehow *do* something about the situation even though we are unable to do anything. By keeping us focused on what *we* must do, the Helpers of the invisible world, that really *can* have an impact on the situation if we ask them, are excluded. Instructions for deprogramming grabbers are given in Chapter 21.

Cases of Discomfort

John had successfully freed himself from the causes of the restlessness leg syndrome he experienced over many years when he went to bed and tried to relax. Nevertheless, he still complained about its sporadic recurrence. The reason for this recurrence was a curse he had put on the bed, making it the culprit. After deprogramming the curse and apologizing to the consciousness of the bed, the restlessness ceased entirely.

In a similar case, a woman who found herself extraordinarily sensitive to the slightest bumps in her bed found that the cause was her childhood identification with the princess in the fairy tale of *The Princess and the Pea*. This identification was a spell and poison arrow she had put both on herself and on any bed in which she slept.

Disharmonious thoughts affect not only our body, but also the consciousness of the things around us. This can have unforeseen consequences, as these examples show.

Microchips and Memory Chips

A microchip is a traumatic memory stored in the *body*, as in muscle tissues, the gut, heart, and sweat glands. It may manifest as lumps, basal cells, obstructions such as arterial plaque, tics, twitches, involuntary sweating, and similar conditions. While they are basically formed of images of the events, they usually also contain any negative conclusions about what happened, guilt, and fears of similar traumatic events occurring in the future.

We use the word "memory chip" to describe a traumatic memory that is stored in the *psyche*. These frequently accompany microchips. They do not normally cause illness, but manifest in other symptoms such as stuttering, and behavioral disorders. For information about deprogramming microchips and memory chips, see Chapter 21, *Methods of Deprogramming*.

A Basal Cell Containing a Microchip

In a case of a basal cell (a type of skin cancer) we addressed on behalf of a friend, Margaret, we found that it contained a microchip. It consisted of a frozen memory of having had a bad sunburn during her teenage years, her conclusion, "I have permanently damaged my skin," and the memory of having already had a basal cell in the same area of skin removed several years before. Fears of getting more basal cells were projections and poison arrows put on her skin that were preventing the affected skin cells from renewing themselves.

A memory chip in Margaret's psyche was also connected with the basal cell. It had to do with her vanity during her teenage years, when she placed excessive importance on looking tanned. The image of looking tanned had caused her to disregard her commonsense, and allow her skin to get burned.

After identifying and deprogramming these elements that had led to the basal cell, and a number of other components shown below that contributed to the problem, the cell began to shrink very slowly. After Margaret reported that she had been feeling it and looking at it in the mirror, to see what was happening, we made her aware that this activity of the ego was halting her healing. She then said a firm No to the ego's activity and turned the matter over to the Cosmos. Six months later, she happened to notice one day that it had disappeared completely.

In researching this problem, we found that a microchip is the body's effort to *contain* the damaging thoughts, and thereby prevent them from spreading to neighboring cells.

The "other components" that Margaret needed to deprogram were a demon of self-blame, blame she had put on the sun for causing the basal cells, and an imp that reverses cause and effect. She also needed to deprogram the words "cancer," and its association with the words "fatal," and "permanent" (as in permanent damage) because such words contradict and block the life principle of transformation and renewal.

An Allergy Caused by a Microchip and a Memory Chip

Katya, age 13, complained about an allergy that made her

99

eyes water and her nose run frequently throughout the day. The symptom was causing her serious trouble at school and during sports activities. We did a systematic inquiry concerning the time, place, and circumstances to determine the cause. We learned that the allergy was caused by an incident that had happened when Katya was 11. She had been at a friend's vacation house. We asked her if she remembered anything unusual about that visit. Katya remembered two things: having seen a "squishy thing in the pond" that had given her an eerie feeling, and having been hit in her back by the sharp edge of a cabinet door that had suddenly opened. The combination of these experiences had left her with quite a shock. She told her mother about it, and remembered that her mother had observed, "You always get hurt when you go there." We identified this phrase as a projection and spell put on Katya. The spell had the effect of creating a fear in her whenever she went back to play at that house. Her eyes and nose watering was her body's attempt to dissolve the frightening spell. While we learned that her body would eventually have succeeded in eliminating the fear, it was possible to end her suffering immediately by deprogramming its cause.

The spell that Katya's mother inadvertently put on her is an example of a generalized conclusion drawn from a shocking experience. The memory of the shocks, seeing the eerie thing in the pond, and hitting her back, had lodged as a "microchip" in her body, and a "memory chip" in her psyche. Both needed to be deprogrammed. Deprogramming them required asking Katya to bring the events back into her mind and to ask the Sage to erase her memory of them.

Erasing the memory of a shocking event means that the negativity and shock contained in that memory get erased. Katya will still be able to remember the outer circumstances, but her body would no longer be afraid. Katya was freed of her symptoms within a day.

13.

Examples of Healing Long-standing or Chronic Illnesses

While this book has been primarily written for people wishing to heal minor ailments, we include in this chapter examples of long-standing and chronic illnesses that were healed by consulting *I Ching, The Oracle of the Cosmic Way*, to investigate their causes. The reader who wishes to investigate a more complex illness will need to learn how to consult the oracle book. The same applies to dismantling the ego program of a long-standing illness described in Part IV.

We have found that even though two people may have the same illness, the precise cause of an illness is unique to each person. The reason is that the sick-making thoughts differ from person to person. What is similar in both people is that which has made them susceptible to that illness.

What is also similar is the damage done to the psyche and/or body by the basic mistaken ideas and beliefs that are shared by virtually all cultures. Once we have an overview of these mistaken beliefs, which are discussed throughout this book, we possess the knowledge needed to identify them.

When we first began researching chronic illnesses, we thought that the best we could hope for was an improvement in the condition we were investigating. With the Sage's help, however, we found that in getting rid of the offending ideas, the illnesses, in many cases, completely lost their basis. Consequently, we now accept the possibility that with Cosmic help and the person's cooperation, there is no illness that cannot be healed. In those cases where the person is unwilling to give up his disharmonious mindset, or is not persistent enough in finding the various layers of mistaken ideas that underlie his illness, healing may be slowed down, or blocked altogether.

Our experiences with long-standing illnesses taught us that

in addition to the "core program" of the illness, other elements had to be uncovered as well. (For a more detailed description of these elements, see Part IV, *Dismantling the Ego Program of a Long-standing Illness*.) It is necessary, therefore, when we address a persistent health problem, to persevere in our efforts to uncover more hidden factors. We need to keep an open mind to the possibility that with perseverance, dedication, and help from the Helpers, they will be uncovered and resolved. The first case, being that of arthritis, is a good example of the results of such perseverance.

A Case of Arthritis

Mary had been suffering from osteoarthritis for some years, with its having affected the neck, back, breastbone, and various joints: fingers, wrists, elbows, hips, knees, and toes. We continued researching this case over two years in which Mary experienced extended periods that were free of all symptoms. Every time the illness returned, the symptoms were in a lighter form, with less pain. Also, after the first session, the symptoms recurred in only one or two body parts. At each recurrence we found one or more additional causes. This made us aware that some illnesses have "layered causes," and that a deeper layer cannot be revealed until the one preceding it has been removed.

This experience led to our later discovery that long-standing illnesses are kept in place by a whole "program" of sick-making thoughts and beliefs. (See Part IV.)

In our first session with Mary we discovered the following spells she had put on herself as a child:

"Arthritis runs in our family."

"When you get old, you get arthritis."

"Arthritis happens even to the nicest people." "I would not want to be like Aunt V," an admired great aunt who had been in bed with arthritis for two years. Mary's identifying with Aunt V inadvertently projected that she might get it too, because people often remarked "what a nice person Mary is." After deprogramming these spells, the symptoms again disappeared.

When the symptoms returned a year later, we found that the

regression was due to a projection of doubt, "How can it be gone so simply? Perhaps it will come back." This was combined with the fear that she might "do something that would undo the work." At this point, we were guided to call on a Cosmic Helper, which we identified as "the Arthritis Doctor."

In addition, the Sage helped us discover that Mary connected the condition, because it had been long-standing, with an imagined "punishment for her sins for having renounced her religion." She imagined that the inflammation in her joints was a "hellfire" she was being made to suffer while still on earth. These poison arrows formed another layer of causes for the arthritis, which together with the doubt, brought the condition back.

When the symptoms returned again a few months later, we found that they were related to pride in having good health again. Mary had boasted to a friend about deprogramming the illness.[1] This loss of modesty on her part had caused the Helpers of Healing to retreat.

Another idea had to be deprogrammed months later when the condition again returned: Mary had said to a friend, "I got rid of the arthritis." This statement implied that the arthritis was the problem, rather than the mistaken beliefs that had caused it. This shift of focus made the illness the enemy, thus hid the fact that it was actually a messenger telling her that she was harboring beliefs that were in conflict with her nature. It also implied a denial of the role of the Helpers in the healing.

The last arthritic attack occurred a year and a half later. Mary had used the expression, "back when I had arthritis." We found that the name arthritis itself was the cause, since it carried images that terrorize the body cells. Both its medical description as "a continuous deterioration of the joints," and its dictionary definition as "an attack on the joints," were poison arrows.

After deprogramming the name "arthritis," with its accompanying images, Mary was finally freed of all her symptoms.

---

[1] We were led to Hexagram 16, *Enthusiasm (Motivating the Helper of Transformation)*, Line 1, which says, "This line also warns the person, who after being helped, interprets this fact as his being 'favored by God.'" Anthony/Moog, p. 222.

Since that time, more than five years ago at this writing, they have not returned.

In addition to the personal causes of arthritis which were unique to Mary's case, we learned that the condition can be maintained by a secondary set of spells put on the joints by blaming them for the discomfort, and by demonizing them as weak.

Asking the Sage later for a correct name to call the condition, we received "disintegrating influences."[2] The Sage made us aware that this name points to *beliefs* that have a disintegrating effect on parts of the body. Joints have the function of holding together different parts of the body through attraction. This natural attraction was blocked by the beliefs unique to this case. The belief, "When you get old, you get arthritis" implies doubt that the body has the means to stay healthy lifelong. This doubt, combined with the fear of getting arthritis, made Mary susceptible to that particular illness. Her fear was amplified through other thoughts and false conclusions that were added on, so that the cells of the joints manifested the fears into reality.

A Case of Hay Fever

In the spring following our first healing experience, a visiting friend mentioned that the spring pollen had triggered her hay fever. Hay fever had plagued her every spring for over thirty years. Knowing that she might be open to asking the *I Ching* about it, we offered this possibility, which she readily accepted.

We asked the Sage, using the *rtcm*, whether the *I Ching* could be of help. The answer was ++. We then asked if a mistaken belief was the main cause, and again got ++.

The mistaken belief came from an event when she was age six, the year when the hay fever had started. We asked her what she could remember happening at that age. She soon recalled a day when, coming home from school, she overheard her grandparents saying, "How shall we tell the child?" They were uncertain about how to tell her that her dog had just died. The hay fever

---

[2]Ibid., Hexagram 58, *The Joyful*, Line 5, p. 619.

started soon afterwards. It worsened during her adult years when a man with whom she had fallen in love, died. Our friend was surprised, never having noticed the correlation between death and her condition.

To help us understand the connection between the idea of death and hay fever, we asked about the statement the grandparents made, "How shall we tell the child?" We found that this question implanted in the child's mind the idea that death is a mysterious unnatural event that threatens life.

Thereafter, at the onset of spring, when all the forms of new life were springing forth, the experience became coupled with death as a threat. She needed to deprogram her grandparents' words, "How shall we tell the child?" and its implied image of death as a threat to life. The hay fever eased within hours. She has been free of it ever since that time, seven years ago.

More and more we are discovering that the failure of a caretaker to help a child process a shocking event implants a fear in the child that later can be the cause of illness.

Aging
Sick-making thoughts are also the causes of a number of health problems having to do with aging. Growing older is, of course, natural, but the concept of "aging," together with all its negative connotations, presents us with a large number of clichés and beliefs that are spells, projections, and poison arrows that turn growing older into a morass of health problems.

When Carol turned seventy in 2000, she began to experience a number of symptoms: stiffness in the back, neck, and joints, increased arthritis, some hearing loss, pains in certain organs, insensitivity to cold, cuts and bruises taking a longer time to heal, not sleeping as well, and more hot flashes than usual. These brought her to consult the *I Ching* to discover their causes.

She was first guided to do a short meditation about what aging meant to her. The first thing that came to mind was a drawing of the "seven ages of man" she had seen in childhood. This drawing shows an arc representing the progress of a man's life from a small baby at the beginning of the arc, going steadily upward through stages of childhood to full adulthood at its peak, and from there downhill in stages of physical decline to the stoop-shouldered, bent elderly person Shakespeare described as, "sans teeth, sans eyes, sans taste, sans everything."

She also remembered that her older cousin suggested a game of imagining what they would be like when they were age 70 (that being "old age" to them). She remembered descriptions by others of shrinking in height, losing one's memory, becoming infirm and dependent on others, one's skin wrinkling, being crippled and blind, and all the images in that drawing of "the seven ages of man." The Sage confirmed to her that the symptoms people have historically connected with aging were the result of just such projections.

She consulted the oracle and received Hexagram 16, Line 3, which states, "Enthusiasm that looks upward creates remorse."[3] She found this was referring to mistaken beliefs that she had adopted in childhood about heaven: that heaven, as a "heavenly place," was "a much more pleasant place to be than on earth"; "heaven as a place of reward, given by a God who, like Santa Claus, only gives it to good boys and girls"; "when you are old, it is time to start looking forward to going there"; "aging is evidence of your body's preparing to exit its earthly existence."

She then remembered her very religious grandmother's referring to her own body as "these old rags of flesh." In her older years, her grandmother had longed to be "beyond this life," "in the hands of the Lord," on whose side she fervently believed she was in the "battle between good and evil." To her, this life was an "evil worldly place of suffering," while "heaven" was a place of relief and vindication. It was clear that all of these ideas, etched into her child-mind in such a monumental way, remained fully viable despite her thinking they were far in her past.

In her questions about looking up to false images, she was surprised to find that cataracts were caused by this wrong kind of seeing, and with looking for fulfillment in heaven. She also found that it was human projections and spells about aging that

---

[3]Ibid., p. 223.

caused cataracts in dogs.

Line 6 of the hexagram states, "Deluded enthusiasm. But if after completion one changes, there is no blame." Since this line often refers to deluded ideas and images one has adopted, she recalled these ideas about aging that needed to be deprogrammed: the phrase heard from an older friend, "getting old is a case of shrinking options"; the image of her great aunt's husband, who had Alzheimer's; the image of the 80 year old daughter taking care of great Uncle Joe, who was 104; and the memory of a woman in the old folks' home, who, although in perfect mental health herself, was surrounded by older people in stages of mental decline. These negative images and statements had also caused her to conclude, "health problems are inevitable as you get old."

Carol understood that by deprogramming these negative images and expectations, the damage created in her psyche and body would stop. This turned out to be true.

Several years later, when another sick-making thought produced a radiating pain in her lower back, it turned out to be caused by guilt for not having a yearly medical checkup. Other mistaken beliefs, including contradictory ones, surfaced at this time: "your body wears out," and the opposite, "if you don't exercise your body, it will stiffen up." "Everything gets harder to heal after a certain age"; "the bones get more brittle and malleable as you get older"; "your body naturally decays"; "one must accept adversity." All these phrases were false thought forms that project themselves into reality.

Researching the fear, "if you don't exercise your body it will stiffen up," Carol got Lines 1, 4, and 6 of Hexagram 58 *The Joyful*.[4] The hexagram was indicating mistaken beliefs that prevent the enjoyment of life. Here is what Carol learned as she asked questions using the *rtcm*.

Line 1: "Contented joy. Good fortune."

Questions: Is the Helper of the ligaments paralyzed by the above fear?+++ Is this fear combined with the idea that the bones get

---

[4] Ibid., p. 612.

more brittle and malleable as you get older?++ Are these two ideas the main ones pointed to in this line for me?++ Are they both connected with the idea of decay?++

Line 4: "Joy that is weighed is not at peace. After ridding himself of mistakes, a man has joy."

Questions: Is a fear of abandoning a scientific view indicated here?++ Is it a spell?+++ Are there two contradictory views operating?++ Is this inner conflict occurring in the ligaments?++ Is one of the ideas that our body suffers "wear and tear with age?"++ Is the idea in conflict with it, "exercising keeps the bone tissues active?"++ Is the pain I experience a cellular fear of movement as a result of these two conflicting ideas?+++

Line 6: "Seductive joy."

Questions: Is this pointing to a belief I have that is seducing me?++ That you can heal yourself by changing your attitude?++ Is the problem that "changes" only deal with the ailment in a superficial way?++ Is it that deprogramming its causes lead to transformation?++ Is the Helper of Transformation blocked by the seductive idea that changing my attitude is sufficient?++

After deprogramming these ideas, Carol's symptoms went away. It became clearer in doing this work with other people that such beliefs and the harmful images that accompany them become lodged in the body tissues. The Sage led us to call their existence in the tissues "microchips."

We also learned that there is a significant difference between the terms "growing older" and "aging." While growing older is natural, the term "aging" carries with it an enormous number of false associations and fears.

One common fear not mentioned here is the specter of death. We have no doubt that all these fears contribute greatly to the health problems connected with the word aging, and with images that depict death as the "grim reaper." Anyone having these fears would need to deprogram them. (Also see Glossary: Death.)

A Case of the Common Cold

Several experiences have shown us that getting a cold can be a sign that we are "fed up" with living up to a particular self-image.

For example, while writing this book, Hanna felt that a cold was coming on one evening. She asked to be shown in a dream, what the cause might be. That night, she had a dream that reminded her of something she had been told when she was five years old: "Next year, when you enter school, you won't be able to play in the mud with your little friend any more—learning means to take life seriously." Hanna remembered how deeply saddened she had been about this statement, but had accepted it as "that's the way things are." She had also equated it with "that is what it means to be an adult—taking life seriously."

Hanna's dream made her aware that she had developed a self-image of "one who is learning and therefore takes life seriously." Making all learning into a serious matter did not allow for humor and lightness, but made it into something heavy. Hanna had a lot of humor outside the field of learning, which made her wonder why she was not able to express humor in writing about what she had learned. Her dream was so clear and liberating that after having assimilated the message, the symptoms stopped soon afterward. Even that day Hanna felt that feelings suppressed for more than fifty years were flowing freely again!

Since this was not the first time Hanna experienced a cold as having the purpose of helping her shed a self-image, it made us realize that having a cold can often have this purpose. The experience also showed us that the body has ways of freeing itself from self-images that suppress our true nature.

Had we failed to recognize this purpose of a cold, and had only focused on the symptom as a nuisance, Hanna may have got another and perhaps more severe cold to get the message across. Or, the ego in her may have "upgraded" the self-image to a new and more appealing opposite self-image, such as "a person who does not take things seriously."

Another Case of the Common Cold

Up to the year 2000, Ann repeatedly had colds. While recovering from one that year, it occurred to her to research its cause by putting the matter to the *I Ching*.

Ann received guidance to meditate for clarity regarding the source of her colds. In her meditation, images returned from a high school science course that showed microbes being spread in a room by sneezing, by handkerchiefs, and by hand-to-hand or hand-to-mouth contact. Another image came of a teacher saying emphatically to any student having a cold, "Don't come near!" She realized that these images were connected with her body's fear of getting colds.

Ann clarified with the Sage that microbes floating in the air are not a cause of colds. After deprogramming the belief and the images, Ann has remained free of the common cold.

Examples of Phrases that have Caused Colds in Other People:

- "If you don't keep a healthy balance in your diet during winter, you will catch a cold."
- "Whenever something is wrong in a partner relationship, one gets a cold."
- "Colds sneak up on you."
- "Coffee (or tea) takes away your resistance to colds."
- "As you grow older you have less resistance to colds." (Another person found the opposite as cause for a cold: "As you grow older you get less sensitive to cold and therefore get chilled before you know it.")
- "The slightest chill makes my nose run."
- "I get a cold every winter."
- "Colds are unavoidable."

In another case, we discovered that the word "cold" needed to be deprogrammed, because its very mention makes the body feel cold and shiver. A runny nose is another way the body expresses shivering.

Another cause of catching a cold had to do with getting "fed up" to the point of burnout on a situation that was requiring a lot of energy. The complete expression was "fed up to the gills," which refers to the breathing organs of a fish. It thus became a metaphor for something obstructing one's breath.

In general, it is good to give a message to one's nose, "You have all the abilities needed to function healthily."

A Case of Hemorrhoids

Barbara was suffering from both internal and external hemorrhoids. In our first session with her the Sage wanted to address a cyst that had formed in the area outside the rectum. We were directed to look at Hexagram 13, *Associating with People,* lines 3 and 6. Line 3 reads: "He hides weapons in the thicket."[5] We found that the thicket was a metaphor for the tissue surrounding the cyst, and the weapons stood for hormones the ego was using to defend the cyst. At this point, Barbara remembered the words: "Hemorrhoids are hard to get rid of." The Sage affirmed that this phrase would need to be deprogrammed, but that there was more we needed to understand about the inner truth of the cyst.

To understand this, we got Hexagram 33, *Retreating/Hiding.*[6] The obvious question was, "what was the ego trying to hide?" Barbara closed her eyes and asked her body. The words came: "Now I am stuck." In a mind-flash, she remembered repeated dreams in which she had the urge to use a toilet, but the toilet was overflowing with excrement. Through asking more questions, we found out that the statement "Now I am stuck" was referring to guilt of some sort. The hint was contained in Hexagram 13, *Associating with People,* Line 6, which reads: "Associating with people in the meadow brings remorse." The text explains that the "meadow" stands for a place outside the city. This was a reference to the hard cyst Barbara had developed further away from the internal hemorrhoids. We understood that we needed to look for the relationship between the outer cyst and the internal hemorrhoids. The word "remorse," became a clue when we replaced it with the word "guilt." Barbara identified it as "guilt for having hemorrhoids."

The question remained: what had caused the hemorrhoids to begin with? In a short meditation we asked the Helpers to show us the answer. One of us saw a brick wall being destroyed by the Helpers. These words followed: "If you have a predisposition for

---

[5] Ibid., p. 193
[6] Ibid., p. 364.

hemorrhoids, you will have them all your life." The brick wall that had been defending this untruth was the common belief, "Hemorrhoids are hard to get rid of." At this point, Barbara mentioned that her father had also suffered from hemorrhoids and had them surgically removed. She had also considered this option before learning about healing illness with the help of the *I Ching*.

We realized that the mistaken belief, "If you have a predisposition for hemorrhoids, you will have them all your life," had caused the condition. It had been guarded by two lines of defense: (1) the phrase, "Hemorrhoids are hard to get rid of," and (2) the guilt for having hemorrhoids, that was hiding in the outer cyst. Three days after deprogramming the above mentioned phrases, Barbara was free of both the hemorrhoids and the cyst.

Seeking to compare the understanding we had received through our questioning with the Sage to the traditional medical understanding of hemorrhoids, we found the following definition in Dorland, *The American Illustrated Medical Dictionary*: "A pile, or vascular tumor of the rectal mucous membrane." We then consulted the "Wikipedia" (a free internet encyclopedia). It gives an extensive list of possible causes, which include: "genetic predisposition, straining during bowel movements, and too much pressure on the rectal veins due to poor posture or muscle tone, constipation, chronic diarrhea, pregnancy, postponing bowel movements. Other factors that can cause hemorrhoids (mostly by increasing rectal vein pressure), especially for those with a genetic predisposition, are obesity and a sedentary lifestyle." As preventive measures the Wikipedia recommends: "drinking more fluids, exercising, avoid using laxatives, and strictly limiting straining during bowel movement."

The conventional approach paints a rather hopeless picture, i.e., that hemorrhoids, under certain conditions, are unavoidable (hereditary), while under others they must be endured (are incurable). The logical conclusion, therefore is that surgical removal is the probable best solution, although there is no guarantee they will not reappear. The preventive measures, furthermore, require that one constantly pay attention to and disciplines the bowel habits. In this approach, the mind is in charge of the body's functions. The *I Ching* approach frees the body from the slanders put on it, and returns it to its healthy way of functioning.

A Case of Sciatica[7]

Suzanne had mild sciatica for many years. She normally took a mild pain killer, and the symptoms were gone in a few days. On this occasion, she experienced a severe bout. It had been more than twenty years since she had such severe sciatica. After taking a prescription pain killer for several days, she felt capable of working with the *I Ching*.

In the research she did all by herself, she found these elements:
- a "dragon of the mind's superiority" (a self-image)
- a self-image of "the person who always takes care of herself"
- a poison arrow of hurt pride for getting sick
- a spell and projection put on her by herself and others: "getting sick means you should take better care of your body"
- "getting sick means I haven't taken care of my body."

Shortly after deprogramming these items, Suzanne felt fine and she has remained symptom free thereafter. It needs to be noted that usually painkillers are not sufficient in themselves to bring such severe symptoms to a swift end.

More research revealed that the sciatica had its origin at an earlier time in her life when she had been severely ill. The fear of not taking care of her body that developed at that time caused her to make a mental pact to manage her body more carefully. This mental pact was the original cause of the sciatica. The yearly bouts of sciatica arose when she became too busy to pay attention to "taking care of herself," and the realization by her body that it was being neglected. The thought that her mind was superior to the body and needed to manage it caused the body

---

[7] Sciatica is pain along the sciatic nerve, located in the back of the thigh; it may also refer to pain in the lower back, buttocks, hip or adjacent areas.

cells to lose confidence in their self-protective abilities, making her susceptible to the bouts of sciatica.

The severe bout revealed this pattern because it came at a time when Suzanne left her old job to set up a business of her own. The new responsibilities required an intense focus, during which time her "taking care of herself" fell into the background. With the self-image of "one who takes care of herself" in place, concern grew in her unconscious that she was neglecting herself, which was revealed in the phrase she found, "getting sick means I haven't taken care of my body." When Suzanne was too busy to pay attention to her body, the body cells let her know their fear by screaming, resulting in the pain of sciatica.

This example shows the danger involved in turning the job of supervising the protection of the body over to the mind. The mind, through this directive, must maintain a constant inner vigilance, out of fear. The ego speaks of taking *pre*cautions. The body, when not interfered with by the mind, is *cautious* by itself, but does not anticipate trouble. The body responds to the now, as needed. Taking precautions means living in fear. As this example shows, the level of fear, which is being maintained in the unconscious, is heightened by any failure on the mind's part to be vigilant.

The *I Ching* made Suzanne aware that she needed to deprogram one more thing: the mistaken idea that the mind needs to manage the body. With this view, the mind manages the body through its *big programs* of exercises, diet, and disciplined meditation. While holding this view, the mind does not fulfill its natural function of *tuning-in to the body's small needs*, therefore the body's small urges to get up and stretch, to drink water when it feels thirsty, to walk around the house, to stop and clear the mind, are neglected. The body, when listened to in this way, will do all the things it needs to do to stay healthy. What Suzanne finally needed to deprogram were the things in her mental list of what she needed to do to take care of her body.

This experience also points to the need for us to deprogram phrases such as "sitting for long hours is hard on your back/

hips/veins, etc." This is especially important in this day and age when we sometimes must sit for long hours at a computer, in cars, and on trains or planes.

This experience reminded us of other cautions we hear from doctors such as, "Be sure to keep up your exercising."

Confronting these mental programs also made us aware that they interfere with receiving the wonderful *chi* that comes when we walk in symbiosis with nature, feeling its harmonies and rhythms. Instead, we keep up a pace for its own sake, and impose an arbitrary distance "we need to achieve." These and other mechanical requirements remove the possibility of being touched by Nature and all its wonders that can occur when we are tuned into Nature.

Damaged Bodily Functions Being Replaced by the Helpers

When Melanie developed a crick in her back, the *I Ching* guided her to start with a meditation. In it, she saw wounded Helpers, which we found out represented bodily functions. To her surprise, she saw these wounded Helpers being replaced with new ones. As the old ones were recycled in a "fire," they turned into new Helpers. Melanie also saw a whole section of her spine being replaced with new parts, as well as her throat, where there were dysfunctional Helpers.

Asking for an explanation about what she had been shown in her meditation, we received Hexagram 36, *Darkening of the Light*, Line 5, which uses the metaphor of a prince who was held at the court of a tyrant.[8] We then asked: Is the tyrant here a metaphor for the ego?++ And the prince a metaphor for the consciousness of certain body cells?++ Are they the ones that are injured?++ Are they wounded beyond repair? - - Are they wounded by fear?- - by slander?++ by neglect?++ Is this saying that the conscious mind is meant to be more caring and sensitive to the body cells?++ Is the slander "The body is not so important?"++ Does the ego think the body can do anything without any consequence to its health?++ Should Melanie ask

---

[8] Ibid., p. 402.

her body, before undertaking heavy bodily work, "is that okay to do?"++ Does she need to apologize to her body for her careless indifference?++ Is it mainly a matter of gaining the body's willing assent?- - Can she ask the body to answer through throwing the coins?+++ Is there more she needs to understand for her back situation? ++

The new hexagram in the research was #46, *Pushing Upward/Being Lifted Up by the Helpers.*[9] We asked, Are you saying Melanie only needs to ask her body when she wants to achieve something through effort?++ Does it have to do with her being too ambitious?++ trying to force results by a certain date?++ her being willing to sacrifice the body to her ambition?++ Have we understood enough?++

After deprogramming the phrase, "The body is not so important," Melanie's back pain disappeared the same day.

We learned from this experience that there needs to be a conscious caring relationship between the mind and the body. This means the mind is not to supervise and manage the body. When we have the attitude that the body is not important, the body tries to get the mind's attention through pain. The body is our equal partner throughout life, worthy of respect and love. If the conscious mind does not live in symbiosis with it, it can become like sitting on top of a bucking horse.

A Chronic Heart Condition

The following case illustrates how a microchip, made up of fears, caused a heart condition to become chronic. Researching Marilyn's heart condition, the Sage guided us to ask her to make a list of the fears she had about her heart condition. She reported the following:
- "I am not good enough to get well."
- "I might become a burden to my family."
- "No one in my family would get joy out of taking care of me."
- "If I become dependent, they may leave me."

---

[9] Ibid., p. 495.

These fears, while not the cause of the condition, formed a microchip in her body that was responsible for her condition having become chronic.

Before deprogramming any of the above phrases, we were guided to ask Marilyn to do a heart meditation. In it, she was to ask the Sage to show her the condition of her heart. Afterwards, she reported: "The Sage was holding my heart and she said, 'It's only a little boo-boo.'" The huge burden had been reduced to a little boo-boo!

With this reassurance, Marilyn was eager to find the original cause. She discovered that a poison arrow had been put on her at an earlier time in her life: "You don't have good genes; several members of your family dropped dead of heart conditions."

At the point of completing this book, a year has passed. Marilyn has reported the following about her condition: "I am feeling much better. I am rarely short of breath and my stamina is much, much stronger. I am conscientious about healthy self-care: diet, exercise, attitude (no poison arrows!!), etc. I still get tired from time to time - but that's just the Sage telling me it's OK to take a break."

This experience describes, as no other can, the caring nature of the Sage. Where the ego creates a mountain of fears and blames our nature for being "defective," the Sage shows us from the Cosmic perspective how easily a situation can be restored to health.

A Case of Food Allergy

The first allergy we worked with in regard to foods was Carol's allergy to the caffeine found in chocolate, tea, and coffee. At one point she could not tolerate any of these substances. In researching it with the *I Ching*, we were led to recall the many negative statements she had heard said about tea and coffee when she was young, as well as those she read later in medical literature. We found that not only did her body consciousness react negatively to the intake of anything possessing caffeine, these foods also had poison arrows on them, which played a role. After deprogramming them, she no longer experienced

117

any difficulties with these foods.

Food allergies, as defined by the *I Ching*, comprise a number of diseases, such as overeating, anorexia, gastritis, and certain other eating disorders. As the *I Ching* has made us aware, there are different causes for each eating disorder. Each, therefore, needs to be investigated for spells and poison arrows put on foods, and on the person's ability to digest them.

There are many sources of spells on food products. For example some growers put spells on produce when they regard it only as "products" and focus on the money that can be made from them. Disregard for any aspect of Nature puts spells on those aspects that can become a part of a food allergy to the susceptible person. The reasons for a given person's susceptibility, which lie in specific conditioning, also need to be investigated.

Among the common conditioning influences are slanders that have caused the body to be seen as "lowly," "the cause of evil," and "stained with original guilt/sin." These slanders demonize the inner senses, making people develop affinities for foods that do not suit them. Conditioning also causes a person to demonize some foods, and to regard others as special. Thus, when a food that has been designated as forbidden by a religion, although it is perfectly suitable for most people, the prohibition affects the body's ability to digest that food. Moreover, whenever people eat it, they feel guilty. This guilt makes the food poisonous to the body. Such disturbances can all play a part in an *allergic reaction*, or be its primary cause.

Because food allergies are often approached with diets, people begin to micromanage what they eat. This interferes with the body's natural ability to be attracted only to what the body needs. As a result, the quantity eaten is disproportionate: either too little or too much, and often not what the body really needs.

A person suffering from a food allergy may need to deprogram the following slanders:

(1) all poison arrows put on the body (such as seeing it as "lowly," or "the cause of evil," or "stained with original guilt/sin")

(2) the image of guilt as an inextinguishable stain (a spell)

(3) the spell created by calling a food "bad for you"

(4) poison arrows of blame put on the body for "being too fat," "too thin," for "having failed," "looking ugly," etc.

(5) the word "weight" (a spell when applied to a person)

(6) the name that has been given to the illness: "overeating," "anorexia," "gastritis," "eating disorder," "obesity," etc.

(7) the spell and poison arrow, "I have to fight my nature."

(8) the list of all the "forbidden" foods

Another cause for a food allergy can be a lack of love from parents during childhood. Love is important nourishment for the body. When persons are starved for love, the body tries to fulfill its needs in other ways, such as by eating larger quantities of food, or sweets, or foods containing carbohydrates. The result is the buildup of fat. Disgusted with the looks of the body, the child either decides to starve, or to live with feeling guilty for "being fat."

Children who decide to starve send their parents the message that they need to pay attention to them. In so doing, they may have put a poison arrow on themselves by concluding, "I am not lovable," and feeling guilty for existing. Deep down, they have given the body the message that the only way out of this dilemma is to die. Illness can be the first step along this path.

Children who decide to live with feeling guilty for being fat may rationalize that mere body size shows that they are not a "nobody," that they are important and that people cannot just "get by" them.

All the spells and poison arrows created from not being loved, as well as any spells listed in (1)-(7) need to be deprogrammed as well as the spell and poison arrow, "If only I didn't have to eat," with the image of the body as the culprit. (See Chapter 21, *Methods of Deprogramming.*)

As for forbidden foods mentioned under (8) that have caused individuals to put on fat, they need to be freed from the poison arrows put on them by listing them as forbidden. The problem is that they produce guilt when eaten. To deprogram them we picture their names written on a blackboard equated with "you may not eat them" and then see that equation being erased.

When they have all been erased, we ask the Helper of Transformation to transform those foods. In addition, we may need to ask the Helper of Dissolution to dissolve any rigid views of foods as good or bad.

To round off the deprogramming indicated above, we also need to remove the poison arrow of blame put on our body for having failed to have the desired look, weight, height, if these are related to food.

A Case of Bulimia

Ann was a teenager suffering from bulimia. As a child she had decided, "I am not lovable, and therefore I am guilty for existing." Because this situation was so unbearable, she *consciously* gave her body the message to die. However, she felt guilty for this death wish because her parents seemed to do "all the right things." The guilt commanded her to live, causing her to stuff herself with food. The death wish commanded her to die, causing her to throw the food back up. The result was that her body became starved. This would have led to her death had she not been guided to look for the causes in her psyche, and removed them.

To return to health, Ann deprogrammed all the things mentioned above under (1)-(8) as well as the following:
- the spell and poison arrow: "I am not lovable, and therefore I am guilty for existing."
- the spell and poison arrow, "If only I didn't have to eat," with the image of her body as the culprit.
- the spell: "I am bulimic."
- the poison arrow: "There is no treatment for bulimia."
- the poison arrow: "My parents are the culprits."

Another cause for her condition was Ann's comparing herself with her overweight mother. Hearing her father condemn her mother for her looks made Ann conclude that if she overate and became fat, her father would not give her the loving nourishment she needed. Accordingly, the following needed to be deprogrammed, as well:
- the guilt spell: "If I get fat, I will disappoint my father."

• the spell and poison arrow: "I will lose his love."

It has now been two years since Ann deprogrammed the above phrases and the images connected with them. During this time she has not had any repeat of the bulimia, or any of its symptoms. Moreover she has maintained a healthy, normal weight. Ann has likewise stayed with the *I Ching* as a daily guide. It has helped her correct numerous areas of her life that tended to make her feel negative about herself.

The Fear of Death Causing Diverse Symptoms

At an earlier time, before she turned seventy, Carol found herself faced with repeated bouts of an inflamed nerve running up one side of her face, combined with a sore throat. The *I Ching* informed her that she needed to look for an idea that was blocking her inner truth. To find out what it was, she needed Hexagram 6, *Conflict*, Line 4.[10]

Carol asked the following questions:

Is this reading pointing to a fate caused by a conflict with my true nature? ++ It then came to her to ask, Is it the fear of death?+++ And of suffering?++ Is it the belief: "Death means suffering?"++ Having not thought of death for a long time, she asked whether it was an old belief from childhood?++ This old fear was that the body would be eaten by worms and devoured by bacteria; it was accompanied by her body's fear that it would be left behind. Another fear was that death would be accompanied by God's punishments, or even eternal damnation, since her grandmother had described abandoning one's religion as the "unforgivable sin."

After deprogramming these beliefs, Carol gave her body the reassuring message, learned from the *I Ching*, that after death, its consciousness would be transformed without any loss of the sense of self. Within two days, Carol was free of all symptoms. (See Glossary: Death.)

This condition occurred over a period of years before Carol addressed it with the *I Ching*. While it did not fit the model

---

[10] Ibid., p. 135.

of an illness having many layers, we include it here because of the unusual fact that it surfaced late in life yet was caused by a single belief that had existed in her psyche since youth. It is an example of how old fears from childhood that rarely come to the surface of consciousness can nevertheless be the cause of mysterious and persistent health conditions.

Estrogen Dominance

There are times when it is necessary to obtain help from medical professionals. At those times the Sage and Helpers can be of great help as this case shows. Through consulting the Sage at every step we can bring aid to our body cells and keep our mind from wanting to manage things. Before seeing the medical professionals, we can also ask the Sage that is in their presence to bring out the best in their unique skills and talents. This prevents us from giving them final authority over our bodies while they are going through their procedures.

In 1995, Emily made a decision to take Hormone Replacement Therapy after her menstruation stopped. After a few years she discovered that progesterone made her drowsy and stopped taking it. She told her doctors at yearly checkups that she had discontinued progesterone and was taking only estrogen. They noted it and said nothing more.

When Emily moved to a new location and went for a checkup in 2005, the doctor reacted quite strongly when she said she was taking only estrogen. It creates a situation some doctors call "estrogen dominance" because the progesterone in its natural state cooperates with estrogen. In its absence estrogen builds up the uterine lining beyond natural limits. The doctor said: "Taking estrogen unopposed by progesterone causes uterine cancer. You probably have cancer now. I want to run tests immediately." By this time Emily was a student of the *I Ching*. She said an immediate inner No! No! No! to the projection from the doctor, but agreed to the tests.

The tests revealed that the lining of the uterus had indeed built up to an unhealthy level and a biopsy of the lining tissues indicated the presence of precancerous cells. These cells simply have a better than average chance of becoming cancerous, but are not cancerous. The doctor immediately repeated her projection: "You probably have cancer. We need to perform a hysterectomy." Emily again rejected the projection; her body's reaction to having a hysterectomy was also one of immediate rejection. The doctor was adamant, and only on the way out of the office did she suggest that in some cases of precancerous cells one could have a hysteroscopy (a procedure that allows a view of the uterus through a fiber-optic camera) while a dilation and curettage (D&C) is being done to scrape all of the cells out of the uterus.

After this visit to the doctor Emily sat down at home with the *I Ching* to ask the Sage: What is the inner truth of the abnormal cells in my uterus? The first thing she learned was that deprogramming the ideas that had caused the condition would have a positive effect in seven days.

To her surprise, she was to begin by apologizing to the Cosmos for having developed a hardened heart. She did this in a meditation in which she sought to visualize her physical heart. She asked the Heart Helper to help and then saw her heart alone and apart from her. There was a big lock on it and signs were plastered all over it saying "Keep Out," "Go Away," "Do Not Enter," "Stay Out." Suddenly the Heart Helper picked up her heart and gently cradled it like a newborn, holding it and rocking it tenderly, clearly loving and protecting it. Emily was overcome with emotion at this point, and cried. Then she asked the Heart Helper to let her take over; she gently took the heart and cradled and soothed it herself. She removed the last vestiges of all that had been plastered over it, and asked for the key to the lock. She opened the lock and threw it away. She asked that her heart be opened and all attendant *chi* be released as well. At the end she asked the Heart Helper and the Helper of Transformation to help her sustain the openness. The Sage indicated that this meditation was to free the heart's *chi* so that it could nourish and heal the uterus before the operation.

Emily was then directed to deprogram ideas that slandered her body and how it looked, and also a Not-Trusting-Life Ego Complex.[11] Over the next few days she had a number of meditations about cleaning out areas of her body. After the first meditation she had a sense that her uterus relaxed.

Emily was guided by the Sage to schedule a D&C with the indication that the uterus needed to be cleared of the lining. She was assured there was no need for a hysterectomy. She was also guided to get assistance from a friend who is a medical intuitive. Together they prepared the uterus for what was about to happen, telling it that there would be a procedure that would clean it thoroughly and that it was not to resist because the procedure would promote its health.

After seven days, Emily felt very healthy and prepared for the operation. She called the day of her operation "Cleaning Day." When she was wheeled to the operating room she inwardly asked the Cosmic Surgeon to work through her surgeon, and the Cosmic Anesthesiologist to work through the anesthesiologist. An operation that was estimated to take 45 minutes was finished in 20, and Emily left the hospital feeling great. She had no pain at all and very little spotting because the uterus had been prepared.

Two weeks later, the doctor gave her the results of the biopsy on the uterine lining that had been removed. There were no more precancerous cells found in the biopsy. Emily followed the doctor's instructions to take progesterone prior to the operation and for four months after. The Sage confirmed that this would be beneficial to the uterus and ensure that the uterine lining would maintain its healthy status. After four months the Sage indicated that the uterus was fine and Emily has not taken any hormones since. She continues to feel very healthy and has experienced neither the emotional nor the physical side effects that according to the medical establishment, are to be expected after stopping hormone replacement therapy.

When Emily later asked the Sage why no precancerous cells were found, it led her to a deeper understanding of the heart meditation. In the meditation the lock represented distrust in

---

[11] This complex is described in Part IV, Section 10, *Ego Complexes.*

her body cells. Taking estrogen without determining that the uterus really needed it was evidence of that. The key was the act of restoring harmony with the Cosmos through modesty, sincerity and renewed respect for the body cells. This unlocked the *chi* that comes directly from the Cosmos. That *chi* also went directly to the affected cells.

The Sage also helped her to understand that the precancerous cells were those uterine cells that had lost the will to live. When Emily reached what is called "menopause" she put spells on herself by thinking of it as an adverse change in her body. When she agreed to take the hormone replacement therapy without consulting her body, she put the spell on it that it was no longer able to function on its own. This cut her body off from its natural Helpers that would support it and keep it healthy. The heart meditation restored her mind-body connection, releasing the healing *chi* that restored her body to health.

Emily's story is an example of how we may collaborate with the medical establishment when it is harmonious to accept their skills in healing. The conditioning we undergo in life sets up a false program that puts doctors and hospitals in positions of authority over our bodies. We then become dependent on doctors and medicine rather than trusting our inner truth. Emily approached the doctor and the operation from a place of inner harmony knowing the support from the Cosmos was present.

If, in such circumstances we fail to consult our body, we may be led to accept solutions that denigrate its integrity.

Conclusion

Some of the cases described above only involved blocks in the symbiosis between the person's mind and body, or between the mind and a particular body part. Other cases had to do with ideas and images that blocked the body's healing abilities. The case of hay fever demonstrated a disturbance in the Body-Cosmos symbiosis.

These cases demonstrate that the causes generally had to do with mental processes rather than physical deficiencies. These mental processes had in one way or another fixed the psyche in such a way as to make the illness inevitable. They have also had the effect of taking away the person's natural protections, thus creating a vulnerability to illness.

While the cases did not require walking through a whole program of sick-making factors, using that program helps us to discover all the root causes of an illness, and the mistaken beliefs that keep an illness alive. A detailed description for investigating the program of a long-standing illness is given in Part IV.

Deprogramming the causes of some of the illnesses discussed above was simple and led to a swift disappearance of the symptoms altogether. In other cases, as with arthritis, the symptoms disappeared with the first effort at deprogramming, but returned later in a lighter form. Each time they recurred, we were led by the Sage to find more causes. This process continued until the last spell, the name of the illness itself, "arthritis," was deprogrammed.

In other cases, the end of the illness came only when the fears of "never getting rid of it," and of "always being subjected to this condition" were deprogrammed. We found that the fear that a condition may be hopeless is a major cause of its continuance. This fear particularly needs to be deprogrammed for people diagnosed with illnesses that have been pronounced "incurable."

In the meantime, we have learned that some conditions return through guilt that sets in for having rejected the sick-making beliefs. This guilt, too, can be deprogrammed.

We now understand that some long-standing conditions have layers of causes that can only be uncovered in intervals, and in an order that keeps them from being reinstalled. Therefore, the guidance of the Sage is indispensable in uncovering these layers, for the Sage guides us to look at them in the order that avoids these problems.

14.

Illnesses caused by Outside Influences

In Chapters 12 and 13 we focused on ailments and illnesses resulting from a person's own mistaken ideas and beliefs. Here, we focus on conditions of ill health caused by what we call "outside influences." These are negative thoughts or statements coming from someone other than ourselves which are projections, spells, or poison arrows. They may be attributes or conclusions one person makes about another, or about his nationality, class, or race. Such thoughts commonly circulate among family members, friends, and fraternal groups, but they also may originate in publicly-made dire predictions of illnesses that threaten a whole nation, or the health of particular groups of people.

Because individuals who are the objects of these thoughts become ill through no fault of their own, they are described in the *I Ching* as having "undeserved misfortune." Since the harm is undeserved, they automatically receive Cosmic help.[1]

It needs to be added that all such sick-making thoughts that harm others create a fate for the person who thinks them. The fate can be ended by recognizing the mistaken beliefs behind the predictions, and deprogramming them. Doing so automatically frees the person affected from his condition.

Chronic Illnesses

Poison arrows put on a person by someone else, sometimes as early as *in utero,* cause many chronic illnesses. Generally speaking, there is no reason for the damage caused by this poison arrow to lead to a chronic condition. That it has become chronic is due to other spells or poison arrows that have been

---

[1] Hexagram 25, *Innocence,* Line 5 says: "Use no medicine in an illness incurred through no fault of your own. Once you ask for help, it will pass of itself." Ibid., p. 304.

added later. An example of such an additional spell is the idea of "original sin/guilt," which injures the person's self-healing abilities. (See *Glossary*: Guilt.)

Thus, when looking for the original cause of a chronic condition, we first ask the Sage if it is due to a poison arrow coming from outside. If the answer is Yes, we then ask whether any spells and/or poison arrows have been added, either by ourselves, the people around us, or by the medical profession. Common among these additional statements is "it is hereditary," or "it runs in our family." It is true that genetic damage can occur to a family's genes if someone in a previous generation has put a spell or poison arrow on the whole family. What makes the damage lasting is the implication that "because it is hereditary, *there is nothing you can do about it*." This implication creates a spell, as does any phrase that gives the impression that "there is nothing that can be done." The spell creates a fear that prevents recovery. The *I Ching* makes it clear that removing the spell and fear, along with the original poison arrow, through deprogramming them, restores the gene(s) to health.

How to Free Ourselves from a Chronic Illness

When we want to free ourselves from a chronic illness, we first need to ask, using the *rtcm*, whether we can simply follow the procedure described below. If the answer is No, we can ask whether the illness needs a more thorough investigation, such as the one described in Part IV, *Dismantling the Ego Program of a Long-standing Illness*.

If the answer is No again, it may indicate that we have doubts about the effectiveness of the approach presented here. Common doubts are, "How can deprogramming help, if nothing else has been able to help me?" and "The approach presented here is not scientifically proven." If we are willing to free ourselves of such doubts, we can deprogram them by using a "bag meditation" as described in Chapter 21, *Methods of Deprogramming*.

If the Sage says Yes to the first question, we can use the following shortcut procedure to find the cause of the illness. We first ask the three basic questions: *From Whom, What, When.* It may help to start with the **When** question because some poison arrows may originate several generations back.

Using an example of an illness that has been called hereditary, we can ask, *did it come from someone in my grandparents' generation? Further back? Two generations back?* Etc. Often the circumstance of its origin is known in the family because it is connected with a deed that was blatantly wrong, or with a perceived injustice that occurred to someone in the family. The words making up the poison arrow may have been pronounced by the wrongdoer or by a bystander. They amount to a curse that affects all future generations of that family until they are deprogrammed by one member. Such a curse is always accompanied by *guilt* that is put on the next generations. Individuals belonging to that family may have been wondering about a mysterious feeling of guilt they have been carrying around.

To deprogram the cause of a chronic illness that has resulted, we do the following deprogramming exercise:

(1) We ask through the *rtcm* whether there is a spell of "original guilt/sin" involved. If Yes, we follow the instructions in Chapter 21, *Methods of Deprogramming.*

(2) We next deprogram the spell "It is hereditary, and there is nothing that can be done about it," using the water meditation described in that chapter.

(3) Lastly, we say No three times to the originator's encroachment into our psyche and into the psyche of every family member. We also deprogram the poison arrow. We then ask the Sage and the Cosmic Helpers to free us from all its effects. Finally, we ask the Helper That Frees People from Guilt to free all the people concerned from the guilt that is part of the poison arrow.

This exercise is repeated daily until the Sage confirms that we can stop. We then thank the Sage and the other Helpers.

Food Allergies Caused by Outside Influences

In Chapter 12 we mentioned that negative thoughts projected onto foods or drinks had caused food allergies. Below, we list the kinds of sick-making thoughts that we have found to be put on food and drink by someone other than the consumer, such as by the producer, distributor, retailer, a person in the consumer's family, by conventional thinking, or by religious taboos.

The following cases are mostly taken from our personal experience. The results of deprogramming the sick-making thoughts often occurred instantly, but never took longer than an hour.

Examples of spells and/or poison arrows created by thoughts or statement:

- Statements that reduce a product to a means to make big money: "This wine will bring us a big chunk of money."
- Statements that turn a product into a cause of ill-health: "This product will make people addicted," or ""You'll get sick from eating that meat."
- Snobbish statements that denigrate a valuable product by calling it "cheap."
- Statements by a producer or retailer that imply a product succeeds only because of its brand name.
- Statements that demonize a food: "Coffee is bad for you."
- Sweeping statements: "Everything needs to be well cooked."
- Religious taboos: "You must not eat..." or "If you eat..., you will burn in hell." (Connecting the consumption of the product with a terrible threat for one's well-being.)
- Statements that forbid consuming a food or drink, causing it to become irresistible and addictive.

Instructions for deprogramming any of the above sick-making causes are in Chapter 21, *Methods of Deprogramming*. The *rtcm* can be used to find out which deprogramming method is appropriate for each thought.

A Toenail Infection

Deirdre shared the following healing experience with us after taking one of our healing courses:

"In the fall of 2005, I noticed an odd discoloration of my toenail on the big toe on my right foot. At first I thought it was a bruise but it got darker and more discolored rather than returning to normal. By December I noticed the nail was not growing. After some investigation via the internet, the conclusion was "nail fungus." All I knew about this condition was it could be difficult to treat.

"My mother has had this condition for several years now. She has used all the pharmaceutical drug treatments, to no avail.

"Several months passed and my nail continued to darken and was inflamed at its base. From the local holistic pharmacy I bought a tea tree/lavender essential oil blend, and apple cider vinegar, both of which are traditionally recommended in a holistic treatment approach. Before using either, though, I checked with the Sage via the *rtcm*: Is it appropriate to use these treatments for the nail? The Sage replied with a definite No. Should I apply anything or take anything internally? Again the reply was a definite No.

"At this point I asked for a hexagram to understand the Cosmic view of the condition. From it I learned that having used a particular antifungal in November had shifted the fungal imbalance from my chest to my toe, driving it deeper into my system. I also found that because I had not been aware of my self-healing abilities, I had disabled them. This blotting out of my inner Helpers was part of a larger pattern I had of blaming Nature for everything that went wrong in my life, including a blockage in my marriage. The Sage indicated, however, that these blockages were really due to my shutting out my feelings and getting stuck in my rational thinking.

"The Sage also pointed to Hexagram 25, *Innocence*, Line 5: 'Use no medicine in an illness that is not your fault.'

"The commentary continues, 'This line is saying that the illness a person is suffering has been caused by a poison arrow coming from someone else, either in the past or in the present, in the form of one or more negative thoughts. When he receives this line, he does not need to identify the thoughts, but only find out who put the poison arrow on him, say the inner No to that person, and then ask the Sage and the Helpers of the invisible world to eliminate it.'

"This was a simple and direct communication. The root of my condition was a poison arrow, the source of which I verified with the *rtcm*. I said the inner No to this person and asked the helpers to continue their healing process with my toe, and any other area of my body or psyche that may have been damaged by this poison arrow.

"I occasionally checked in with the Sage as to whether I should apply any treatments and consistently got a clear No. Finally I realized that the Helpers were handling things and I could trust that and stop asking!

"In June I began to notice the nail was different. The middle section was still discolored but the top of the nail, and the lower third were now a lighter, more normal color. Gradually the middle section decreased, and by July I noticed the nail was slowly growing out a bit. I had not trimmed that nail in a year.

"I also worked on my self-healing capacity and deprogrammed obstructions I later found that were blocking the Helpers that were important to my overall healing process.

"In this regard, I found that a threat of punishment was involved dating back to seizures of epilepsy as a child.

"The seizures occurred because I had concluded that my feelings were dangerous to the household order, and that there was not room in the family for them to be expressed. I feared that something awful (abandonment or death) would happen if I felt, knew, or expressed my true feelings. Instead of feeling, I learned to shut down, and literally would faint and black out at unusual times. I had also concluded that life was definitely not safe, and my feelings were what drew the danger. Hence I developed a whole other way of relating to my world and life to create a sense of safety. It was to rely only on rational thinking.

"I still wanted to check the progress periodically, and had to remind myself that the Helpers were handling this and I didn't need to supervise or follow up. This need happened less after I deprogrammed the doubt I had.

"My conclusions had slandered the Cosmos and Nature, including my own nature. They were spells and poison arrows that had made my self-healing abilities non-functional."

By the time this book was printed, the nail was not fully healed. As Deirdre reported, "the lower quarter of my nail has risen off the nail bed and a healthy new nail is growing underneath. It appears to be pushing the old nail off the nail bed at the pace at which a nail grows, i.e., slowly."

This experience shows how a simple health problem that could be healed swiftly, because it was due to a poison arrow coming from outside, can develop into a long-standing condition when we blame Nature for the problem, as Deirdre had done. It also shows a common mistaken attitude toward fungi that will be examined in Chapter 16. In this particular case, Deirdre did not need to identify the content of the poison arrow. It is important during one's investigation to ask, using the *rtcm*, whether the content of the poison arrow needs to be identified.

15.

Causes for Other Health Conditions

In this chapter we present additional health conditions we have encountered and what we learned about their causes, even though we were not always engaged long enough to learn the outcome. We include them to broaden the reader's understanding. The symptoms investigated are listed in alphabetical order.

While we give information regarding the sick-making thoughts that needed to be deprogrammed in the specific cases listed, the reader needs to do his own investigation to find the sick-making thoughts that apply to the issue he seeks to understand, since the causes are unique in each case. We give instructions for deprogramming in Chapter 21.

Heart Palpitations: For an adult man with heart palpitations we found that they were caused by a memory chip. It contained the memory of the smell of the paper store in which his first school books were bought. This smell had been combined with the terror of authority instilled in him when he first went to school. Later in his life, the man developed heart palpitations whenever he came in contact with that odor, and also when he was confronted with educational and other institutions that represented authority to him. The fact that he had become a professor did not protect him from that terror as long as it was stored in the memory chip. To our surprise, we also found, as part of the memory chip, a projection and poison arrow the man had put on himself: "My only protection is to become a professor myself." The *I Ching* shows us that true protection comes only from the Cosmos. We lose it when we think that we can protect ourselves.

We were first made aware of this man's heart palpitations when we accompanied him to a paper store that incidentally had the same smell as the one in his childhood. Through the *rtcm*, we found that this smell triggered the heart palpitations. We further learned from the *I Ching* that his inner sense of smell had been made dysfunctional by his terror of authority. Because the man was a guest who was only passing through, we were not able to complete the deprogramming with him.

High Blood Pressure: High blood pressure can indicate that a person's body cells have been made unable to process sunlight, which is necessary to produce nourishing *chi* energy for all body and brain cells. The processing of sunlight occurs through photosynthesis in the cells, as we know from plant biology.

This disability is due to spells or poison arrows put on the person's bodily nature by sayings, such as:
• "Human nature is divided into good and evil"
• "Human nature is defective"
• "Humans have a lower and a higher nature, with the higher nature needing to be developed, and the lower nature needing to be suppressed or overcome."

The person needs to find out which of the above spells or poison arrows he has accepted into his psyche, and deprogram them. This is not to say that all people who have these spells put on their nature suffer from high blood pressure. The effect of spells may show in many forms.

Hot flashes: Hot flashes are due to subliminal worries, anxiety, fears, shame, and feelings of hopelessness. Hot flashes and nightly sweats can occur both in women and men. They are primarily a response of the psyche to the activity of a demonic element called a "grabber."[1]

The hot flashes connected with menopause can be caused by slanders such as "the body is a bother and nuisance." The hot flashes are "floods of tears" the body sheds for all the slanders that have been put on it, and for its inability to cope with all the things we ask it to endure. Each slander is contained in a mi-

---

[1] For a more detailed description of the grabber see Appendix 2: *Demonic Elements in the Psyche that Cause Illness.*

crochip that also contains self-blame. Another example of such a slander is the poison arrow, "the body is a set of mechanics." (Other causes of issues that can arise in menopause are described in a separate entry below.)

Hot flashes in a man can result from questioning the purpose of his life. Doing so creates an anxiety that he may die without having found his life's purpose. When examining his respective thoughts, he first needs to look for any guilt for things he may have done in his life. (See Glossary: Guilt.) He also needs to understand that the word "purpose" implies fulfilling a self-image garnered from the image book of the collective ego. The *I Ching* makes us aware that the true purpose of our life is to fulfill our uniqueness. No special intention is needed.

In an actual case, the hot flashes a man was experiencing came from a memory chip of having been intimidated in youth by playmates who were from an upper class position, who made him feel inferior. From that time on the memory chip came into play whenever he was in the company of persons whom he saw as superior to him. The memory chip caused him to constantly see himself through their eyes as evaluating him, and making him feel embarrassed about his supposed inferiority. To free himself, he deprogrammed the memory of the original incident, the image of himself as inferior, and the fear of being put down.

Menstruation Pain: Most pre-menstrual or menstrual pains are cries of alarm to make us aware of the presence of one or more projections, spells, or poison arrows in our psyche. The sick-making thoughts are to be found in the area of mistaken beliefs about womanhood, and include curses. Examples: "menstruation is a curse put on all women"; the image of menstruation being connected with original sin; "women are inferior to men"; "during menstruation women are more powerful; they can do irrevocable harm to men"; "menstruation is dirty, despicable"; "women should be segregated during their menstruation." All these phrases, can cause pre-menstrual pain or cramps during menstruation, or too much blood flow.

Menopausal Troubles: The word "menopause" is an example of the creation of words that make no sense. The word "pause" suggests that menstruation has come to a pause, but will be resumed at a later point in time. This is obviously incorrect, because menstruation is coming to an end, even though haltingly. The correct name would be "completion of menstruation," meaning that menstruation has completed its function in the life of a woman. The word "menopause" needs to be deprogrammed as a spell, because it is an incorrect description of a natural process.

Other disturbances are created by worries: the worry of losing one's childbearing function, of no longer being seen as a "functioning woman," of becoming unattractive to men, of approaching death, and the like. All these worries are mental images projected onto the body as "a problem." In reality, these images are slanders to which the body responds with illness, or symptoms of ill-health, all of which show the power of disharmonious thoughts.

Yet other problems are caused by the regret of not having given birth to a child. Such regrets often come from thinking that "a woman is only a real woman when she has had a child" (a poison arrow). Such an idea is a standard put on women by conventional thinking; it is not in harmony with Cosmic standards. The Cosmic standard for a woman, just as for a man, is to bring to expression her uniqueness; it is not that of fulfilling a role given to her by society.

All worries and mistaken ideas about a woman's role need to be deprogrammed with Cosmic help, because they interfere with the ability of the body to complete the transformation of a natural function of the body, i.e., reproduction.

Another cause of menopausal troubles are worries or regrets a woman has about not having found her life's purpose. This is often true for women who have considered their only purpose in life to be bound up in their role as a mother; menopausal trouble may arise when their children are grown up and leaving home. Thoughts such as, "it is too late for me to do anything worthwhile with my life," give rise to hopelessness. Such thoughts need to be firmly rejected and deprogrammed, otherwise they may lead to serious illness.

A mistaken belief that exists in some schools of Chinese medicine is the idea of treating an imbalance of Yin and Yang in menopausal women by "balancing" them. The *I Ching* makes it clear that it is not a matter of balancing, but of *harmonizing* them. Yin and Yang are names for the dark and the light that together make up *chi* energy. However, they have been given a large number of false connotations by the Yin-Yang School of China, which concluded that the light and the dark were *opposite* forces, and that all things in the universe can be categorized in terms of opposites.

Trying to balance Yin and Yang does not solve the problem, and can actually add to it, since seeing them as "opposites" causes them to fight each other. The dark and the light are the two *complementary* aspects of *chi* that through complementing each other bring about transformations. The dark and the light return to harmony when the wrong mental ideas projected upon them are deprogrammed.

Bipolar Disorder: Although mental disorders are not the subject of this book, the Sage wanted us to mention this disorder here. It is the result of the attempt on the part of the person who is suffering from a spell, to counter its effect by putting another spell on himself. Example: The original spell may be the statement: "I was born defective." The counter-spell is, "I have to prove that I am worthwhile." The existence of these two spells in his psyche throws him from one extreme to the other— from despair to ambitious striving. This condition can be remedied by deprogramming both spells; however, other spells that have been added as a result of the condition also need to be identified and removed.

Migraines: Migraines are long-standing conditions that run on a more complex mental program than acute headaches which are caused by a single projection, spell, or poison arrow. In addition to a primary cause, the program also contains a secondary cause consisting of fears.

One primary cause is false sympathy for someone else who is sick. False sympathy means that one person sees another as helpless. He "wracks his brain" about what may be causing the other's condition, and what needs to be done about it. This worrying is caused by a rationalizing demon that has been re-playing the same thought over and over, causing the pain in a synapse in his brain. In addition to killing the demon, he needs to deprogram the negative thoughts he is projecting onto the sick person by seeing him as helpless.

Another primary cause occurs when a person suffers from guilt whenever his true feelings do not conform with what he is expected to think, feel, or do. This guilt also prevents him from saying an inner No to inappropriate expectations. Getting a migraine gives him an excuse to not have to conform to what is expected of him. Using the migraine in this way leads to its becoming a chronic condition.

Often what prevents a person from saying an inner No is the self-image of the "good son/daughter," who is rewarded for not saying No. Deprogramming that self-image can free up the person's ability to say an inner No to all situations in which his feelings say No to expectations put on him by others. Saying the inner No provides him with an inner protection.

Another case is that of a person who wants to free himself from guilt. Because he has been taught that his animal nature makes him guilty, he believes that the problem can be resolved by leaving behind his animal nature through becoming a spiritual person. The migraines he experiences are triggered by the fear of dying before having completely freed himself of his guilt, and of having to burn in hell forever. A demonic element called the "changeling" is involved that drives him ever further away from his connection with his body.[2] His striving to overcome his bodily nature causes his body cells to fear that they will be sacrificed. In this situation he needs to deprogram: the concept of guilt; the spell, "I am guilty because I have an animal nature," together with the image of hell fire; the poison arrow, "to free myself from guilt, I have to overcome my animal nature;" the self-image of the spiritual person; and the changeling.

A migraine can also be caused by a person's guilt for having done something and believing that he cannot free himself of its taint. He may feel indebted to the one he wronged, or have feelings of guilt of an undefined nature. This creates the fear of "being stuck forever." This fear gives a demon free room to replay over and over the thought of having wronged someone. Often, this replaying goes on in the subconscious, or in the back-of-the-mind, so that it is only barely noticeable. The result, in either case, is the migraine. To free himself, he needs to deprogram: the concept of guilt, feelings of guilt for what he has done, and any self-blame spells or other projections or poison arrows he may have put on himself, such as, "I can never be forgiven," or "I deserve to be punished." In addition, he needs to apologize to the Cosmos for his deed.

A migraine can also be caused by a person's feeling wrongly indebted to his parents for his life. This makes him feel guilty for never doing enough to pay them back, although he constantly tries to do so. It is as if he were walking on a treadmill; it is this treadmill that is causing the migraine. At the same time, the migraine serves to "protect" him from having to do ever more. The *I Ching* refers to this kind of situation in Hexagram 21, *Biting Through*, Line 6, as "His neck is fastened in a wooden cangue, so that his ears disappear." [3] (The explanation given in this line is that the wooden cangue is a means by which the Cosmos forces us to look within our own psyche for something that causes us to act compulsively against our own nature.) The person with the migraine needs to look for a poison arrow put on him from outside. While the cangue is in effect, it prevents him from doing more harm, both to himself and to the Cosmos through his compulsive actions. To free himself he needs to deprogram the concept of guilt, and the poison arrow, "You owe your life to your parents, and you can never do enough to

---

[2] For a more detailed description of the changeling see Appendix 2: *Demonic Elements in the Psyche.*

[3] Anthony/Moog, p. 272.

pay them back." The *I Ching* makes us aware that the idea that children owe their lives to their parents comes from the collective ego. Even the Cosmos does not hold it to be a debt that it has given a person life.

In another case, the guilt a person feels draws others to take advantage of him. The dynamic works as follows: the guilt creates a hole of insufficiency in him that makes him want to fill it. Others sense this and seek him out to enlist him in their projects, and to do work that will add to their ego's claims of achievement. Having this pressure put on him thrusts the person into an inner conflict, because there are others, too, who would also need his help, but he cannot satisfy everyone's demands. This inner conflict of loyalty to one that cannot be extended to an equally deserving other causes a situation of despair because whatever he does, he only creates more guilt. This is another case in which the migraine "protects" him from "having to do it all." Such a person needs to free himself from the concept of guilt, and to say the inner No to expectations put on him, and to his belief that he is unworthy unless he serves others.

Still another cause for a migraine can be the spell and poison arrow, "Only a miracle can save me." This mistaken belief keeps us waiting for a miracle instead of asking for help.

Paralysis Affecting a Nerve: The nerves are part of our body's protective system and are directly connected with certain inner senses, which the *I Ching* calls our "metaphorical senses." By that we mean, for example, our sense of simplicity, our sense of caution, our sense of what is appropriate and fitting, as well as many other metaphorical senses mentioned elsewhere in this book. All these senses are part of our animal nature. When our animal nature has been demonized by spells or poison arrows (i.e., "our animal nature is evil, or the source of evil," "our animal nature is our lower nature," and "we are guilty because we have an animal nature") our metaphorical senses are rendered dysfunctional. The *I Ching* describes this condition as, "A one-eyed man is able to see. A lame man is able to tread." The word "lame" indicates that one or more of the person's metaphorical senses are paralyzed.[4] When not paralyzed, our metaphorical senses guide us safely through every situation without the necessity to think through each step. When they are paralyzed, we are forced to rely only on thinking to make our way through life. This means we lean on the rules provided by society. Since every life situation is unique, rules are hardly ever truly appropriate to any situation. Furthermore, when we relate to situations in a way that is crassly inappropriate, we create a fate. The fate can come in the form of a paralysis affecting a nerve. It can be ended by deprogramming the poison arrows that have paralyzed the metaphorical senses in question.

Paralysis Affecting a Muscle: Paralysis of a muscle can be caused by the paralysis of the metaphorical senses of danger and appropriateness. When functioning normally, these metaphorical senses have a direct connection with all the muscles throughout the body. We recognize this in "body language." When these senses are healthy, our body language is totally appropriate to the situation; when not, we behave awkwardly or inappropriately. Our natural impulse to flee or to withdraw from a dangerous situation is also a direct expression of the guidance we receive from these metaphorical senses. However, when we adopt the poison arrow that "our bodily nature is defective," our sense of danger becomes paralyzed. When we adopt the belief, "You need moral rules to define appropriate conduct," our sense of appropriateness becomes paralyzed by that poison arrow because it denies that we know through our natural makeup what is appropriate conduct. When we conduct ourselves according to moral rules we are likely to create fates. The paralysis of a muscle can be such a fate. Deprogramming the poison arrow that has paralyzed the metaphorical sense in question ends the muscle paralysis.

Parkinson's Disease: When a close relative showed symptoms of trembling on reaching his late seventies, we asked the Sage if

---

[4] Ibid., Hexagram 10, Line 3, p. 172.

we were permitted to look into the cause and deprogram it on his behalf. The answer was Yes.

The cause was an incident when he was age 17, and his father put him in charge of a section of workers in his business. During this time an older worker, insulted at having someone so young put over him, and who could report his performance to the boss, threatened to kill him and his father if the young man ever said anything bad about him. That experience, together with his mother's comment, "Be careful, one day he might succeed," settled into his body as a microchip. Other incidents later in his life when he had become the owner of the business himself, included dangerous encounters with other workers during union riots. These added to the content of the microchip. The trembling had to do with the memory of feeling terrorized, and thinking he must always be on guard. After deprogramming the microchip on his behalf the tremor disappeared almost completely.

Stuttering: Although stuttering is not a physical health condition, the Sage advised us to include it in this book, since it can be thought of as a neurological problem. We learned that stuttering can have its roots in two conflicting commands given to a child, such as: "You shouldn't say anything unless you have something important to say" and "To be polite you must not leave people just hanging there in silence." The second spell commands the child to do the very thing the first spell forbids. In this combination, they constitute a double bind, or lock in the psyche, that paralyzes the child's ability to meet situations from his inner truth.

Uterus (Heavy Bleeding): The healthy function of the uterus is not only to provide the environment for a pregnancy, but also to renew the woman's life force throughout her life. Heavy bleeding indicates that a spell has been put on the renewal of her life force. Examples of such spells are: "The uterus only has the purpose to enable pregnancies." "When a woman no longer has her period, her uterus is useless." Heavy bleeding can also be due to the woman's having given up on life, as in thinking, "my life has no purpose," "I was never meant to live," or, "I am guilty for existing."

Another cause of heavy bleeding can be related to the curse put on Eve by the biblical God: "Because you have seduced Adam, you have incurred eternal shame"; or the image of God's finger pointing at Eve, accompanied by the words: "You, Eve stand for all women." These curses need to be deprogrammed as a memory chip and a microchip.

16.

Understanding Infections

The Cosmic definition of infections gave us a surprisingly different perspective regarding their causes. This new perspective could only be understood after we were made aware of the *Guilt Toward Nature Complex* described in Chapter 9.

The conventional understanding is that bacteria, fungi, or germs are the cause of infections, and therefore need to be fought. However, all bacteria, fungi, and germs are parts of Nature, and our healthy relationship with Nature is a positive symbiotic one, not one of enmity. All our experiences of healing with the help of the *I Ching* have confirmed that illness is caused by beliefs that are in conflict with Nature. Moreover, healing can occur only *with the help of Nature*, not by fighting it.

Fighting Nature, as in fighting bacteria, fungi, or germs, only results in the creation of resistances on their part that grow ever stronger. This is observed in the way bacteria have become increasingly resistant to antibiotics over the years. The *I Ching* teaches that when we meet with such resistances, it is time to reflect on what thoughts or attitudes have created them, because it is a clear sign that we are unaware of, or are not observing a Cosmic Principle of Harmony.[1]

All attempts to discover new ways of destroying bacteria are futile. Nature is stronger because it is part of the Cosmic Order.

Bacteria and Fungi

Many wonderful things have been discovered in recent years by the scientific community about bacteria and fungi. Our body would not be able to function without them. We would not be able to make bread, yogurt, cheese, and wine, and all foods that involve fermentation without fungi. Things go wrong in

---

[1.] Anthony/Moog, p. 432. Hexagram 39, *Meeting Obstructions*, Line 1: "Going leads to obstructions. Coming meets with praise."

all these fermentation processes when we demonize fungi and fail to respect their importance. Bacteria, likewise, have a totally beneficial function in Nature, even when they have been demonized. In the following paragraphs, we will focus only on what we have learned about *bacteria*. However, the same principles can be applied to investigating the effects of demonizing fungi.

We demonize bacteria when we project generalized fears on them, such as:[2]

- The fear projected on all bacteria: "Bacteria cause infections." "Bacteria need to be killed."
- The fear of bacteria in water: "I might get an infection from swimming in that water." "That water contains bacteria."
- The fear of bacteria in the air: "When someone has a cold, you must not get too close, because of the bacteria." "Bacteria fly through the air invisibly and can attack you." "They can come in through your breathing and make you sick."
- The fear of bacteria in the ground: "You need to wash your hands after touching the ground, because it's full of bacteria."
- The fear of bacteria in our own body: "They are dangerous." "They can cause sickness."

The fears listed above become true only when we look at bacteria with suspicion and distrust, meaning, when our natural symbiosis with them is disturbed through the poison caused by the demonizing ideas.

All of the above fears come from the false idea that our body has no natural protection. We do not need protection against Nature; rather, we need protection from the poison arrows that demonize Nature.

The common belief that bacteria are the primary *cause* of infections has never been examined in the light of the fact that mistaken beliefs have damaging effects on the consciousness of those things in Nature we demonize.

The Sage reminded us that bacteria, like everything in Nature, are compressed Cosmic Consciousness. Like everything in Na-

---

[2] For deprogramming such fears, see Part IV, *Section 6, Fears Connected with the Illness.*

ture, they have a function that needs to be understood as part of the harmonious cooperation between the various parts of the whole organism of Nature. However, when we project any fear or demonizing thought on them, their nature is disturbed, and sometimes even perverted. When this happens, a Cosmic Principle of Harmony is set in motion whereby the demonized bacteria become part of the immune system of Nature as an arm of Fate. At this point a bacterium becomes what is referred to as a *virus*.

This Cosmic Principle makes sure that the demonizing idea (the fear) runs into the barrier of Fate—that barrier being the manifestation of the condition feared.

What we observe in an infection is a dynamic that has three basic parts: (1) the news of an incipient "infecting agent," such as a flu virus; (2) the creation of vulnerability to infection by the fear of that virus; and (3) the fact that the body has been rendered defenseless by a variety of slanders put on our animal nature in childhood.

In a totally healthy person, the body cells' own protective system is fully capable of deflecting many poison arrows coming from outside. However, due to the poison created by the slanders mentioned under (3), this system is weakened. Once weakened, the cells fear they can no longer protect our body from harmful thoughts coming from outside, such as the news mentioned in (1). The cells attempt to make the mind aware that the news contains poison arrows that if believed, would open the body up to harm. The mind, however, under the flattery that it knows better than the body what is wrong, disregards the body's message. Then, when the damage occurs, the mind looks for an outside culprit to blame. This is generally something in Nature. The blame the mind puts on Nature is yet another poison arrow that damages the body, because the body is part of Nature. At this point numerous poison arrows are in play. Together, they create the defeat of the body cells. This conglomeration of defeating elements cause the infection, not the virus.

The part of the body that gets infected in this process is the specific part that is considered to be vulnerable to becoming infected, such as the nose, the hands, or the urinary tract.

The bacteria found by doctors at the "scene of this crime," are those that come from Nature itself to rectify the damage done by the slanders against it. These are the demonized bacteria that now serve the function of Fate. Because the main function of bacteria is to decompose things, they come in this case to decompose the harm done to the body cells in the area infected by the poison arrow. They have followed the sensual track of the poison arrow back to its source in the person. There, they go straight to the affected cells, assess the damage, and begin to free the cells from the poison. The infected body cells, knowing their beneficial intention, welcome them in. Seen from the outside, however, we mistake them as the cause of the infection, whereas they are really Helpers.

It is true that it may take too long if we were simply to wait for the bacteria to cope with all the poison in the affected body cells. And, indeed, the bacteria need more help. The Sage has made us aware that an antibiotic salve can be helpful for reasons not known to science. One can ask the Sage which kind of antibiotic is to be used.

Plagues and Pandemics Caused by Projections

Once we saw that demonized bacteria act as part of Nature's immune system, we were not surprised to find that the viruses connected with plagues and pandemics are also *demonized bacteria.* They become demonized by the human fear that Nature will retaliate for the harm that humans have done to Nature. Guilt, whether individual or collective, draws these diseases to those who take it on.

People do not realize that Nature does not retaliate. It is their false fear of Nature's retaliation that comes back to them as self-punishment. A related fear comes from the mistaken belief that "God punishes us for our sins/mistakes." Deprogramming these two fears frees us from their negative influences.

The *I Ching,* in Hexagram 25, *Innocence,* stresses the importance of keeping our minds innocent and free from expectations or projections. This includes negative predictions about what might happen in the future. Making such predictions comes from the hubris that makes humans think they are brilliant enough to predict the future. That same hubris blinds them to the fact that it is those very predictions that actually cause lethal plagues.

17.

Addictions

What we are referring to as an "addiction" is the constant urge to fill a hole in the psyche that is accompanied by a depressing feeling. This hole may be felt physically in the center of the chest, or under the navel; it is accompanied by the feeling that something is lacking. Some people describe this as "feeling low." The ego exploits this hole by seducing us to fill it with substances or diversions that create a "high." These activities only succeed as long as the high lasts. At the end of every high cycle, the person experiences a deflation as the hole empties out. Alcoholism, drug addiction, bipolar conditions, and workaholic or goal-oriented addictions all follow this model.

From the Cosmic perspective, at the heart of addiction are the three major forms of guilt described in Chapter 9: guilt toward God, guilt toward Nature, and guilt toward self. This guilt makes us believe "we can never be good enough" and "there's no use in trying."

Guilt, combined with the belief that we can never be good enough, creates the twins of self-doubt and self-hatred. These elements create a constant urge to compensate by seeking approval outside of ourselves. The collective ego provides all sorts of ways in which this approval can be achieved, such as success through making a lot of money, working tirelessly to acquire titles or fame, or even the high moral regard of others. Once such goals are attained, they prove to be hollow since they only fulfill a self-image. For those who find the obstacles erected by class or environment too difficult to overcome, the solution is sought in numbing substances that temporarily fill the hole in their self-esteem. The only real solution is to remove from the psyche ideas and beliefs that take away our self-esteem.

While guilt continuously gnaws at the hole, self-hatred causes it to become infected with poison. Self-hatred results in craving for approval. But since the approval comes from the same authority (the collective ego) that has taken away our self-esteem, we find ourselves trapped by the mistaken belief that the collective ego is the only legitimate source of esteem. When we are healthy and whole we are nourished from within and therefore have no hole that needs filling.

Since many addictions circle around what is taken into the body, it is easy to see that they are related to our various sources of nourishment. The Guilt Toward God Complex disturbs our relationship with the Cosmos, the source of our life force and love energy. The guilt and self-hatred this complex creates forces us to look outside ourselves for substances that give the impression that they can supply us with the life force and love missing in our lives.

The Guilt Toward Nature Complex blocks our ability to take in nourishment from Nature in the form of *chi* energy. We receive this energy when we are in harmony with nature, just by being present in Nature. It gives us physical and emotional strength. Foods also contain *chi* energy, but this energy is blocked when we have guilt toward Nature. This leads some people to overeat in general, or to eat excessive quantities of certain foods.

The Guilt Toward Self Complex blocks our ability to gain the inner nourishment that would come from self-esteem. This nourishment is sweet and fulfilling. Lack of it leads us to ingest foods or substances that are sweet and filling.

Regardless of the obsessive habit: the use of drugs, eating or not eating, smoking, excessive reading, watching sports or television, working, religious or political zeal, the root cause is the same—the hole in one's original self-esteem created by self-doubt, guilt, and self-hatred. The yearning for the substance or activity reawakens as its dulling effect wears off. In the case of the workaholic or zealous caretaker, it wears off the minute the body would like to rest. Eventually, a crisis appears that forces the person to recognize that his real need is for self-esteem. It can come in the form of a fate, such as a dangerous accident, collapse of a body function, failure of one's relationships, loss of job, or other losses.

Initiation into Adulthood as the Cause of an Addiction

An addiction to smoking or drinking can also have its roots in a feeling of inferiority instilled in childhood. When the child reaches the teenage years, there is a susceptibility to anything that dulls that feeling. Often the addiction begins by his imitating an adult who is using an addicting substance; the teenager believes that this is "grown up behavior" that makes him an adult. Sometimes, a parent sets the example for the teenager, as the following case of a woman who stopped smoking with the help of the *I Ching*, shows.

Ending a Long-standing Smoking Habit

Gaby, a resident of Munich, wrote to us telling how she had stopped smoking with the help of the *I Ching*.

"I had been smoking since I was 15 years old. In my 'best times' I consumed about 50 cigarettes per day. When I decided to do the necessary deprogramming, I had the vague feeling that I wanted to stop, although I did not know how it could work. (I had made two unsuccessful attempts, one through acupuncture.)

"Someone told me to try hypnosis, but the psychologist who worked with hypnosis told me that the process would only function in small steps considering that I was such a strong smoker. I would need at least 12-14 sessions. I decided that was not my way. On my way home I reflected for the first time why I was smoking. I suddenly had an inkling that the *I Ching* could also help me with this as it had helped me with my relationship issue.

"I realized that my first experience of serious smoking coincided with the death of my father. While he was in the hospital, my mother wanted to be near him, so she spent the nights at our city apartment. I don't know why she chose me, and not my two sisters, to accompany her. She was a strong smoker, so for her it was only normal that she would smoke even more under the stress of the circumstances. Every time she lit a cigarette, she offered me one, too. This is how I came to accept that smoking might help me to cope with stress, and to see smoking as an important way of relating to my mother. Smoking enhanced our communication, because when I smoked with her, my mother would talk with me like an adult.

"After having brought this whole situation back to mind, I wrote down what my mother had put on me at the time:

'Smoking helps to cope with stress; it creates a bond between us. Like me, you cannot stop any more.' She had also put on me: 'You are like me.' Later, I put the false assumption on myself: 'I cannot enjoy, cannot communicate, cannot think, cannot relax without cigarettes.'

"I deprogrammed all these projections and spells according to the instructions in *I Ching, The Oracle of the Cosmic Way* [the German edition]. The deprogramming took three days (once per day). On the night of the second day I stopped smoking. After that I have never again had the desire to light a cigarette, and I would now call myself a non-smoker, although it doesn't bother me when other people smoke in my presence.

"Looking back at this experience, I cannot help but notice the seeming paradox: the simplicity with which a rather complex situation was ended. After all, a mother-daughter relationship is a rather complex thing."

Freeing Oneself from an Addiction, or Helping Another Person Become Free of One

Once we understand the origin of addictions in self-doubt, self-hatred, and guilt, each of us holds the key to helping ourselves or another person to become free from an addiction. If we want to help another person, we first need to ask the Sage whether that person is in a state of readiness to be helped. If Yes, we ask whether it is correct for us to do any deprogramming on his behalf. If Yes, we can proceed to deprogram: the Guilt Toward God Complex, the Guilt Toward Self Complex, the Guilt Toward Nature Complex, and any of the spells and poison arrows listed below.[1]

• The poison arrow, "Nature is divided into good/evil."
• Spells put on Nature, such as "Nature cannot be trusted," or "Nature is an enemy."

---

[1] See Chapter 21, *Methods of Deprogramming.*

- The poison arrows by which the person has demonized the substances to which he has become addicted
- Phrases about the substances: "they are powerful," "it has power over me," or any self-image that associates using the substance with sophistication or bravado
- Spells put on foods as "bad for you" (include conventional sayings about these foods)
- Spells put on certain foods, on fat, or on carbohydrates
- Any self-blame spells, such as for "being fat" or "malformed"; blaming the body for being a "problem"
- The word "addiction" (itself a spell); also the spells, "I have an addiction," or "I am an alcoholic, drug addict, workaholic, codependent," etc.
- The spell, "addictions are hard/impossible to cure."
- The self-image of the "loser," being forever an alcoholic, or otherwise crippled, allergic, or helpless against the addictive substance
- Any self-image taken on around eating, such as that of "being fat," or "you are what you eat."
- The self-image of being "unlovable"

People with addictions may also have a "ball of conflict." This ball is formed by seeing life, the Cosmos, oneself, one's body, or the addictive substance as a *culprit*. To become free of a ball of conflict, we need to say No three times to the false concept of "culprit," and then turn the whole ball of conflict over to the Helper of Dissolution.

A ball of conflict has a circular logic that by its own nature is illogical. There is no way to resolve it except to dispose of it as illogical. A ball of conflict is not to be taken apart or inspected for any phrases, for in looking into these balls one can find neither a beginning nor an end point.

18.

Pain as a Messenger

Whether a pain comes in an isolated form or accompanies an illness, its main purpose is to wake us up to look for its cause. It is telling us that in some way the cells in the area of the pain have been injured. It also tells us that we need to identify and free them from the cause of that injury.

Pain is an expression of the cells' alarm. If there is no visible cause, then we need to look for a projection, spell, or poison arrow (or combination of them), that has been put on us either by ourselves or by others. If there is a visible injury, we need to be aware that the external event with which it is connected has a deeper cause. This deeper cause is a false thought form that has manifested into reality. If we only seek to "kill" the pain, we miss the message it wants to give us; getting rid of it alone is like turning off our valuable alarm system and natural safeguard without seeking why it has come on. For this reason, if we approach the Sage with the intention of only getting rid of the pain, the Sage is unable to help us. That fact, however, does not mean that we are supposed to endure pain and suffering.

We take the message seriously when we look for the cause of the pain in the form of a projection, spell or poison arrow and deprogram it. Then, the alarm system has done its job unless something else still needs to be identified. When this is the case, the cause can be one of the following possibilities:
- we have not uncovered the complete cause
- the phrase(s) we have identified does not correspond closely enough to its original wording or meaning
- a phrase is still missing
- guilt, pride, or other ego emotions have been connected with the cause, which need to be deprogrammed
- we may have put blame on the pain itself
- we may have blamed the Cosmos for giving us the pain, or for making life a painful experience

We have learned that there is a Helper that can be called upon to relieve the pain before we have identified and deprogrammed its cause. However, this can only be a temporary measure, since, if we do not follow up and deprogram the cause, the pain will return. This Helper is the Helper of the consciousness of the body part that is in pain. For example, if the pain is in the hand, we ask for the Helper of the Hand, and then turn the matter over to that Helper.

When we understand the helpful function of pain, it becomes clear that the use of pain medicine does not remove its cause; it merely suppresses it. In certain cases, it is acceptable to use some pain medicine if it relieves the acute pain to the degree that we feel able to look for its deeper cause. If the pain returns, it is a sign that we need to resume our search for the complete cause.

Different Types of Pain

Nerves surrounding the cells that are affected by injury or by harmful thought forms convey the pain as an alarm. Pains can have other sources as well, as in memories of injuries, and ego emotions that have become connected with those memories. We have found four different causes of pain that can be deprogrammed:

(1) Pain caused by false thought forms whether they have manifested as an accident or a disease. Included are phantom pains that often accompany amputations. They are caused by a memory chip.

(2) Pain due to a freak-out of the cells in the proximity of an injury, or near tissues that have just been operated on, rather than the damaged tissues themselves, which are still in shock. These neighboring cells fear that whatever happened to the injured cells might also happen to them.

(3) Pain mechanically produced by the mind's taking over the alarm function of the body cells.

(4) Emotional pain

When the pain is identified as either (1) or (2), we can ease the pain by reassuring the injured cells and those surrounding them that we are going to ask for Cosmic help that will free them from the grip of the false thought form(s), and that we will make any other necessary corrections. In regard to pain mentioned in (2), it is also helpful to tell the cells that the injury or surgery that happened is over and there is no further threat. This is a language the body cells understand. It is like speaking to a child that needs loving reassurance that help is on the way. In doing this we can picture the injured body cells as wounded and frightened children whom we comfort and give our loving attention. We can then ask the Helper of the affected body part to help all the cells involved.

In the case of phantom pain, all the memories of the event which caused the injury need to be brought into consciousness, along with the conclusion drawn ("I have lost my hand, leg," or the like) and any guilt for what happened. These, together with any pride for having made a sacrifice, need to be deprogrammed as a memory chip in a water meditation. (See Chapter 21.)

The pain of headaches caused by feelings of guilt is relieved when we have identified and deprogrammed the guilt.

Pain that is mechanically produced by the mind (3) results from the mind's having taken over the body's natural function of providing the alarm that pain is meant to serve. This occurs through certain thoughts that express *shoulds* or *musts*: "I must not (should not) over-exercise," "I must watch my bodily functions," and "I must regularly have medical checkups." (The latter phrase turns the alarm function over to the medical profession.)

When our mind usurps the alarm function, we may experience pain for no reason other than that the alarm system, being turned on, is left running. Thus the pain occurs when we believe we might have overstressed our body or have not fulfilled a particular "should." Pain may also be caused by mentally keeping on the lookout for health problems.

Emotional pain (4) is caused by the body cells becoming starved for *chi* (love) nourishment. This kind of pain manifests as a depression containing a component of bitterness. Guilt, initiated by the ego, causes this starvation through siphoning off the flow of Cosmic *chi* to the body. The guilt is caused by the doubt that we have the right to enjoy life. It is guilt about being healthy while others are suffering, having food when others are starving, and being well off in comparison to others. The guilt carries with it the commands: "you have no right to enjoy anything while others in the world are deprived of it," and "You have to sacrifice what you have." The sacrifice, however, allows the ego to appropriate the *chi*.

Emotional pain is often experienced by people suffering from cancer or cirrhosis of the liver or other illnesses involving starved tissues.

The Role of Images in Relieving Pain

Carol's experience with a broken collarbone, related in Chapter 4, revealed to us the role of images in relieving pain, long before we had learned about healing with the help of the *I Ching*. Carol had unknowingly internalized the image of the bone as crooked and the doctor's comment that "it would always hurt some." After seeing the bone as straight in meditation, she experienced no more pain.

As this example shows, the body consciousness responds to negative images with pain, and is relieved by correcting those images.

Pain has also been relieved by visualizing, in short meditations, the painful area as being bathed either in a white or colored light, such as blue or green. The *rtcm* can be used to determine what kind of light is best in a given circumstance to visualize.

(Deprogramming the causes of pain identified in this chapter is explained in detail in Chapter 21, *Methods of Deprogramming.*)

Part III

Freeing Yourself from an Ailment or Illness

19.

Using the Retrospective-Three-Coin-Method (*rtcm*)

Carol Anthony discovered the Retrospective-Three-Coin Method (*rtcm*) in 1994. In a few emergency situations, she simply tossed three coins to get Yes or No answers from the Sage. The answers always proved to be true, and this prompted her one day to ask the Sage, tossing ten coins for the answer, "Is this way of getting a yes/no answer acceptable?" Carol took the head side of a coin as meaning "Yes," and the tail side as "No." Nine of the coins came up heads. From that time on, she used it as a retrospective method to ask whether she understood the *I Ching* messages correctly, as well as many other questions to clarify her understanding of the *I Ching* text. Much later, she happened to re-read Richard Wilhelm's introduction to his translation of the *I Ching* and saw that the *I Ching* had developed from just such a method of putting Yes/No questions to the oracle.[1]

Since three coins are used to develop a hexagram, it was only a small step to use the same three coins to ask questions to clarify the *I Ching's* messages. Using three coins gave four possible answers: a definitive Yes (three heads), a relative Yes (two heads), a relative No (two tails), and a definitive No (three tails).

Because Carol initially used this method to clarify the meaning of hexagrams she had received, she called it the "Retrospective Three-Coin-Method" or "*rtcm.*" Prior to using the *rtcm*, and like most other users of the *I Ching,* Carol relied on the existing interpretations, or what she intuitively understood from the hexagrams, or what understanding of them came through

---

[1] Wilhelm, Richard, *I Ching, or Book of Changes*, Princeton U. Press, 1950. In his Introduction, Wilhelm writes: At the outset, the book of Changes was a collection of linear signs to be used as oracles. In antiquity, oracles were everywhere in use; the oldest among them confined themselves to the answers yes and no. This type of oracular pronouncement is likewise the basis of the Book of Changes. "Yes" was indicated by a simple unbroken line (—), and "No" by a broken line (- -). Page xlix.

meditation. The *rtcm* sometimes verified her intuition and sometimes verified the traditional meanings. At other times it replied No to both. At such times she put forth hypotheses of what the meaning might be until she received Yes as a reply. Sometimes the Yes meant only that the question asked was true, but at other times it was to be taken as an indicator of the direction in which her questioning was to proceed, so that a much bigger realization could become clearer as she went. She began to understand that the method gave the Sage space to explain the Cosmic view of an issue. By this was meant the "inner truth" of the issue that showed why something was successful (because Cosmic Principles of Harmony were respected) and why it failed (because those principles were disregarded). Asking about why a person was going through difficulties, such as bad health, the Sage invariably pointed to the inner thoughts either of that person, or those around him that were creating his misfortunes. *Never* did the Sage point to the apparent external factors that are commonly pointed to as the cause. This fact made her aware that the oracle's answers are always to the inner truth of situations, and that its hexagrams and lines can only be understood correctly if they are taken in this light. Through the use of this method, the Sage's messages were no longer a matter of guesswork. Moreover, the *rtcm* gave the Sage the space it needed to answer beyond what was written in the traditional *I Ching* text.

Having had this experience, we have usually recommended that the use of the *rtcm* be limited to clarifying the messages received from hexagrams. The reason is that the ego is often waiting on the side, ready to jump at the chance to usurp the answers given by the *I Ching* and to interpret its messages within the framework of the ego mindset.

For the purpose of this book, however, the Sage said Yes to the *rtcm* being used independently of consulting the *I Ching* to investigate the causes of an ailment or minor illness. This is possible because we are making the investigator aware in this chapter of the tactics and traps the ego uses to interfere.

Investigating a long-standing illness, however, requires using our book, *I Ching, the Oracle of the Cosmic Way*, and a greater understanding of the ego-program described in Part IV, *Dismantling the Program of a Long-standing Illness.*

To aid the reader in the use of the *rtcm*, we discuss some dangers here and later in this chapter that would lead to its misuse and to incorrect answers. These dangers include getting answers to ego questions that are inspired by hope or fear, such as, "Is my illness fatal?" A simple Yes answer to such a question has the potential to damage the will of our cells to live; therefore, using the *rtcm* requires a system of checks to be sure we are not asking questions from the ego.

Used properly, the *rtcm* enables us to communicate with the Sage in such a way that our mind understands the answers coming from our inner truth. This is possible by putting forth hypotheses to find out in which direction we need to search. When we find the direction, we then ask questions to find out what the sick-making ideas are. The manner of questioning is similar to that asked by children in playing the "hot/cold" game. Receiving three heads tells us our question is "hot" on the trail that leads to understanding the problem. Getting two heads means our question is "warm," meaning relative to our subject, and a good enough answer to proceed further. Getting two No's is a simple negation. Three tails, on the other hand, can mean a number of things. It can tell us our question is not to the point, and therefore, is "cold." It can also mean one of the following:

- that our question contains a word, such as "culprit," that has no Cosmic basis and therefore cannot be answered
- our question comes from an ego-based attitude, or ego-based idea, such as "Is she on my side?" (The Cosmos does not take sides.)
- our question is based on an assumption that is outside the Cosmic view (See below: *When You are Stuck in the Questioning Process.*)
- we have asked the same question previously, but did not like or accept the answer (This is called "begging the question," which causes the Sage to cease answering.)

When we do not like the answer, it means the ego is asking

the questions. Further questioning draws a string of confusing answers. At this point we can ask, "Is the ego in me asking the questions?" The Sage will answer this question. If the ego is involved, but we then return to a respectful and sensitive attitude, the Sage will return to answer us.

Keeping a Record of Your Questions and Answers

Because begging the question is a frequent error, it is important to keep a written record of one's questions and the answers received. Keeping the record in a computer is particularly valuable for times when we need to revisit the work we have already done on an illness.

What are the specific uses of the rtcm *in the context of this book?*

We use it:

• to determine whether something specialists or friends told us, or what we accept as conventional wisdom, is actually true. This question needs to be asked especially when a prognosis is given. However, we need to be aware that the Sage does not simply replace a bad prognosis with a good one. It will say, "You have the potential to get well, if you bring yourself into harmony with your nature."

• to work with the Sage to reveal our own *inner* truth of a situation, and what needs to be done on the *inner* plane to put us back into harmony with it.

• to avoid merely assuming we have understood something correctly, or as a check when we think that what we have learned is the magic bullet, the once and for all answer. We ask, "Have I understood this correctly?" or "well enough at the moment?"

• to ask questions to determine the WHAT, WHEN, and FROM WHOM. (See *Guidelines* listed below.)

• to assess whether we will be able, simply through using the *rtcm*, to successfully identify the cause of an injury, ailment, or illness (Example: "Can the simple use of the *rtcm* lead me to a good enough understanding of my health condition?" If

No is the answer, we ask, "Do I need to consult *I Ching, The Oracle of the Cosmic Way?*")
- to determine which deprogramming method is appropriate for the particular circumstance
- to determine whether we need to correct our attitude toward the Sage, or to find any other obstructions that are getting in the way of communicating with the Sage (See *Problematic Questions* below.)
- to ask what the No-answer we have received means, as in, "do you want to say this (or that) by giving me a No?"

Getting inwardly prepared to ask questions with the rtcm

Before starting to ask Yes/No questions and throwing our three coins, it is important to attain inner neutrality. Lack of neutrality unconsciously distorts the answers. What distorts the answers are preconceived ideas we already have about the way things work, a "doubting Thomas" attitude, the desire to hear a particular answer, or fears that the answer will require us to do something that is incorrect or would harm us. The answers will also be distorted if we approach the Sage with an arrogant attitude that we know it all already. In this case, the Sage is unable to come to help, since we do not have an open and receptive mind.

Even if our mind is not open and receptive due to fears and doubts, so long as we are not arrogant the Sage will help by working around them so that in the end they can be dissolved. (The Sage's response will be swifter if we set aside any arrogance from the start.) Inner neutrality is achieved in a short meditation in which we ask the Sage to intervene with the ego in us for the duration of our inquiry.

Some Guidelines for the Questioning Process

To free ourselves from an ailment, the correct approach is to look for the sick-making thought that caused it.

From Whom:

Begin with identifying the originator of that thought: If we are the originator, we can go to the next question below. If the thought comes from someone outside ourselves, we can start with those closest to us: Is it a member of my family? If not: A friend? Someone from work? A group? The culture I belong to? Or, Is it from something I have read? Heard on the radio? Seen on TV? Once we identify the source, it is easy to remember the kinds of negative thoughts that were expressed.

What: *The actual sick-making thought*

If the sick-making thought has not come to mind easily, we can ask our body, in a short meditation, what the thought is, because our body knows. We simply ask our body, "what thought or image has made you sick?" When we have inwardly heard the thought, we verify with the *rtcm* that the wording or phrasing approximates the original sufficiently to be deprogrammed. We also ask whether there is more to find. Usually this refers to a related thought or an image.

Is the sick-making thought a projection, spell, or poison arrow or is it a demonic element?

Once we have found the phrase(s) and/or the image of the sick-making thought, we need to find whether it is a projection, spell, or poison arrow, or a demonic element (demon, dragon, or imp), or what we have described as a microchip or memory chip. (See Appendix 1 and 2: *Kinds of Sick-Making Thoughts* and *Demonic Elements in the Psyche.*)

When: *The time element*

It is always helpful to find out when the sick-making thought was put on us. We can start with questions such as, "Is it an old item?" "Did it happen recently?" The following possibilities exist: at conception; *in utero*; at birth; 0-6 years old; 7-10, 11-20; up to the present. We can pin it down to the exact year by asking further questions. When we identify the year, we often remember the upsetting thing that happened to us, the conclusions we drew from it, or the damaging things people said about us at the time.

The End of the Oracle Session

The end is determined by asking, "Is this all I need to know now?" If the answer is Yes (++ or +++), thank the Sage for the help received. If the answer is No, ask the Sage for further clarification in a meditation or another hexagram.

If, however, we have the idea that we must continue in spite of being exhausted, the coins will say Yes to our question, "should I continue?" This happens because we require that of ourselves, not because the Sage requires it of us. We need to be aware that we can become trapped by going against our commonsense.

General Guidelines

A good way for using the *rtcm* is to follow the path outlined by questions that receive either ++ or +++ answers, and avoid deviating into new, uncharted paths. For example, if we have learned that the damaging thought was a conclusion we drew, it is not helpful to then ask if the damaging thought came from someone else. We also need to check periodically whether the ++ answer is leading us to the source, or is only saying Yes because our hypothesis is true. Therefore, we need to ask when any hesitation enters our mind about an answer, "is this answer to the main point the Sage wants to make?" At all times our questioning needs to proceed toward the *main* point the Sage wants to make. We generally know when a question is beside the main point; nevertheless, the ego likes to pull us aside simply to satisfy a curiosity. Such questions, however, invariably lead to confusion.

The Sage communicates with us often in the form of hunches. Following these hunches is very valuable in using the *rtcm*. However, when we have been cut off from our feeling nature for many years because we doubt or do not trust it, it will require practice at asking questions with the *rtcm* before our ability returns to full strength. If we find the *rtcm* initially a bit difficult, we can temporarily free up this ability by saying, No, No, No to the poison arrow, "You can't trust your feelings." We may need to repeat this procedure every time we find ourselves allowing our mind, rather than our feelings, to dominate. To deprogram this poison arrow for good, we need to follow the instructions in Chapter 21, *Methods of Deprogramming*.

Problematic Questions

- Questions about the future that imply it is a pre-written script, cannot be answered by the Sage. Such questions are based either on hope or on fear. An example of a hope-based question is: "Am I going to get well?" The actual answer to this question is, "Yes, if you bring yourself into harmony with your nature," and not because it is written in the stars. Bringing oneself into harmony entails finding out the sick-making thoughts that are disturbing that harmony, and deprogramming them with Cosmic help. An example of a fear-based question is, "Am I going to be permanently disabled?" Such a question implies that no help is available from the Cosmos. The coins will only reflect our fear, since the question cannot be answered by the Sage.

- Questions that reflect our wanting assurances: "If I do this, will I have success?" This question falsely implies that we can make deals with the Cosmos, slanders its self-respecting nature, and goes against our own integrity. If, however, we are asking this question from a sincere effort to gain a greater understanding about how the Cosmos functions, there is no problem. If we are unsure about our attitude, we can ask with the coins whether our question comes from the right place inside us.

- Questions that reflect a slavish dependency on the Sage. The Sage will not make decisions for us that we can make by following our commonsense. Example: "Is it time to get out of bed now?"

- Questions that deprecate our own nature. Examples are "Am I a bad person?" "Am I defective?" "Is there something wrong with me?" The fact that we ask such questions shows that we have adopted negative judgments about ourselves that have created self-doubt. *All of these are untrue for any person,* and therefore need to be deprogrammed as poison arrows. (See Chapter 21. *Methods of Deprogramming.*)

- Cross-questioning occurs when we ask the same question twice because we did not like the first answer, or doubted it. However, asking the same question again is not a problem if and when we truly do not understand the answer.

• Questions that arise from the fear of making a mistake, such as "Will I be punished if I do not follow the Sage's advice?" These questions can come from the belief that the Sage is difficult to communicate with, or that the Sage punishes us if we make a mistake, or the fear that we might be communicating with a devil. Such fears can stop us from asking questions altogether.

The Sage teaches us that making mistakes is part of the learning process. What counts is that we approach the Sage with sincerity and are willing to correct our mistakes.

Questions to Ask in Healing an Illness:
In anticipation of healing an illness, we need to ask:
• "Is there anything in my attitude that would create an obstruction to the healing process?"
• "Have I or has anyone else put a projection, spell, or poison arrow on the successful outcome?"
• "Is there anything I need to do on the outer plane to make it possible for the healing to occur, or to accelerate the healing process?" (Example: the use of herbal remedies.)

Helpful Questions to Check Where We are in Our Questioning Process:
• "Am I still on the right track?"
• "Is there more I need to understand in this matter, now?"
• "Do I need to look for something to deprogram?"

• "Is it time to proceed to the deprogramming?"

When Answers are Contradictory or Confusing:
• "Am I begging the question?" (to be asked when we receive confusing answers)
• "Have the answers been coming from the ego because my questions were inspired by the ego?" (If you receive a Yes you can go back over each answer to ask which ones have been coming from the ego.)

When We are Stuck in Our Questioning Process

- "Does my question contain an incorrect presumption that prevents me from understanding the Sage's answer?" (An example is when we ask the Sage what needs to be done with a presumption that all help involves external procedures. However, the Cosmic Way is to correct things first and foremost on the inner plane, in the realm of consciousness. Usually, this is sufficient to end the illness.)
- "Does my question contain an incorrect word?" Sometimes we use a word that would mislead us, so it may be useful to ask this question. (If Yes, we need to look at ideas or words in our question that we take for granted as true. We can ask the Sage, pointing to each word, if an incorrect presumption is involved.)
- "Have I used a word in my question that has no Cosmic basis?" If yes, use the *rtcm* to find out which word.
- "Is my approach too mental?" If Yes, "would it help if I ask my body to put forth the questions?"
- "Would it be helpful to ask the Sage to bring the right questions to my mind?"
- "Is there an obstruction in my attitude?"
- "Is it better to stop asking questions, and do something else?" "Sleep on it?" "Meditate and ask for help?"

Among such obstructions are the following:

- Having doubts about the answer, even before asking
- Having already decided to do something, then asking the Sage just to get a confirmation
- Presuming that the Sage will protect us from harm no matter what. The fact is that we are protected by the Cosmos as long as we are sincere in our efforts to correct ourselves. This includes making the effort to free ourselves from our fears surrounding the illness. (See Part IV, *Dismantling the Ego Program of an Illness.*)
- Is a demonic element (demon, dragon, or imp) causing the difficulty? Here are two examples:
    1. A dragon of fear of what the Sage is going to say. This will

only cause the coins to reflect the fear; the answer is not coming from the Sage.

2. An imp of idle curiosity about someone else's health problem; this causes the Sage to retreat. (To free ourselves from imps, demons, and dragons, see Chapter 21. *Methods of Deprogramming.*)

What to Do When the Sage has Retreated

We encounter this situation frequently when we are still in the beginning stage of learning how to use the *rtcm*. We know this is happening when we receive either a series of No answers, or contradictory answers. The reason for this situation may be that we have fallen into one of the dangers listed above. It is part of our learning process to make mistakes. Once we become aware of a mistake and correct our attitude, the Sage is once more available to us. We need to remember that the Sage retreats in the face of arrogance, or when we have an attitude of superiority, as when we treat the Sage as a servant that can be commanded. It also retreats when we become ambitious, as in seeking to be the "most spiritual." If we suspect from a series of No's that the Sage has retreated, we can ask directly whether that is the case. The Sage returns to answer that question, or any other question in which we attempt to correct ourselves.

In some cases, correcting our attitude can be done by saying an inner No to the incorrect attitude, such as saying, "No, No, No to my cross-questioning," or, "No, No, No to my thinking I know better," and then apologizing to the Sage. In other cases, a demonic element (demon, dragon, or imp) may be interfering with our communication. The Sage will help us in our search as long as we are sincere. Here is a list of commonly encountered demonic elements that can interfere in our questioning:

• an imp, demon, or dragon of "knowing better"
• an imp, demon, or dragon of impatience
• an imp, or demon of distraction
• an imp, or dragon of ambition
• an imp, or dragon of spirituality
• a demon of servile behavior

To free yourself from these demonic elements, see Chapter 21. *Methods of Deprogramming.* Then apologize to the Sage without ceremony, and refrain from blaming yourself. That is all that is needed to correct the mistake.

20.

Investigating a Minor Ailment

Investigating the cause of an ailment or illness has the goal of attaining the inner truth of a matter. This inner truth is generally composed of projections, spells, poison arrows, or self-images that have damaged the cells and our natural protective abilities. Attaining this inner truth requires that we first suspend our use of the language of medicine.

The investigation is carried out by communicating with the Sage through the use of the *rtcm* for all steps involved.

However, before beginning your investigation, you need to find out whether the condition falls into the category of a minor ailment. Using the *rtcm*, ask whether you can follow the procedure shown below, or whether you need to follow the procedure described in Part IV for a long-standing illness. If you receive No to both questions, it may indicate that you, or the person on whose behalf you are questioning, are too blocked by skepticism to engage the help of the Helpers. If so, follow the conventional medical approach.

Skepticism implies that you "know better," and therefore your mind is closed. A new experience of healing will not occur under such circumstances. Deeply rooted skepticism toward help coming from the invisible world can only be overcome by a modest attitude, e.g., you need to open your mind enough to allow for a new experience.

Suspending Beliefs and Disbelief

One of the first obstructions we may encounter are doubts that we can be helped by "something that has not been scientifically proven," and that involves "invisible Cosmic Helpers."

For this approach to healing ourselves, it is not necessary to believe in anything, but it does require that we *suspend both our beliefs and our disbelief.* Only by doing this can we create the necessary receptivity to have a new experience.

This way of healing does not require us to do anything that is against our commonsense. We are only presented with what our body knows. The following examples show how sudden pains resulting from small injuries can be stopped. They serve as a starting point to have an almost instant healing experience.

Awareness of the Difficulty Created by Guilt and Related Words

It needs to be noted at the outset that the ego has a vested interest in making us fear investigating the causes of an illness, since the investigation will certainly point to those phrases and images that make up the ego. To discourage us, it makes us fear that we will find that we are guilty of causing the illness. The fear of being guilty is so great, that unless we can see that guilt is part of the logic of the ego, we will turn away from the investigation. We need to realize that guilt has no Cosmic validity. (See Chapter 9, *The Origins of Guilt.*)

We may not think of guilt when we use the word culprit, and other words that imply that guilt is a valid concept. However, many people view themselves or others as culprits. They may have adopted this idea due to feeling unwanted as children. The idea of there being such a thing as a culprit implies that evil is part of the Cosmos and part of Nature. In itself, the word culprit contains the great human arrogance of judging the goodness of the Cosmos. Use of the word culprit causes us to focus on ourselves or others as intrinsically evil, rather than looking for the thoughts that slander our true nature, and distort our actions.

When we look for the cause of an illness, we need to look for any intimation that we may see ourselves as culprits, since this idea contains guilt. If we find this to be the case, we need to deprogram the concept of guilt and any other guilt-related complexes mentioned in Chapter 21, *Methods of Deprogramming.* Note: It is also important that we do not make the ego into a culprit, since this puts us back into the camp of ego logic, where we must fight evil. Doing so makes the ego into a dragon force that is impossible to overcome.

How to Find Relief from Sudden Pains

The pains we are speaking of here can be a sudden headache (not migraine), or a sudden pain in any area of our head, neck, back, or other body part.

It is our experience in most cases (except for headaches discussed below) that such sudden pains are caused by a sick-making thought or image coming from another person or group. That person or group can be near or far away. The pain serves to make us aware that a projection, spell, or poison arrow has just injured our psyche and body. The sooner these false thought forms are identified and deprogrammed, the faster we feel relief.

If we keep getting these sudden pains, it indicates that we need to look for something in our own psyche that lets in or draws these false thought forms to us. For example, we may have harbored harmful thoughts about the same people who are sending them to us. The harmful thoughts we have been sending them can be identified and deprogrammed in the same manner as the ones we are receiving.

The following is a schematic for your investigation. Record your questions and answers:

Question 1: Is the cause coming from outside myself? If Yes, identify the person(s): Start with those persons closest and work your way outward. Is it anyone from my family? If No, anyone from work? A friend of mine? Someone in this country? Etc.

Question 2: Is the harmful thought a projection, spell, poison arrow, or any combination of these? (See Appendix 1, *Kinds of Sick-Making Thoughts.*)

If the answer is No, ask, whether it is a demon, dragon, imp, or any combination of these. (See Appendix 2, *Demonic Elements in the Psyche that Cause Illness.*)

Question 3: Is a changeling involved? If Yes, write this down because it will need to be deprogrammed as well.

Next step: If the harmful thought is a projection, spell, or poison arrow, identify its word and/or image content by closing your eyes, and asking the Helpers, without trying to specify which ones, to bring the phrase(s) and/or image(s) to mind.

Examples of such thoughts coming from other people: "She should really do something for her health." "I wish he would suffer the same as I have." "He is just as strong-headed as his father." "She is getting old" (accompanied by "typical" images of old age).

Common themes of such thoughts are:
- the three w's: wishing, wondering, and worrying
- phrases containing the word "should"; their purpose is to suggest that the receiver is under a moral obligation, and to instill feelings of guilt
- phrases that inspire fears (they are often accompanied by a threatening image)
- thoughts that wish the other ill
- judgmental thoughts
- envious thoughts

If the harmful thought is a demon, dragon, or imp, identify the ego-emotions that they create in you. Examples: feelings of vengefulness, hatred, blame, resentment, annoyance.

Check with the *rtcm* whether you have uncovered everything necessary to free you from the pain. Write down what needs to be deprogrammed so that you can repeat the deprogramming as long as needed. (See Chapter 21, *Methods of Deprogramming.*)

Headaches

Headaches are mostly caused by the ego in ourselves, through its putting pressure on us to feel guilty or blameworthy. We may be blaming ourselves for not keeping up the pressure to get things done, or for not keeping up with a time requirement. These stress-producing thoughts are often accompanied by a demon or dragon of guilt.

The fact that we have unconsciously taken on guilt indicates that at some point in our lives we have taken on a self-image such as that of the dutiful daughter, son, husband, wife, mother, or father. Guilt follows automatically when obligations associated with the self-image are not fulfilled, or are neglected or delayed.

To make sure that the guilt does not return, we need to ferret out that dutiful self-image and deprogram it, along with the dragon or demon of guilt that accompanies it. Since guilt is a conditioned response coming from the ego, it needs to be clearly distinguished from remorse, which is a natural feeling that follows making a mistake. (See Glossary: Guilt.)

The Activity of a Free-Floating Changeling

An acute headache or other physical symptom can also be caused by a demonic element we call a "free-floating change-ling." This changeling is one that remains active after we have deprogrammed an ego element to which a changeling has been attached, but has not itself been deprogrammed. The changeling then becomes free-floating. It can be compared to a free radi-cal—always on the lookout for something to attach itself to. It thus becomes a mischief-maker in our psyche. It shows itself in physical symptoms that crop up in various places in the body either all at once or successively. When we suspect that this may be the cause of the problem, we can ask, through the *rtcm* whether it is the case.

Crystallized Fears

Among the causes of bodily pain are fears that have crystallized in a given body part. The body part, through the pain, seeks to inform us of the damage the fear is causing.

We learned about this while investigating a case of diaphrag-matic hernia. The pulsing of the heart beat on the left side of the person's chest was dismissed by a doctor as a diaphragmatic hernia. It was the cause of severe pain and difficulty in breathing if the person slept on his left side for only a short time. Our in-vestigation revealed that the small area where this pain occurred contained three crystallized fears. The first was that if he lay on that side, he would suffer the experience. The second fear was that the pulsating artery might get strangulated in the hernia; the third was the fear that because the condition was not determined by x-ray or other means, it might be an aneurysm, which was common in his family. All these fears concentrated in that one spot, and were activated whenever he lay on that side.

Deprogramming was followed by a meditation in which the fears were dissolved by a Helper. A changeling was also connected with it; therefore, it too needed to be deprogrammed. After the deprogramming, the problem gradually went away. It was also necessary during the healing time that he deprogram any impulse to watch to see if it had healed.

Crystallized fears are not caused by spells and poison arrows put on us by others, but by the paralyzing effect of our own fears. Among the most potent of these fears is that of not being able to get free of the pain, the fear that there is no remedy for it ("it is hopeless"), and the fear that it will get worse, or may lead to death. Even if we find that the pain was originally caused by poison arrows coming from others, we may have added these fears once the condition became persistent.

Microchips

A microchip contains the bodily memory of a traumatic event. It can cause allergies and other ailments. When the *rtcm* confirms that we need to look for a microchip, we need first to find out how old we were. Then we review the circumstances that come to mind for that year. We can ask who else was involved in creating the traumatic memory. A microchip contains the things that were said, images connected with the event, and conclusions we drew from the experience, such as, "there is no help," "I will never be able to get over this," "I can't trust anyone," "I am a bad person," "I am guilty," or "I need to be punished." Fears are often part of a microchip, as in, "I have been damaged for life." We always need to ask whether guilt in one form or another is part of the microchip, and whether a changeling is involved.

A microchip is something the body produces to *contain* the traumatic memory. It acts as an envelope that protects the other cells in that part of the body from its negative effects.

Small Injuries

Small injuries can be caused by a thought coming from ourselves or another person. Such a thought can be "I am clumsy." Coming from another, the thought can be their wishing us ill.

178

A small injury is a warning to make us aware that something disharmonious is present in our psyche due to one of these causes. It can also be due to adopting a self-image, or putting a projection and poison arrow on someone else. The warnings given by small injuries are meant to cause us either to review our thoughts or to review events which may have caused others to attack us. If we do not heed them, the shocks become more severe, such as those produced by a car accident, or a broken leg or arm, or a worse injury or illness.

Question 1: Is the cause coming from outside myself? If Yes, follow the line of questions described above under "sudden pains." If the answer is No, proceed to the next question.

Question 2: Is this to make me aware of a self-image I have taken on? If Yes, identify the self-image by closing your eyes and asking the Helpers (unspecified) to bring the self-image to mind. Examples: The self-image of "one who, thanks to the *I Ching*, or to some other source, has superior knowledge," or "one who can now take it for granted that due to his working with the *I Ching*, Cosmic protection is a given." (In the latter case, the ego has appropriated the work and taken away his modesty. Modesty is the source of our Cosmic protection.) A quite frequent self-image is that of the Sage, or of the Sage's right hand man.

If the cause of the small injury is not a self-image, we can ask whether it is an ego-attitude, such as an exuberant enthusiasm, or overconfidence. It can also be that we are blaming the Cosmos for some reason. In such cases we need to identify the thoughts behind these attitudes. They come from demons, dragons, or imps in the psyche that need to be identified, along with the incorrect thoughts they have created in us. Example: "The *rtcm* didn't tell me the truth." This thought comes from a dragon of blame. Or, "I don't need to use the *rtcm*, I know it already." (This comes from a dragon of overconfidence, together with an imp that says, "why bother?") Overconfidence may also contain expressions such as, "it's silly and unscientific to throw coins," or, "my commonsense tells me." The ego often calls such thoughts "commonsense," but they come from the conventional view of things, not our natural commonsense.

A small injury can also make us aware that we have put a projection or poison arrow on someone else, and that this has created a fate for us. If this is the case, we need to identify the thought that has created the projection and/or poison arrow. Examples are blaming, resentful thoughts, and thoughts by which we have given up on another as hopeless, or the thought, "that will never change."

When We Do not Heed the Warnings of Small Injuries

When we have not paid attention to the warnings mentioned above and are now faced with a more severe injury or illness, we need to remember that it is not too late to correct ourselves. The moment we identify the mistaken idea or belief, or the self-image that caused our fate, we start to feel the relief. The next step is to deprogram it.

It is part of the caring nature of the Cosmos that our fate is not a punishment, but a means to make us aware of our mistake and to bring us back to our senses. Furthermore, a number of Cosmic Helpers are active in the situation to help us do this. Cooperating with them to remove the *cause* of our mistake requires only that we identify the cause, and deprogram it. The next chapter gives instructions for deprogramming.

21.

Methods of Deprogramming

To free ourselves or others from conditions of ill health, it is necessary to understand what we mean by deprogramming. We learned these methods over an extended period of time, and always in connection with actual cases.

Our first experience of healing the nodules in Hanna's chest showed that her healing entailed deprogramming beliefs she had accepted during childhood that were in conflict with her true nature. In a meditation, she was shown that she needed to vote "No" to having accepted their validity. We later found that this No had the effect of reversing her former acceptance, much the way a -1 in mathematics eliminates a $+1$.

Over time we found that deprogramming needs to observe a certain order. The reason is that certain Helpers necessary to healing need to be freed as the first order of business. We also learned that in some cases, deprogramming can be undone by certain other aspects of the ego such as guilt or doubt, if these are not removed first. The order laid out in this book makes it less likely that the reader will run into such problems.

It is also our experience that deprogramming sick-making thoughts cannot be carried out in a ritualistic way that excludes our feelings. This is because Cosmic Helpers only respond to feelings; they are not able to respond to a purely mental or mechanical approach. For this reason, rituals are counter-productive.

How Deprogramming Initiates Transformations

Deprogramming is the process of *saying No* to words, phrases, and images to which we have previously said Yes, either consciously or unconsciously. Saying a firm No to them reverses the Yes, and thereby removes them from the psyche. Saying No to traumatic images and memories also removes those from the psyche and body, where they are stored.

Deprogramming requires the aid of Cosmic Helpers referred to in many places in the *I Ching* as "friends," and "specialists in their fields."

Generally, it takes three days in which we repeat the deprogramming and another three days for the Helpers to carry out the transformations in the realm of the atom, which is the realm of consciousness. When a transformation leads to healing, the cells that were injured by the false thought form are returned to normal. The results are not always visible after six days, even though the transformation has taken place. In some cases the results are noticable only weeks later.

The process of deprogramming consists of two parts: (1) saying No to the word, phrase, or image in question, and (2) asking the Helpers to complete our effort. The reader will notice that the methods given below for deprogramming differ slightly from this description. The reason is that quite a number of people have been deprived of their ability to say No, either partially or totally, due to childhood conditioning. The methods described below allow the Helpers to say the necessary No on our behalf.

As mentioned above, it is necessary to communicate with the Sage via the *rtcm* for all steps involved in deprogramming. How the *rtcm* is to be used wisely is described in Chapter 19.

Deprogramming Demonic Elements

Deprogramming demonic elements in the psyche means that they are to be killed. This task is carried out by certain Helpers such as the Helper that Kills Imps, the Helper that Kills Demons, and the Helper that Kills Dragons. Some people hesitate to ask for something to be killed because they believe they are killing off parts of themselves. Or, they hesitate because of the commandment, "thou shalt not kill." They need to realize that demonic elements are parasites in the psyche that are created by false thought forms that have taken on a life of their own. They use the idea that they are part of our nature, and the commandment not to kill, to give them safe haven in the psyche. So long as they exist, they imprison the Helpers of our true nature. The reader who wants to free himself of them may first need to deprogram the belief that they are a part of him, along with the phrase, "thou shalt not kill."

Deprogramming on Behalf of Another Person

Basically, it is always possible to deprogram on behalf of another person, but we need to ask the Sage whether it is wise and correct to do so at this given time.

Deprogramming Guilt

Because of the fact that guilt can undo your deprogramming, it is recommended to begin by deprogramming anything related to guilt: the false concept of guilt, the spell of "original guilt/sin," and any feelings of guilt surrounding the illness.

If guilt is not deprogrammed successfully, it will undo the deprogramming already done of any mistaken ideas, beliefs, or self-images that have guilt invisibly connected with them.

Before deprogramming guilt, you need to be clear about the definition of guilt. (See Chapter 9.) If you deprogram the three ego complexes described there (The Guilt Toward Self Complex, The Guilt Toward Nature Complex, and The Guilt Toward God Complex), you do not need to deprogram (1) and (2) below.

(1) Deprogramming the false concept of guilt

To free yourself from the *false concept of guilt as an inextinguishable stain on your nature* do a mini-meditation in which you ask the Helper that Frees People from Guilt to free you from the concept of guilt; also ask the Cosmic Doctor to do what is necessary to erase the effect the guilt has had on you.

Ask each following day whether you need to repeat this procedure until the answer is No. Then thank the Helpers.

(2) Deprogramming the spell of "orginal guilt/sin"

Picture the phrase, "humans are born with original sin/guilt," and the image of an inextinguishable stain on human nature as being *dunked in water until the stain is removed*. Ask once each following day whether you need to repeat this meditation; if so, repeat it until the answer is No.

(3) Deprogramming feelings of guilt

Whenever you find that you feel guilty of something, say No three times to your feeling guilty of whatever it is, and ask the Helper that Frees One of Guilt to free you from it.

If you have a whole list of things you feel guilty of, do the *Mini-Meditation Using the Image of Water* described below, dunking the whole list in the water.

Mini-Meditations

Sick-making thoughts are deprogrammed in a mini-meditation that should not exceed three minutes. In the following, we shall describe three different kinds of meditations that use the image of water, fire, or a Cosmic vacuum cleaner bag. When we put the sick-making thoughts or images in the water, fire, or vacuum bag, and hand them over to the Cosmos, the Cosmic Helpers free us from their harmful effects. We always need to ask the Sage, through the *rtcm*, which of these three means, water, fire, or the vacuum bag, is appropriate for the specific thing we want to deprogram. The deprogramming occurs in the realm of consciousness. No part of our nature or psyche gets injured or harmed in this process; on the contrary, they get freed from an oppressive energy.

(1) Mini-meditation using the image of water

Microchips, some poison arrows and some self-images are best deprogrammed by picturing splashing water on them, or dunking them in water.

To deprogram a microchip it is necessary to identify the traumatic event in question, with the help of the *rtcm*: This includes the things that were said, the images connected with the event, the conclusions drawn from the experience, and any guilt taken on. Picture dunking the memory and guilt in water; then ask the Sage to take care of the matter. Ask once each following day whether you need to repeat this procedure; if so, repeat it until the answer is No. Then thank the Sage for its help.

If the same traumatic event has also created a memory chip, both the microchip and the memory chip can be deprogrammed together in the manner described above.

To deprogram a poison arrow picture the phrase as a fiery arrow that you splash with water until it is extinguished. Then ask the Helper that Takes Care of Poison Arrows to take care of it. Ask each following day whether you need to repeat this procedure until the answer is No. Then, thank the Helper.

To deprogram a self-image, picture it as a mask that you splash with water until it has lost its fiery quality. Then ask the Helper that Takes Care of Self-Images and the Helpers (unspecified) to take care of it. Ask once each following day whether you need to repeat this procedure until the answer is No. Then, thank the Helpers for their aid.

2. Mini-meditation using the image of fire

When this method is indicated, do a short meditation in which you picture putting the phrase, image, or mask into a fire. Then ask the Sage to take care of it. Ask once each following day whether you need to repeat this procedure until the answer is No. Then, thank the Sage for its aid.

3. Mini-meditation using the image of a cosmic vacuum cleaner bag

This method is used to deprogram memory chips, preconceived ideas, poison arrows, and spells (when indicated), as well as imps, demons, and dragons. In a short meditation picture a Cosmic vacuum cleaner sucking up into a bag whatever you have identified. Ask once each following day whether you need to repeat this procedure until the answer is No.

Deprogramming Other Demonic Elements

To deprogram a changeling ask the Sage to bring in the specific Helper needed to kill the specific changeling you are dealing with.

When a free-floating changeling needs to be killed, ask the Helper that Kills Free-Floating Changelings to kill it.

To deprogram a doubter ask the Helper that Kills Doubters to kill it.

To deprogram a nightly grabber first sit up to become fully awake. You then need to ask, using the *rtcm,* if a grabber is operating. Or, you can recognize it by noticing that it has grabbed your mind's attention by putting forth one after the other, only subjects that will make you feel hopeless and helpless. Or, it introduces worldwide problems that you personally cannot solve. You then need to say No, No, No! to both the grabber, the subjects it brings to mind, and to the torturous game it is playing with you. You next need to ask the Helper that Kills Grabbers to kill it. During an imaging meditation, mentally participate in killing it. You also need to ask the Helper of Dissolution to do whatever else is necessary to free you of it. After that, ask the Sage to clear out your mind, and help you return to sleep.

Deprogramming an Ego Complex
Ego complexes are deprogrammed by using a fire meditation in which we picture the spells written on a piece of paper that is then burned. Self-images are pictured as a mask that gets burned. Then we ask the Sage to kill the changeling that has been guarding the complex, and to extinguish any other elements that belong to the complex. We also ask the Helper of Transformation to complete the process, and the Helper of Healing to heal the damage done by the complex to our psyche and body. We ask each next day whether the procedure needs to be repeated until we get No for an answer.

It is important to turn any doubt in the validity of the deprogramming process over to the Cosmos before undertaking the deprogramming.

What to do when Some of Your Deprogramming has been Undone by Guilt or Doubt
When you notice that symptoms have returned, it may mean that your deprogramming of spells, poison arrows, or self-images has been undone by guilt connected with them that was overlooked at the time. Do not despair: find out what you feel guilty for, and deprogram this guilt according to the instructions given above. Next, you can ask the Helper that Deprograms Re-

installed Things to deprogram them again on your behalf. You do not have to know what those things are. Ask each following day whether you need to repeat this procedure until the answer is No. Then thank the Helper for its aid.

If you find that *doubts* in the effectiveness of the deprogramming have undone your work, you need to ask for help to deprogram an "imp and dragon of doubt in the effectiveness of deprogramming." Follow the instructions for the "Mini-meditation using the image of a vacuum cleaner bag." (See above). Next, ask the Helper that Deprograms Reinstalled Things to deprogram them again on your behalf. You do not have to know what those things are. Ask once each following day whether you need to repeat this procedure until the answer is No. Then thank the Helper.

Deprogramming the Program of a Major Illness

Deprogramming the whole program of a major illness is not something you can do within a week. You need to allow enough time for each part that gets deprogrammed to be transformed by the invisible Helpers. What they do happens outside your conscious awareness. The following is a rule of thumb: allow three days for repeating your deprogramming effort, then allow another three days for the Helpers to do the necessary transformations. If the Sage indicates that your part of the deprogramming process has been successful after only one time, you can proceed to deprogram another part. If after a time your ailment remains, you may need to inquire whether there has been some block in the deprogramming effort brought about by guilt, doubt, fear, a human-centered view, or other ego attitudes. Persistence in your efforts to find the problematic attitudes succeeds.

Over time, as you deprogram more and more faulty ideas, you will simultaneously be freeing blocked Helpers that will make your deprogramming more effective and easier. This will allow the Sage to show you new deprogramming methods and procedures as your relationship with the Sage becomes freer and more creative.

187

22.

Causes for Regressions and
Hindrances to Healing

We will first address the causes for a regression of the ailment or illness that sometimes occurs. Generally when this happens the symptoms return, but in a milder form.

However, the return of a symptom may not actually indicate a regression, but the surfacing of another layer of causes for the illness. Our experience is that when an illness has layered causes, we cannot get to all its layers at once. The Sage leads us to remove one layer at a time, and in an order that prevents true regressions.

What we address here are true regressions. These are caused by ego interferences that we allow after a healing has taken place. By interferences we mean that the ego surfaces with its doubts, fears, guilt, bragging, or other appropriations of the success. Therefore, when a symptom does recur, it is necessary to ask, using the *rtcm*, whether it is a true regression or yet another layer of causes that is now surfacing.

The ego awakens the very moment we notice that the illness has either disappeared or that the condition has much improved. This is because it realizes that its power over us is threatened by the success of our relating to the Helpers.

Ego interferences come in many forms, as we list below. They can be tiny, fleeting, and barely audible inner voices that suggest, "how do you know the illness has not only become hidden from view, and will return?" "In the final analysis, you are going to get fooled." Listening to these voices gives them validity, causing our deprogramming to be put in doubt. This in itself causes the illness to partially return.[1]

---

[1] If we are consulting the *I Ching*, we may be warned of an ego interference by receiving Lines 4 and 6 of Hexagram 63, *After Completion.* Line 4 reads, "The finest clothes turn to rags." Line 6 says, "He gets his head in the water, danger." Anthony/Moog, p. 663, 666.

Once we have said a firm No to such back-of-the-mind thoughts and made a clear decision to follow our inner truth, all conflict ends, the Helpers are freed, and we are able to get well. That decision is not made just to get free of the illness, or to gain the help of the Helpers; it is made because our inner truth is the only thing that can free us from within and fulfill us. All future success follows from recognizing the necessity to make this inner decision.

When we become aware that a regression has taken place, it does not mean everything is lost. We can seek out the offending thoughts and deprogram them. In all cases, the cause lies in the activity of the ego rather than a failure of the Helpers. We close our connection with the Helpers the moment we allow the ego to enter the scene.

Common Causes for Regressions

The following is a list of the most commonly encountered kinds of ego interference. We distinguish between (a) incorrect attitudes toward the Helpers and the Cosmos, (b) incorrect attitudes coming from the human-centered view, (c) guilt, (d) a false image we have of the illness, and (e) influences coming from a demonic element called "the doubter."

(a) Incorrect attitudes toward the Helpers and the Cosmos

- The ego causes us to talk about the healing in such a way as to expose the Sage and the Helpers to ridicule. This happens when we talk to people who might not be open to the possibility of there being Helpers.
- The ego calls "complete healing" an illusion. It is a common assumption that some illnesses are "incurable." One example is a comment made in AA about alcoholism, "You can't turn a pickle back into a cucumber." That is true for a pickle, but people are not pickles.

(b) Incorrect attitudes coming from the human-centered view

- The ego tries to appropriate the healing by discrediting the role of the Helpers. It does this by crediting the healing to everything but the Helpers: "I did it (all by myself)." "I would have gotten better anyway. It was only a matter of time." "It

189

was due to my good constitution." "It happened because I deserved it," "I had a right to be healed," "It was good luck," "My healing was a miracle."

- We take on the self-image of the one who has "made it," meaning survived the threats posed by the illness, and the self-image of the one who makes a new beginning. We can understand how these two self-images are counter-productive when we realize that they are self-congratulatory. They show how the ego has seized the success and now wears it as a badge of its achievement.

- We resume a careless and egocentric lifestyle, or continue to indulge in the same or similar thoughts that led to the illness.

Regarding the idea of miracles; this idea comes from the ego's inability to think in terms of *transformations*. What it cannot explain in its own terms is categorized as a "miracle." Behind the belief in miracles is the attitude of the small child who has been taught to look up to his parents as the ones who "can fix everything." That image is combined with the idea that we have to make a special effort to get what we want from the Cosmos. Such ideas put projections and spells on the Helpers that block their abilities to help. What the Helpers do is never a miracle, it is simply the normal way in which the Cosmos and Nature operate. Because healing through the Helpers removes that which depresses health, health spontaneously returns.

(c) Feeling Guilty or Feeling Privileged for Having Been Healed

- The ego tries to reverse the healing process by making us feel guilty for having been healed, with the phrase, "I don't deserve to be healed," or it encourages us to compare ourselves with others who are still sick, in a compassionate way, and thus makes us feel guilty for being better off.

- The ego encourages us to feel privileged through having an association with the Sage, and thus causes us to brag.

(d) A False Image We Have of the Illness

- Certain ways of referring to the disappearance of the health condition can cause it to return. When we say "I'm glad it's gone," the statement implies that we are looking at the illness as an *enemy* rather than as the messenger it actually was.

• We make illness into the standard of normalcy. We make this mistake when we notice that we have not been ill for awhile and say such things as, "I haven't had a headache in three months." Such a statement implies that not having had a headache is a fluke, and that having headaches is to be expected. The regression does not occur when health is the standard and illness the fluke.

The collective ego leads us to expect to be ill. We need only consider the large quantity of advertisements for medicines that are said to prevent illness, to know this is true. The assumption is that the enormous capability of the body to be vigorous and to easily throw off the threat of disease does not exist. When our view of our body's capability matches what our body is truly capable of, we feel great vigor and experience few invasions from outside. Restoring our true standard requires deprogramming all the low standards we have accepted for ourselves.

(e) Influences Coming From a Demonic Element Called the "Doubter"

A doubter is a demonic element caused by a poison arrow that dissolves the natural attraction between psyche and body and lodges in the heart. Examples of such poison arrows are the phrases: "You can never trust anything unless it has been proven," "change is the rule of life," "ups are inevitably followed by downs," "nothing lasts," and "there is always a loophole through which the illness can come back." These very thoughts *create* the hole! The role of doubts in causing the very thing they doubt is frequently overlooked. They are projections and poison arrows, in the presence of which the Helpers must withdraw.

When the doubter is active, one doubt is followed by another, thus creating hopelessness. The doubter invariably calls into question anything that cannot be seen with the outer eyes, because it is also based on the belief that you can only believe what you can see.

Examples of other phrases used by the doubter are: "The healing is a trick that will evaporate, because the Cosmos is a trickster," "You can only tell for sure after five years," "You can convince yourself of anything, but it will still be there, when you turn around," "Maybe the problem has only been masked or covered up but will crop up later."

Such doubts cause us to expect the problem to return. That expectation is the very projection that causes it to return. The seed phrase behind all these statements is the generalized mistaken belief that "good things or good experiences don't last." The *I Ching* makes it clear that duration, not change, is the way of the Cosmos. So long as these incorrect beliefs are held in the psyche, the success of the healing may be reversed.

Deprogramming Causes for Regression

In reference to (a) and (b) mentioned above, when the cause is an incorrect attitude or a self-image, these need to be deprogrammed in a mini-meditation by saying No three times to each phrase and/or image involved, and picturing each being sucked into a Cosmic vacuum cleaner. Tie up the bag and turn it over to the Helper of Transformation and the Helper of Dissolution. Ask once each following day whether to repeat this procedure until the answer is No. Then, thank the Helpers for their help.

In reference to (c) above, regarding feeling guilty or privileged for having been healed, the imp that causes these feelings needs to be killed. In a mini-meditation, ask the Sage to kill this imp. Check whether other demonic elements are also involved, such as a demon, and/or dragon of guilt, or a dragon of privilege. All these need to be killed by the Sage. Ask once each following day whether to repeat this procedure until the answer is No. Then, thank the Sage for its help.

In reference to (d) above, when the cause is a false image you have of the illness, deprogram this image in a mini-meditation by saying No three times to the image, and picturing it being sucked into a Cosmic vacuum cleaner. Tie up the bag and turn it over to the Helper of Transformation and the Helper of Dissolution. (This is a one-time exercise.)

In reference to the doubter (e) above, say No three times to its doubting activity and to the phrase(s) and image(s) it puts forth. Then ask the Sage to kill it. Ask once each following day whether to repeat this procedure until the answer is No.

Be aware that the doubter may be accompanied by another demonic element called "the changeling." This changeling would undo the transformations achieved by the Helpers. Use the *rtcm* to check whether a changeling is also active in the situation. If yes, ask the Helper that Kills Changelings to do so. This is a one-time procedure.

Hindrances to Healing

Allowing the ego to interfere while the healing is still in progress either blocks or hinders the Helpers. This happens in a variety of ways that include actions, observations, comments, or arguments, such as:

(a) Allowing the ego to keep its eye on the healing process either to judge its efficacy, to measure its progress, or to comment on the deprogramming procedure. This happens when we allow it to comment: "Thoughts cannot be that destructive," "There must be another cause," "How can invisible Helpers heal something that is visible," "Nothing is happening that I can see," "I'll believe it when the tests show it's true," "You can wait forever, and it won't happen." "Where are the Helpers, anyway?" "Healing can't be that easy."

(b) Watching for a miracle to happen. As mentioned above, under Causes for Regression, healing the Cosmic way is through transformations in the consciousness of the cells, not through magic, or "miracles." Expecting the healing to take place overnight or within a specified amount of time, and complaining when this does not occur, is an interference of the ego that prevents the completion of the healing.

(c) Arguing: "How can deprogramming free you from an illness that even doctors cannot heal?"

(d) Spells that inhibit healing. Among these spells are:

- Mistaken beliefs that denigrate or deny our *inner* senses which are part of the Helper of Transformation. Example: "Only the eyes see the truth." "What you see is all there is." "The truth must be obvious."
- Mistaken ideas that put down our feelings and/or elevate our ability to think. Examples: "Feelings don't count." "Feelings cannot be trusted." "Thinking is superior to feeling." "Humans

193

are special because they have the ability to think." "You get to the truth through thinking."

• Mistaken beliefs about the way Nature functions. Example: "Nature works through changes."

(e) Pride that inhibits healing. The ego may put up a pride-induced resistance to being dependent on Helpers while at the same time reminding us how dependent we are on it.

Cooperating with the Helpers means we are making a conscious choice between the ego and the Helpers. It means welcoming the Helpers as a part of ourselves, and not looking at them as an alien force. It means recognizing their unique abilities to help us return to harmony with ourselves and with the Cosmos. It is good when we consciously affirm this fact by saying Yes, Yes, Yes to the world of invisible Helpers.

The Helpers work best when, after doing our share of deprogramming, we turn the matter entirely over to them, and go on with our daily lives. When we notice, often weeks or months later, that we are back to health, it is time to thank the Helpers for their aid.

(f) Self-images that inhibit healing.

Examples: The self-image of the one who survived the threats posed by the illness, and the self-image of the one who makes a new beginning.

We can understand how these self-images are counter-productive when we realize that they are self-congratulatory, indicating how the ego has seized the success and wears it as a badge.

Deprogramming Hindrances to Healing

As soon as you become aware of any ego-comments, expectations, arguments, or self-images referenced in (a)-(f), say No three times to them, and picture them being sucked into a Cosmic vacuum cleaner. Tie up the bag and turn it over to the Helper of Transformation. (This is a one-time-only exercise.)

If there are spells present that inhibit healing (d), make a list of them. Then, after saying No three times to each one, picture the whole list being sucked into a Cosmic vacuum cleaner. Tie up the bag and turn it over to the Sage. Ask once each following day whether to repeat this procedure until the answer is No. Then, thank the Sage for its help.

When ego pride hinders the healing (e) the "dragon of pride in human independence" needs to be killed. Say No three times to this dragon and ask the Helper that Kills Dragons to do so. (This is a one-time procedure.)

Check whether you have put any spells or poison arrows on the Helpers. If so, deprogram them by saying No three times to each one, and use the bag meditation as described two paragraphs above.

In all cases where there seems to be a hindrance to healing, or where a regression to earlier symptoms has occurred, the cause always lies in the activity of the ego. While we have listed as many obstructions as we have encountered, the list may not exhaust all possible kinds of ego interference. We need to persist in our efforts to uncover the causes and allow for new discoveries. Learning to work with *I Ching, The Oracle of the Cosmic Way* makes it easier to identify hidden causes.

Checking Whether any Deprogramming has been Undone

After having deprogrammed the causes you have found for a regression, or that have hindered your healing, you then need to check with the *rtcm* whether your previous deprogramming has been undone by the ego's interference. When the answer is Yes, you need not despair. You can ask the Helper that Deprograms Reinstalled Things to deprogram them again on your behalf. You do not need to recall what those things are. Repeat this request until you receive No to continuing.

Part IV

Dismantling the Ego Program of a Long-standing Illness

Overview of the Ego Program

Long-standing, serious, or chronic illnesses run on a "program" the ego has installed in the psyche. Like a sophisticated computer program, it has defensive, maintenance, upgrade, and reinstalling features. Thus, once one or two false thought forms start an illness, other ego-elements are added over time. Some keep the illness in place, others make it worse. Some protect the ego from being discovered as the cause of all the trouble. In such ways the program of the illness enables the ego to live off the energy created by the fears, worries, and stress it causes the host.

To fulfill these purposes, the ego uses a number of language tricks to blind the sick person (a) about the cause of his condition, (b) to facts about the treatment, (c) to facts about the prognosis, and (d) about the sources of help that are available to him. Instrumental in this activity is a demonic element created by the ego that we have called the "changeling." The main job of the changeling, once a person has become seriously ill, is to develop a whole program in the psyche that insures that from that moment on, the person's life revolves around the illness. The changeling is instrumental in developing and guarding every aspect of the program of the illness described here. We will mention the changeling whenever it needs to be included in deprogramming parts of the program.

If we forget to deprogram a changeling that has been connected with an ego complex or such, it becomes a mischief-maker in our psyche. Like a free radical, it seeks something neto pair itself with. We then speak of it as a "free-floating changeling." Such a free-floating changeling can be recognized by physical symptoms that crop up in various places in the body either all at once, or successively. (See Chapter 21 for instructions how to deprogram a free-floating changeling.)

In this chapter we liken the program of an illness to a "forbidden ancient city." The forbidden city is a metaphor for the extreme effort the ego makes to conceal its sick-making program in our psyche so that we continue to view the ego as our wise counselor and friend. In this way, the ego can siphon off our life force without our notice.

We will show in the following sections which role each aspect of the forbidden city plays in the program of the illness, and point to those parts of our true nature that have become blocked or made dysfunctional. We will also show which specific mistaken beliefs or images have made this possible. The reader can follow the schematic presented below to uncover the inner components of a long-standing illness; the process is designed to enable you get to know your own natural makeup better. You can use the schematic to check, using the *rtcm*, which elements apply to you, or to a person whose illness you are investigating, so that those elements can be deprogrammed. (The use of the *rtcm* is described in Chapter 19.)

A Visual Image of the Program of an Illness

The forbidden city consists of the main kinds of sick-making thoughts and images that comprise the program of the illness. A wall and a moat defend its core elements. Atop the wall with its gates, are watchtowers. Suburbs and an extended city stretch outside the walls. In the distance is a crossroads with a signpost; hovering above the whole scene is a hawk.

- *The core city* represents the original mistaken beliefs that caused the illness.
- *The gates* into the city represent slandering or flattering ideas that are disabling our self-healing abilities, thereby making us susceptible to illness.
- *The defensive walls* represent unconscious resistances to getting well caused by the ego's finding gain in our being ill.
- *The watchtowers* represent certain preconceived ideas about illness that support the resistances to getting well.
- *The moat* represents fears connected with the illness, such as the fear of becoming guilty for wanting to get well.
- *The suburbs* represent projections, spells, or poison arrows, and others' explanations of the illness. Included are the mechanical descriptions of the symptoms given by doctors.
- *The extended city* consists of mistaken ideas about the way the body functions, and about the Cosmos and its Helpers.

- *The signpost* points to beliefs that make us look in the wrong direction both for the cause of the illness, and for help to get well.
- *The hawk* that controls the whole landscape from above represents the concept of guilt that is often connected with being ill, which keeps us caught in the illness.

Our examination of the above elements of this program will not be in the order shown above, but in the order needed to successfully free ourselves from all the components of the program. Following this order, step by step, is recommended as the most economical and strategic way to proceed, because with every step, Helpers are freed that are needed to help with the next step. By proceeding in this way, we avoid being attacked from behind, or being obstructed in our progress by preconceived ideas or fears.

When an outside influence is the cause of the illness

An exception to the above occurs when the primary cause of the illness is due to an outside influence, i.e., a poison arrow that has been put on us by another. In this case only those aspects of the program described in Sections 1-8 may apply. They apply because the illness has become chronic due to other sick-making thoughts having been added to the primary cause by ourselves and others.

Because the illness was caused by an outside influence in which we have had no part, Cosmic Helpers have been at work all along to break the primary poison arrow that makes up the core of the program described in Section 9. The Helper of Transformation has also been busy on our behalf by transforming it bit by bit until it is broken.

What we still need to find out is who has put the original poison arrow on us and say No three times to that person's having done so. Then we need to ask the Helper of Deprogramming to deprogram it. We do not need to identify the content of that poison arrow. (Also see Chapter 14, *Illnesses Caused by Influences Coming from Outside.*)

1. Hidden Resistances to Getting Well (The Defensive Walls Surrounding The Forbidden City)

Before we can successfully deprogram the root causes of an illness, we need first to deprogram any hidden resistances to getting well; otherwise these resistances will reinstall the core elements of the program.

It may seem odd that we can have a resistance to getting well. Having such a resistance does not mean we do not want to get well. Rather, on becoming ill, the ego quickly finds advantages in this fact. Below is a partial list of "gains" that are implied in an illness. These gains support the ego in us, while leaving our body to suffer. It needs to be added that certain resistance factors can even be among the reasons for becoming ill in the first place.

Resistance to getting well mainly has two sources: self-images and guilt. Both either injure or capture those of our natural functions which protect us from illness and help us heal. The imprisonment of these protective and healing functions is one of the reasons that an illness becomes chronic.

Examples of self-images that create resistance:
- the "brave person," and the "one who can endure endlessly" (the self-image of the hero)
- the "one who deserves the pity of others" (the self-image of the victim)
- the "one who accepts the scientific view of illness" (the self-image of the objective person) A person with this self-image would feel guilty if he stepped outside the medical framework to heal his illness. ("What will my doctor think?")
- the "person no one notices" (who believes being ill is the only way to gain notice, or be cared for by others).
- the "one with the interesting case"
- the "one with a mysterious illness" (a dramatic self-image)
- the "one who sees suffering as redeeming others" (the scapegoat self-image that gives one's life a noble purpose)

The following are examples of self-images that are a primary

cause of illness, because to fulfill them, the person must be ill:
- the self-image of "being helpless," or the "one who is disadvantaged by Fate"
- the "saintly person" is a self-image based on the belief that self-sacrifice, even death, will make one a saint in heaven. This includes persons with the self-image of the devoted caretaker who sacrifices his needs and well-being for the benefit of others; it may also include "the one who willingly carries his cross"

These self-images are often adopted to punish us for the guilt of not having lived up to an absolute standard of goodness; thus they serve as a form of redemption.

Ego-resistances to freeing ourselves from a self-image:

Because the ego gains so much from our investment in a self-image, it uses a number of language tricks to either keep the self-image in place, or to quickly replace it with an upgraded version once we make the effort to free ourselves of it. These language tricks are the work of the "changeling" mentioned above. The following three aspects of the changeling fulfill these functions:

"The identifier" uses the verbs "to be" and "to have" to make us identify with the illness. For example, when a person is diagnosed with an illness, the identifier shifts his identity from being "a healthy person," to one who "has cancer," or "is a cancer case." (Remember that our body cells identify with whatever we identify ourselves with; in this case, they identify with the illness.)

"The excuser" upgrades the illness into something the ego regards as useful to its ends, such as a device to gain attention, love, and care that we may feel has always been missing in our life, or to fill a gap in our life that cannot otherwise be filled.

"The blamer" seizes the illness to attain power over others, by holding them to blame for making us sick. For example, if we believe our parents made us sick as a child, we may unconsciously resist getting well, so that we can continue blaming them, or making them feel guilty.

Since the fear of becoming guilty for wanting to get well is connected to many of the above self-images, we also need to ask whether the fear of becoming guilty is connected with any self-images we identify as applicable to ourselves.

The Body's Attachment to a Self-Image

In deprogramming self-images, we are confronted with the fact that all self-images have been adopted as a protection against being seen as deficient. After adopting a self-image, the body soon adapts to that self image and becomes attached to it. For example, the body of the person who has adopted a heroic self-image will endure and suffer silently to support the image of the "brave person."

Thus, a part of that person's resistance to giving up the self-image actually comes from his body cells that have become habituated to playing their part in this charade. Consequently, the idea of "getting well" can arouse the body's fears that it will no longer be viewed as the hero, and will now be reduced once again to being seen as "deficient." Part of deprogramming a self-image, therefore, requires deprogramming those slanders put on us in childhood that have made us feel deficient:

• "You are not good enough"
• "You are deficient"
• "Something is wrong with you"
• "Why are you not like everyone else?"

(You can add any others that may apply.)

To free ourselves from any of these slanders and self-images, we first need to deprogram any guilt described below. Exact instructions as to the order in which deprogramming is to be done are given at the end of Section 3 below.

2. The Role of Guilt (The Hawk)

Guilt, if not deprogrammed, greatly diminishes our self-healing abilities. It therefore keeps us ill for longer periods of time than necessary. Guilt also reinstalls the things we have deprogrammed by making us fear that if we turn our backs on our time-honored beliefs, we will become guilty. This fear may not be conscious when we decide to deprogram a self-image or mistaken belief, but we can take its existence for granted because of the way we have been made to accept mistaken beliefs during childhood training. We have discussed the role of guilt in illness in Chapter 9. When investigating a long-standing illness, we need to check with the *rtcm* whether any or all of the three guilt complexes described there need to be deprogrammed.

3. The Causes of Susceptibility to Illness (The Gates in the Wall Surrounding the Forbidden City)

Slanders on our self-healing abilities are among the factors that make us *susceptible* to getting ill. They injure our wholeness, causing "holes" in our natural protective system. When our self-healing abilities are fully functioning, they protect us from getting ill. Some of them also have the ability to heal us when other parts have been rendered dysfunctional through slanders. These slanders are contained in a limited number of commonly held mistaken ideas about our human animal nature:

• "Human animal nature is the source of evil."
• "Humans are born guilty because they have an animal nature."
• "In and of yourself you are insufficient to cope with life."
• "There is no help for you from the Cosmos."
• "You cannot trust your feelings."

In the light of all the wonderful things we have learned from the *I Ching* about the completeness and total goodness of our nature, these statements are slanderous. Such ideas damage the genetic combinations in our DNA that in their totality protect us from getting ill, and help us heal. Deprogramming them corrects this damage.

Our Self-Healing Abilities

The functions that make up our self-healing abilities are contained in the DNA of every body cell. The DNA is our Cosmic operating system. It possesses its own repair program, which begins its work when other parts of our DNA become injured by slanders put on our true nature. However, even this repair function can become injured or captured by the ego. Because this injury can only happen through our free will, it is always possible to return to health and harmony by correcting our mistaken thinking.

Injury to our DNA and its repair program is caused by the *fear of becoming guilty.* As mentioned above, this fear sets in when we attempt to free ourselves from self-images that have the approval of the collective ego. This fear further blocks our self-healing abilities. We have described the origins of guilt and the three ego complexes formed around guilt in Chapter 9. Deprogramming the guilt complexes that apply to us is the first step in freeing our self-healing abilities. (You can make sure through the *rtcm* that your deprogramming of guilt, or the fear of becoming guilty, has been successful before deprogramming the slanders mentioned in Section 1. These slanders can be deprogrammed in a water meditation. (See Chapter 21.)

When we receive confirmation through the *rtcm* that the slanders have been successfully deprogrammed, we can start deprogramming any self-images identified in Section 1. For this purpose, a bag meditation is used. If we have found that the identifier, excuser, or blamer aspects of the changeling are involved, we also deprogram these by saying No three times to each phrase they have put forth, and by asking the Sage to bring in the Helper needed to kill the changeling-aspect in question.

After any self-images have been successfully dealt with, the slanders that have made us susceptible to illness, mentioned in Section 3, can be deprogrammed. The deprogramming usually needs to be repeated over a period of three days. We can check with the *rtcm* each day as to whether we need to continue.

4. Beliefs Pointing in the Wrong Direction (The Crossroads with the Signpost)

On learning that we have become ill, we may feel that we are at a crossroads where we need to make a decision about what *outer* action is to be taken. By this subtle shift from *inner* to *outer* action, the ego is put in charge of taking care of the illness. Once we have understood that the causes are to be found by looking within, we no longer find ourselves at such a crossroads, as the example of the nodules in Chapter 1 showed. If any outer action needs to be taken to support our inner efforts, it will be shown in the process of consulting the Sage.

If we have been conditioned to think only in terms of outer action we will be presented with a signpost that distracts our attention from looking for inner causes in the forbidden city. Written on this signpost are the various scientific definitions of the illness. Although they seem to present us with different options by offering different causes, these definitions have in common that they put the blame for the illness on Nature, either our own nature, or some agent coming from our natural environment, such as bacteria, or fungi. Nature also gets the blame when the cause is sought in foods, or substances to which we have become addicted or allergic. As we discussed in Chapter 17, addictions are not caused by substances, but by particular ego complexes. The same ego complexes cause the infections for which bacteria and fungi get the blame. (See Chapter 16.)

Because they blame Nature, medical therapies lead us away from discovering the core program of the illness. Moreover, these therapies often add more elements to the program.

The following elements may need to be deprogrammed:

• "To cure an illness you need to take outer action."
• "The first thing to do is to see a doctor."
• "All illnesses are caused by Nature—either your own nature, or something coming from your natural environment, such as bacteria or fungi, or by substances to which you are allergic or have become addicted."
• "Illness has to be treated with medicine."
• "Some illnesses require interventionist therapies, such as radiation, the ingestion of chemicals, or genetic manipulation."

To deprogram any of the above false thought forms, follow the directions given in Chapter 21.

5. Preconceived Ideas about the Illness: Prognoses, and Expectations Concerning the Future (The Watchtowers)

The Watchtowers represent that part of the ego program that predicts how the illness is likely to develop and how the illness will impact the person's future life. Such ideas have particular weight because they are backed by scientific proofs. *However, we need to remember the power that projections, predictions and expectations have to create the very conditions they project.* When this is taken into account, we can see that the projections are the very things that supply these proofs given by science.

The defensive walls that surround the core program of the illness (the core city) are made up of the resistances created by certain self-images, which combine with the fear of becoming guilty for getting well. These fears are, so to speak, the mortar that holds the walls together. The watchtowers on top of the walls protect the whole structure by presenting the threat of a dire future, a threat which keeps the host person dependent on the collective ego for help. The ideas that make up these watchtowers consist of things that have been said about the illness by doctors, health care workers, medical literature, family members, and friends. They can also be conventional ideas, such as the "seriousness" of the illness, the kinds of complications that accompany it, and how it is expected to progress. Included are pictures taken of the sick cells during medical examinations. While the pictures showed the inner truth of the condition at the time they were taken, they need to be totally released as something belonging to the *past*, otherwise the ego will seize them and replay them before the person's inner eye, inducing yet more fears. The ego will also use those pictures to boast about the seriousness of the condition. If these pictures are not deprogrammed, their remaining in the psyche can reinstall the program.

One common expression that belongs to the watchtower section of the program is "It is better to expect the worst; then when things turn out to be better than you thought, it is a relief."

This list gives examples of mistaken ideas that belong to the watchtower part of the program, taken from actual cases we have worked on:

A woman with a heart that had become enlarged (known as "dilated cardiomyopathy")

- "The diagnosis must be true"
- "My heart is defective"
- "The disintegration of my heart is inevitable"
- "It will lead to my death"
- "I must take medicine in order to feel better"

A middle-aged man with a back injury from his high school days:

- "If I eat right, exercise right, and have the proper posture it will go away"
- "I can't live a normal life"
- "I have to live with periodic pain"
- "It's my cross to bear"
- "I have to limp along in life because my body doesn't work right"
- "I'm always going to be weak there"
- "It will affect my relationships with others and my ability to do what I want"

A woman with "laryngopharyngeal reflux"

This is a condition in which a small amount of stomach acid and enzymes make their way into the larynx or voice box. The woman in question found these fears produced by ego speculations:

- "The disease is chronic; I may never get rid of it"
- "The disease can cause cancer if the larynx is not treated"
- "Cancer of the larynx could leave me mute"
- "If I'm mute I can't do my job"

To investigate the program of an illness, it is desirable to make a list of any preconceived ideas we have about the illness, as well as those we have accepted from doctors, family, friends, or what we have read about it. We add any "final conclusions" that foresee a dire future, or that describe the way the illness will affect our life. We also include any images stored in our memory that depict the result of medical examinations, be they in the form of images of sick cells, or of dramatic figures resulting from blood or similar counts.

Deprogramming our preconceived ideas and stored images

The *I Ching* makes it clear that in deprogramming preconceived ideas, we need to mobilize our whole will. To do so we do a meditation in which we see our list written on a piece of paper that is then burned. We then ask the Helper of Breakthrough to deal with the changeling that guards these ideas.[1] We also ask the Helper of Dissolution to dissolve the rigid structures produced by these ideas in our psyche. We need do this only one time.

In a separate meditation we burn any stored images, and ask the Helper that Extinguishes Images to extinguish them. We then ask the Sage to kill the changeling that has been guarding them. We repeat this exercise daily until we receive confirmation through the *rtcm* that we have done what is necessary to permit the Cosmic Helpers to complete the deprogramming.

The *I Ching* informs us that the force of will lies neither in physical nor mental power, but in the irresistible strength it develops when our will aligns with our inner truth. This alignment breaks the ego's resistance to our getting well.

6. Fears Connected with the Illness (The Moat)

The moat that surrounds the forbidden ancient city represents certain fears connected with an illness. These are different from the fears mentioned above, and from those that may actually have caused the illness.

Before we can address the question of how to deal with these fears, we would like to share a discovery that has given us a

[1] See the description of the changeling in Appendix 2, *Demonic Elements in the Psyche.*

whole new understanding of the general nature of fears. This discovery has had an enormously liberating effect on us and on those with whom we have shared it.

The General Nature of Fears

When writing *I Ching, The Oracle of the Cosmic Way*, we often noticed how our human-centered view had turned the Cosmic reality on its head by excluding the invisible Helpers from our view. Over and over, we were guided by the Sage to reverse our perspective to see that many negative things we had taken to be "natural," were slanders on the Cosmos, on Nature, and on our own true nature. Among these was the idea that "fear is natural."

The Sage's lesson on the true nature of fears started with a mind flash informing us to ask our biggest fear to tell us how it began. We emptied our minds from all preconceived ideas about the origin of fears and listened within. To our surprise, the voice that replied was the voice of our body. It told us that its biggest fear was to be abandoned by our mind. This fear, as we later learned from the Sage, is true for all people. It has its origin in an early childhood event in which we have concluded that *following our feelings leads to punishments and other unpleasant events.* With the feelings thereby discounted, the body is to all effects abandoned by the mind. This revealed to us the intimate connection that exists between body and mind and the big fear that is created in the body when the mind is led to conclude that the body is "inferior," or "bad," or when the mind looks at the body as an enemy to be fought. The slanders put on the body by the mind also separate the body from its symbiotic relationship with the Cosmos. This happens, as explained in Chapter 11, through doubt splitting the consciousness of the body cells apart, so that only a small part of that consciousness remains connected with the Cosmos through our DNA.

In addition to the body's biggest fear of being abandoned by the mind, its other big fear is of becoming ill and dying. The body's fear of becoming ill is created by the mind's denial of the body's great self-healing abilities; its fear of dying is created by the mind's belief that the body is mortal. (See Chapter 10.)

We have mentioned that it is the body which possesses, through its DNA, the Cosmic operating system for our whole being. The *I Ching* calls this our *inner truth*. It is also through the body that our life energy is continuously supplied. These, and many other bodily functions, which are Helpers of our animal nature, are to be highly valued, and not dismissed as mere mechanisms without consciousness. All parts of the body know their functions and do them, when unobstructed, with the utmost efficiency.

The existence of what we would call a "big" fear always indicates that a particular helping function of our animal nature has been denied by our conscious mind. In being denied recognition, that Helper is like an unemployed worker that wants to do its job; however, it is prevented from fulfilling its function. Knowing that it is needed but unable to help, it becomes agitated in trying to get the attention of our conscious mind. *It is the agitation of this Helper, together with the body's recognition that it has been rendered vulnerable through being deprived of its own vital resources, that we experience as fear.*

With this understanding, we no longer need to feel helpless when confronted with a big fear; once we find the name of the unrecognized Helper, and consciously validate its function it can resume its functioning in our body. This brings joy and relief both to us and to that Helper.

Fears, then, are the body's knowledge of "what might happen should a threat occur" while it has been rendered helpless by a mistaken belief.

The most common fears in the context of illness are:
• the fear of contracting a particular illness
• the fear of dying
• the fear of suffering
• the fear of being disfigured or crippled
• the fear of staying disabled
• the fear of being stuck in an illness

Asking our Body about the Cause of the Fear

We ask our body to inform us of phrases and/or images that are causing the fear. Our body knows the slanderous phrases and images because they are stored in the body.

Let us say, for example, that we have identified with the *rtcm* that we have the fear of staying disabled by the illness. We now ask our body, "what is causing my fear?" It may say, "There is nothing that can be done" (a comment made by a doctor), or, "I will always be dependent on others" (a conclusion that we have drawn). Blotted out by these phrases is the Helper of Healing.

Deprogramming a Fear Coming from the Body

We follow these steps to deprogram fears of the body:

Step 1: We become aware of the fear, such as the fear of staying disabled by the illness.

Step 2: We ask our body: "What phrases/images are behind this fear? We listen carefully to what our body replies. (In the above example, the body's reply was, "There is nothing that can be done.")

Step 3: We identify the Helper that has been blotted out by the phrase or image that has caused the fear. That phrase or image was identified in Step 2.

We now ask the blotted out Helper to give us its name. It will be happy to tell us. In the above example it was the Helper of Healing.

Step 4: We say No three times to the phrases and/or images our body told us in Step 2.

Step 5: We ask the Helper we have identified to free us from the fear-inspiring image identified in Step 1. In our example it was the image of staying disabled by the illness.

Steps 4 and 5 are repeated over several days until we learn through the *rtcm* that we can stop.

Fears Coming from Our Mind

While fears coming from our body are often the *cause* of an illness, the false fears that come from a particular demonic element in our mind can *trigger a latent illness*. We call this demonic

212

element "the projector of fearful images." It is an aspect of the changeling. We can use the *rtcm* to obtain clarity about whether a particular fear comes from the body or from the mind. If it comes from the mind, two things need to be deprogrammed: (1) the changeling mentioned above (for this purpose we ask the Helper that Kills Projectors of Fearful Images to kill it), and (2) the fear it has inspired (it is a projection and poison arrow).

The Effect of the Mind's Fears on the Heart

The main function of our heart is to distribute harmonious Cosmic energy throughout our body, including our mind. We depend on this energy, called *heart-chi,* for nourishment and health. Our lungs, the organ that renews the air we need as part of our Cosmic nourishment, join the heart in this distribution task. When we are in harmony with ourselves, our heart beat and breathing correspond to a rhythm in Nature that is felt as peace and joy.

Since our heart is the center of our feeling consciousness, we feel feelings most strongly through our heart. We are speaking here of caring and loving feelings, feelings of joy and peace, and also of sadness. These true feelings must not be confounded with ego-emotions such as alienation, hatred, vindictiveness, inferiority and superiority. The latter are the result of mistaken ideas and beliefs that create an inner conflict between the ego and our true self. Ego-emotions result from the ego's using the mind to stimulate false feelings, such as hoping, doubting, wanting, and fearing. These feelings are then fed to the heart, thus hijacking the heart to feed the ego's need for energy. It is important to realize that the ego feeds on negative as well as positive emotions.

We have all had the experience of ego-emotions getting us into trouble. However, in its customary way of shifting blame away from itself, the ego uses this experience to make its most consequential judgment: "You cannot trust your feelings." In doing so, it puts the blame on our true feelings as the troublesome aspect of our nature. This obscures the fact that the trouble was actually caused by ego-emotions.

The judgment that "you cannot trust your feelings" puts a spell on our true feelings, leaving the neurons in our body without the guidance provided by our feelings of inner truth; as a consequence, the neurons must now look to the thinking mind for guidance. This enables the ego to become the decision-maker in the psyche.

As a result of the spell, "You cannot trust your feelings," the healthy relationship between the heart and the thinking mind is disturbed, leaving the mind starved for the nourishing *heart-chi*. In this situation, *the mind begins to fear that it will die*. It no longer knows what is causing its fear, but projects it onto life itself. As described in Chapter 10, mistaken beliefs about death have their source in this experience of a mind that has separated from the true feelings of the heart. All fears connected with illness have their source in these mistaken beliefs about the origin of death.

When a person's heart is hijacked by the ego, he can be compared to someone lying in a sickbed being nourished only through tubes, as in intensive hospital care. A person whose heart is not hijacked by the ego finds himself in a regular bed getting a good night's rest and waking up in the morning nourished by the *chi* that has come from his heart.

The *I Ching*, in Hexagram 27, *Nourishing*, speaks of the difference between "looking for nourishment from the summit and seeking nourishment from the hill."[2] Seeking nourishment from the hill refers to nourishment that comes from our true feelings. The hill suggests green pastures that are full of nourishing herbs. The summit, representing the mind when it has become isolated from the feelings, is a place covered with hoarfrost.[3] The summit is the place where mechanistic explanations of life are to be found. All they have to offer in the face of life-threatening fears are hopes, which by their very nature are devoid of nourishment. Offering us hope is the ego's way of coping with fears. We scarcely notice, in this process, that hope is only the

---

[2] Anthony/Moog, p. 317, Hexagram 27, *Nourishing*, Line 2.
[3] Ibid., p. 94, Hexagram 2, *Nature*, Line 1, "When there is hoarfrost underfoot, solid ice is not far off."

backside of the coin of fear.

The fear of getting a life-threatening illness, as we all know from experience, deprives us of feeling at peace. This indicates that *our heart fears for us*. It is sending our mind the message that it needs to consciously recognize the existence of certain Helpers of our nature. We feel peace returning to our heart when we recognize these blotted out Helpers and deprogram the slanderous beliefs that have caused our fear.

A fear resulting from an illness in the past can be stored in certain body cells. Such a fear can produce inexplicable pains, which, in turn, can give rise to more fears of becoming ill. Coupled with the fear that we might die, this situation creates a poison arrow that triggers the old fear created by the illness in the past; this old fear can cause these body cells to lose their will to live. The thing needed to brace their will is *heart-chi*, which is why freeing our heart from the prison of the ego is so important.

The Effect of Fears on the Body

We have just described a circumstance in which certain body cells can lose their will to live. Two factors come together to make this possible: the first is the presence of a dormant fear created by a previous illness that has been stored in body cells; the second is the fear of getting a life-threatening illness. The latter is often taken in from ads, the media, or other people who spread statistics that speak of the "risks" of contracting illness. When we give credibility to a statistic for a certain kind of illness that supports our existing fear of getting that illness, the illness starts to manifest. Additional fears diminish our natural protection against further projections, spells, or poison arrows coming from the people around us who have the same fears.

An example is the fear of getting a life-threatening influenza if we have stored a fear from a previous but less severe flu. When we then listen to a fear-inspiring news report about a newly discovered flu virus that "has already taken several lives, and threatens to spread," the mechanism described above sets in. The Sage has made us aware that the poison arrow created by this set of circumstances weakens those body cells where the fear of the previous illness is stored. This leads to the development of the disease. Another factor in the situation is that the poison arrow is also put on the bacteria in animals that are viewed as carrying the disease. As was pointed out in Chapter 16, these bacteria are drawn to the origin of the poison arrow. Our body does not fear what comes from Nature; it only fears the poison arrows coming from the ego mindset.

7. Freeing the Heart, our Source of Inner Nourishment (The Suburbs)

The suburbs represent obstructing beliefs that make it impossible for the heart to fulfill its function of nourishing our whole being with *heart-chi*. These beliefs are the same as those that have separated the thinking mind from its natural relationship with the heart. The Helpers that keep our heart supplied with the life energy that comes from our inner truth become blocked when we accept the spell that "we cannot trust our feelings of inner truth."

As a result, our heart becomes the storehouse for the mind's fears, trivialities, guilt, and self-doubts. The *I Ching* refers to them as "the mud at the bottom of the well."[4] The presence of such mud causes the heart to shrink, harden, or thicken, or to thin and widen. These effects were shown in a heart meditation.

Doing a Heart Meditation

To see the condition of our heart we recommend the following meditation: we sit in an upright normal position on a chair or cushion, and close our eyes. We then ask the Helper of Mind Cleansing to remove clutter from our mind so that it becomes receptive. We next ask the Helpers to show us the condition of our heart. We may find that it is injured, or locked-up, or contains worms, or shows some other kind of problem. We then ask

---

[4] Ibid, p. 521, Hexagram 48, *The Well*, line 1.

the Helper of our Heart to free it from the ego-elements that are causing these conditions. We then simply observe what happens. If we feel moved to help, we follow our heart. At the end of our meditation, we thank the Helpers for their aid.

The Renewal of our Life Force

The nourishing life force that comes to our heart from our inner truth is normally renewed through our symbiotic relationships with the Cosmos and with Nature. It can also be renewed by love coming from the Cosmos, as in the sexual expression of love with our love partner, or when we give sexual expression to this love directly, without a love partner. Cosmic love does not require a love partner. When we are not connected with the Cosmos, the expression of sexuality does not renew our life force.

Being in harmony with Nature also connects us with Cosmic love. If we are unable to feel the Cosmic love that comes through Nature, it means there is a block in the form of one or more mistaken ideas about Nature, as when we believe that humans are the centerpiece of creation.

The Function of our Body Cells in the Renewal of our Life Force

The fact that we live in a body indicates that our lives are part of the way the Cosmos has structured life. To fit into this structure, the Cosmos provides us with a specific bodily makeup that allows us to receive life force. We receive this force automatically so long as we have not separated from the Cosmos.

In this context we refer to a particular group of cells known as *germ cells.*[5] Germ cells are not restricted to the reproductive cells with which we normally associate them, but comprise all the cells that make up our sexual organs. People tend to think they are only instrumental to the procreation of children. However, the *I Ching* has made us aware that they are also instrumental in renewing our life force throughout our lives in a body. *The*

---

[5] germ cell: "an egg or sperm cell or one of their antecedent cells." Webster's New Collegiate Dictionary.

harmony of our body and psyche, including our thinking function, depends on this life force.

When our bodies and our sexuality are free of spells, our life force is renewed through the attraction of *the light force* by *the dark.* (See Pattern 3, p. 13.) The dark aspect of the physical body, as a whole, attracts the light force of Cosmic love.

The light force can enter the dark of the physical body only through our germ cells. The Helper of Transformation then unites the light force with the dark through transformation. This creation of life force takes place in the genes of the germ cells.

The following mistaken ideas prevent this renewal of our life force. If through the *rtcm* we find that we hold them, they need to be deprogrammed.

(a) Slanders put on the light and the dark:

These slanders block the attraction of Cosmic light to the body, and thus prevent the Helper of Transformation from renewing our life force.

- Seeing the light and the dark as opposites and/or as opponents
- Seeing the light as "higher" and the dark as "lower"
- Seeing the light as welcome/preferable/good, the dark as fearful/undesirable/evil
- Seeing our animal nature as connected with the dark and our "higher" nature with the light
- Equating the light with heaven as paradise and the dark with the earth as hell

(b) Slanders put on love

- Categorizing love as being either "divine/agape/platonic" or "earthy"
- "Love does not last"; "love is for fools"; "true love does not exist"
- "Love must be unconditional" (loving also the ego)
- "To have love is our right" (the Cosmos owes us love)

(c) Slanders put on our sexuality (in the form of images)

- Seeing it as stained with guilt, dirty, lowly, bad, evil
- Seeing it as "getting us into trouble"
- Seeing sexuality as a thing to enjoy in itself, separate from

love and sensitivity
• Seeing one gender (male or female) as superior to the other
• Seeing sexual love as owed
(d) Slanders put on life as an entity (in the form of images)
• Seeing life as pain and suffering, as a bad experience, or as a dog-eat-dog experience
• Seeing life as unjust, or a bad joke
• "Life has no purpose"
(e) Slanders put on our body (in the form of images)
• "The body is vulnerable, weak, inert, needy, incapable of defending itself"
• "The body is the source of evil"
• "The joys of the body are evil"
• "Certain parts/functions of the body are disgusting"
(f) The name given to the illness
• its Greek or Latin or other medical diagnostic name
(g) Spells or poison arrows that undermine the will of the cells to live
• Diagnoses such as "This is a terminal illness."
• Statements such as "You will always have this condition/pain/problem"
• "You don't have good genes"
(h) Slanders put on the Cosmos
• "The Cosmos has abandoned us"
• "The Cosmos is indifferent to our suffering"

Deprogramming the Above

To deprogram, we assemble all the slanders and false statements found in this section into a list. As we write them down, we take some time to reflect why they are slanders on the truth. When that is not immediately obvious, it is helpful to consult the Sage by asking to be pointed to a particular hexagram in *I Ching, The Oracle of the Cosmic Way* for clarification.

We check with the *rtcm* whether we also need to deprogram the spell, "you cannot trust your feelings." If Yes, we add it to our list. Our whole list can now be deprogrammed in a "bag meditation." In this meditation, we picture each image or phrase being sucked into a Cosmic vacuum cleaner. We then tie up the bag and turn it over to the Helpers (unspecified) and the Helper of Dissolution. We ask once each following day whether we need to repeat this procedure until the answer is No. Then we thank the Helpers for their aid.

8. Joint Approach:
Replacing the Mechanical View of the Body
(The Extended City)

The extended city is that part of the ego program that contains obstructions erected to the *process of healing*. It is also where it is necessary to engage the cooperation of the various Helpers of our nature to complete the healing. In the *I Ching*, this coopera-tion between our conscious mind and the self-healing abilities of the body is called "Joint Approach."

Joint approach also refers to the interconnection and coopera-tion that goes on between cell parts for each cell to function. The renewal and healing of the body takes place on the cellular level through the body cells' ability to divide and thereby produce new cells. It is through this dividing activity of the cells that injured, old, or inoperative body cells are replaced with new cells. Healing thus takes place within the cells, in the realm of the atom, which is the realm of consciousness. The role of consciousness in this process involves the conscious assent of the mind to relinquish those parts of the ego program it has adopted.

To enable a joint approach to healing, the mind needs to understand that the way it thinks can either bring us pain and suffering, or joy and happiness. Pain and suffering result from thoughts that contradict the harmonious ways in which our whole being is set up to function. Joy and happiness result when the mind understands these harmonious ways of our natural program, and supports them.

The first step in the *normal* process of healing involves the removal, through deprogramming, of the sick-making thoughts in the realm of the atom. This process of correction usually takes three days. In Hexagram 18, *Recognizing and Correcting the Causes of Decay*, the *I Ching* speaks of "before the starting point three days; after the starting point three days."[6] The second set of three days refers to the activity of the Helper of Transformation, which is also known as the Helper of Completion. We have mentioned that the Helper of Transformation can be partially blocked by poison arrows. They are the same poison arrows that have caused the illness. Fortunately, this Helper can be activated temporarily by deprogramming the poison arrows that caused us to become susceptible to illness in the first place. They are referred to in section 3 above. If we have already deprogrammed them, the Helper of Transformation is free to do its job.

9. The Core of the Program of the Illness (The Core City)

The core of the program of the illness consists of its primary cause(s) in the form of mistaken beliefs or self-images, and the ego complexes derived from them. This core is the part of the program the ego most hides from us; thus, it is likened here to the center of the forbidden city.

The primary cause of the illness is usually a projection, spell, or poison arrow that slanders life, human nature, the nature of the Cosmos, or our relationship with the Cosmos. Knowing this means we need not search far and wide for the cause.

The following is a rather comprehensive list of possible primary causes (spells and poison arrows) that over time have become components of larger structures we call ego complexes. These ego complexes are described in Section 10. If we wish to investigate a specific illness we will first need to identify its specific cause from the following list using the *rtcm*. Once we have identified all that apply to our illness, we go to Section 10 and select those ego complexes that are referenced to the

---

[6] Ibid, p. 235.

causes listed here.

(1) Slanders on the nature of the Cosmos

a) "The Cosmos is divided into good and evil"
b) "The Cosmos uses power," or "the Cosmos is all-power-ful"
c) "The Cosmos is indifferent, and leaves us to our own re-sources"

(2) Slanders on life

a) "Life is unfair"
b) "Life sucks," or similar statements

(3) Slanders on human nature

a) "Humans are born guilty"
b) "Human animal nature is the source of evil"

(4) Self-images, such as

a) The "saintly person" who believes that self-sacrifice (even death) will make one a saint in heaven
b) The "sinner"
c) The "one who willingly carries his cross"
d) The self-image of "being helpless," or "the victim"
e) The "one who is disadvantaged by Fate"

(5) Slanders on the relationship between humans and the Cosmos

a) "Humans are the special creatures of creation"
b) "Humans have to do it all"
c) "Humans have been given the task to control Nature"
d) "I deserve to be punished because I have sinned"

All the above slanders cause damage to our DNA because they cast a doubt on the fundamental goodness of the Cosmos, of life, and of human animal nature. This damage can remain dormant for many years, and at some point attract a "trigger" that causes them to manifest as illness.

Here are the most common triggers:

• Fear of getting a particular illness
• Fear of becoming the victim of an epidemic going around
• Guilt for something one has done and for which one expects to be punished in one way or another

Although this list of core mistaken beliefs and the ego complexes they spawn may seem long, it is short when one considers the catalog of symptoms and causes of illnesses listed by the medical profession. Most importantly, the core mistaken beliefs are quickly recognized and become deprogrammable once we have become familiar with the main Cosmic Principles of Harmony. By possessing the methods needed to deprogram them, we become independent of having to take outer action. The help is there, at all times in our own bodily knowledge, and in the hexagrams of the *I Ching,* to address the most complex-seeming illness. Does it take some study? Yes. Does it take some perseverance to get past the interfering ego? Yes. But, once we learn the kinds of thoughts and tricks the ego plays, we no longer need to be vulnerable in terms of health. Sincerity in asking the Sage for help to do this work always brings a reliable response.

10. Ego Complexes

We have now covered the primary sick-making causes that are at the root of our separation from the Cosmos, Nature, and our own nature. They are responsible for blocking much of the help we would ordinarily attract to us from all quarters.

We present here the ego complexes that are relevant to the primary causes mentioned above, and some others that are often related to illnesses. Note that they are keyed by letters in parentheses to the primary slanders listed in Section 9 that give rise to them.

Since ego complexes often contain an assemblage of beliefs and images that can be deprogrammed as one unit, it can be tempting to approach deprogramming them in a superficial way, which would not be effective. We need to go through the beliefs and images that are contained in the description of a complex, feel which of them apply to us personally, and allow ourselves to perceive how we have based our actions on them. We use the *rtcm* when we are in doubt whether a belief applies to us. (To Deprogram an Ego Complex see Chapter 21.)

The description given for each complex is not necessarily exhaustive. Other beliefs or self-images may need to be identified that pertain to us individually.

The Primary Causes (1a)-(1c) listed in Section 9 have created the False-Cosmos-Complex:

The False-Cosmos-Complex is based on the following slanders:

• "The Cosmos is divided into good and evil"
• "The Cosmos uses power," or "the Cosmos is all-powerful"
• "The Cosmos is indifferent, and leaves us to our own limited resources"

Its subsidiary false beliefs are: "The Cosmos is divided into opposing forces," "The Cosmos is indifferent to human suffering," "The Cosmos is indifferent to its own creation."

[Note: The belief that the Cosmos is divided into good and evil falsely implies that evil is an integral part of the Cosmos. The *I Ching* makes it clear that what is called evil is wholly created by the collective ego, out of its dichotomous thinking. *The Cosmos, as an integrated system of harmonics, does not include the ego and the parallel reality of demonic consciousness the ego has created.* When we accept the view that evil is part of the Cosmos, we allow the collective ego to shift the blame for the suffering *it* creates onto the Cosmos.]

Along with the gift of creativity, humans are given freedom to imagine and to think. The purpose of this gift has ever been to benefit the Cosmic Whole. However, humans have used this freedom to turn that gift to their own glorification, thereby defying the limits that pertain to human existence. When human limits are defied, Fate sets in to help bring people back to their true nature. Fate is also the instrument by which the collective ego and its parallel reality are contained. It stands like a wall around the Cosmic Harmony that keeps it undisturbed. Myths that evil exists to test human virtue are simply false. Evil has no Cosmic function. The ego uses the argument that evil has a purpose only to justify and maintain its own existence.

The collective ego similarly uses the false belief that the Cosmos is all-powerful to justify its own use of power. The *I Ching* shows us that the whole idea of power contradicts the Cosmic Way. The Cosmos operates through transformations in the atomic realm where the resistance implied by the concept of power does not exist. Transformations are initiated through the force of attraction between the complementary aspects of the Cosmos. This attraction is felt as love.

The slander that the Cosmos is indifferent to all the parts of itself that make up existence, is a false view gained from the narrow perspective of only looking at the outer appearance of things. In many of its hexagrams, the *I Ching* shows us the loving and caring nature of the Cosmos. However, for the reasons given above, it does not give its love and care to any aspect of the ego.

The Primary Causes (1a) and (1c) in Section 9 have also created the Judgment Complex:
   The Judgment Complex is based on the spells:
 • "Humans have the right to judge things"
 • "Humans have the duty to judge things"
 • "Humans are the only ones with the ability to judge things"
 • "We must act according to our judgment, and use power to correct situations"; "power enables us to survive"
 • "You have to be ruthless, willing to cheat, and if necessary, to steal the pennies from your dead mother's eyes"
 • "There is a higher power; you need to have it on your side"

The Primary Causes (1b) and (1c) in Section 9 have also given rise to The False-Nature-Complex:
   The False-Nature-Complex is based on phrases such as:
 • "Nature is wild and dangerous"
 • "Nature is chaotic and therefore needs to be ordered "

225

- "Humans have rights over Nature"
- "Nature is man's enemy and therefore must be controlled"
- "We are dependent on Nature even though it is cruel and merciless"
- "Nature is impersonal"
- "Nature is fearsome, awesome, and therefore unknowable"
- "Predator animals are evil"
- "Death is the opposite of life"
- "Death is evil"

Since our own nature is part of Nature we will also need to deprogram all thoughts that slander it as evil, bad, inferior, disgusting, or phrases that imply that we are separate from Nature. Examples include:

- "My own nature is wild and dangerous"
- "My sexuality is bad (and makes me guilty)"
- "The functions of my lower body are disgusting"
- "Our nature is divided into good and evil"

The Primary Causes (2) in Section 9 have created the Not-Trusting-Life-Complex

The Not-Trusting-Life-Complex. The following are typical phrases belonging to this complex. If this is the complex pointed out as the primary cause of the illness, we need to find which phrases are stored in our psyche and add others, if necessary:

- "Life is unfair," or "life sucks"
- "Life is a series of ups and downs, good times followed by bad times"
- "Sometimes we get what we need, sometimes we don't" (This complex causes us to extend our distrust to the Helpers and the Cosmos.)
- "Life is suffering," or "Life is a vale of tears"
- "Life is not meant to be a bed of roses"
- "Life cannot be trusted," or "Life sometimes hands you raw deals"
- "Life requires a lot of us" (patience, continuous effort, facing and conquering our fears without knowing how, etc.)

Seeing life as a hostile entity imprisons the Helpers that would otherwise happily carry us through life.

The Primary Causes (3a) and (3b) in Section 9 have created the Guilt Complex and the Redemption Complex:

The Guilt Complex is based on the spells:
- "Humans are born guilty"
- "Humans are guilty because they have an animal nature"

The complex is accompanied by the image of guilt as an "inextinguishable stain put on our nature." *As long as a person is under the Guilt Complex, WHATEVER he does that hints of his true nature will make him feel guilty.* When freeing ourselves from this Complex, we first need to make sure that we have freed ourselves from the *concept of guilt* (see Chapter 21), because otherwise we will feel guilty for having deprogrammed the Guilt Complex.

Possible other components of the Guilt Complex are:
- "What I feel is wrong"
- "I am unlovable"
- the self-image of being a sinner who has to suffer for his sins (carry the cross)
- "To free yourself of your guilt you have to redeem yourself in the eyes of God"

The Redemption Complex. This complex is created as a "way out" of the Guilt Complex and the Punishment Complex. It is based on the spell: "You must redeem yourself by sacrificing your guilty animal nature."

The Primary Causes (4a)-(4c) in Section 9 have created the Punishment Complex:

The Punishment Complex. If the self-images of "the saintly person," or the "one who willingly carries his cross," or that of "the sinner" were indicated as the primary cause of the illness we are investigating, we also need to deprogram the Guilt Complex and this complex, as it is based on the Guilt Complex.

The Punishment Complex can be described as the image of a "Supreme Court of Justice" that has installed itself in our psyche. It is composed of the following demonic elements: a supreme judge, a prosecutor, a defender, a jury that judges us from conventional standards, an eye-witness who says "it is obvious that you are guilty," and a torturer.

We need to realize that it is the ego that fulfills all these roles in accusing, judging, and torturing us. The ego has declared the true self to be guilty even before it has entered the court. The court exists within us until we deprogram it.

When deprogramming this complex, it can be pictured as a painting of the whole court building with all these figures in it, which gets thrown into the fire.

The Primary Causes (4d) in Section 9 have created The Victim Complex. It is also connected with The Inferiority and Superiority Complexes:

The Victim Complex (or Helplessness Complex)

The self-image of the victim/helpless person gives rise to these false beliefs:

- "There is nothing that can be done about these conditions or this situation"
- "Everyone has turned against me, even God"
- "I am a victim of circumstances"
- "I can't even help myself"

These self-deprecating ideas sound soft and self-pitying as they whine in a back-of-the-mind monologue. However, as soon as they get the conscious attention of the mind, they swiftly turn into a demanding, commanding demon that urges that someone must do something, anything, about the situation. It justifies its demand by saying, "God (or the Cosmos) owes me for letting me down." When we are under the influence of this complex we attempt to instill guilt in others to make them share their possessions, their time, and their energy. Then when others help, they invoke a fate because they fail to say No to the ego in us, and because they also act on the belief that there is no help from the Cosmos for us. Such thoughts lock us into our poverty and prevent us from asking for help from the Cosmos.

The Inferiority Complex. If we have found that the self-image of "the helpless person" is the primary cause of the illness, we

also need to deprogram this complex. It is based on the spells:
- "You are not good enough in and of yourself; no matter how hard you try you will never be good enough"
- "You are born defective"

These ideas create a hidden negative image of the self that demands the attainment of a compensatory positive self-image; it thus leads to the development of the Superiority Complex.

The Superiority Complex. This complex is based on the spells:
- "Humans are the centerpiece of creation"
- "Humans are the pinnacle of evolution"
- "Humans are superior"
- "Humans are special"
- "Everything in the Cosmos is created to serve humans"

The Inferiority and the Superiority Complex need to be deprogrammed as a unit, otherwise the remaining one will re-install its counterpart.

The Primary Cause (4e) in Section 9 has created the Susceptibility Complex (also called the "Achilles Heel Complex")

If the self-image of "the one who is disadvantaged by Fate" is a primary cause of the illness, we need to deprogram this complex, which is based on the poison arrow, "Every human is born with a fatal flaw (a weak place)." This causes us to fail at the moment we might attain our biggest success. The ego's idea of how we are to cope with this supposed fact of life also needs to be deprogrammed as it insures continued failure: "There are two ways of dealing with this fact of life: either you accept it or you fight it. If you want to make peace with the gods you had better accept it."

The Primary Cause (5a) in Section 9 has created the Superiority Complex described above.

The Primary Cause (5b) in Section 9 has created The Helper or Duty Complex:

The Helper or *Duty Complex.* This complex is based on the slander, "Humans have to do it all" (a belief that rules out the Helpers). It is also composed of the following mistaken beliefs, some of which may apply to us, and some may not. We only need to deprogram those that do:
- "Nobody is there to do it but me"
- "Everything depends on me"
- "If I don't do it, things will collapse"
- "People can't take care of themselves"
- "I am a person of responsibility" (implying a responsibility that has no limits)
- "You are responsible to your parents, siblings, children, friends, neighbors (without measure)"
- "It is my duty to sacrifice my needs to those of others (without limits)"

The Helper or Duty Complex can include a person's taking responsibility for everything that goes wrong in the family, or taking responsibility for all the things humans have done to the planet, other species, etc. The person blames himself for failing to be there "at the right time," or for failing to do the "right thing." This also leads to blaming the Cosmos for "making us inadequate," or "flawed."

A slightly different version of this complex starts with the phrase: "I am the one to help because I am the best qualified." This idea has behind it the flattering idea that "the superior man has a duty to help." All these ideas initiate "the grabber," a demonic element that presents our mind with unsolvable problems, and then embroils it in investigating the many aspects of the problem until we realize that our inquiry leads only to a dead-end because the problem cannot be solved, at least by us. (See Appendix 2: *Demonic Elements in the Psyche* for a more detailed description of the grabber. Instructions for deprogramming the grabber are given in Chapter 21.)

The Primary Cause (5c) in Section 9 has created the Wild-Nature Complex and the Power Complex:
The Wild-Nature Complex is based on the mistaken idea

that Nature is wild. The ego formulated this idea to separate us from Nature and from our own nature. It is the basis for the further mistaken idea that "humans have been given the task to control Nature."

The Power Complex contains these additional false beliefs:
• "Power is the way of nature"
• "Power enables us to survive"
• "There is a higher power; you need to have it on your side"
• "If you don't have power you are vulnerable"

Other ego complexes that may need to be deprogrammed

After identifying the ego complexes above that are the primary causes of the illness we are investigating, the following ego complexes can play a supporting role to keep the illness alive. Therefore, we need to check with the *rtcm* whether any of them also need to be deprogrammed.

The Hero Complex. This complex is a derivative of The Superiority Complex mentioned above. It is handed down from ancient beliefs in the hero as having the purpose of fighting evil in the world, even though attaining the title of "hero" often requires the sacrifice of one's life (or life-energies), health, or well-being.

The catch in this idea is that for there to be a hero, there must also be something to fight (the dragon/evil). When we have this complex, we look constantly about for a counter-part to fight, whether in the form of personal, sports, business, religious, or cultural competition. The quest may be carried out entirely vicariously through compulsively reading novels about heroic exploits or seeking out the negative news in newspapers and commenting on how the world is "going to the dogs."

The ultimate heroism is achieved through overcoming something, either through fighting or "bearing with," or through endless waiting and persevering. All these qualifications of the hero entail going beyond the limits of ordinary commonsense. They generally embroil us in conflict and sacrifice of our true self.

If we have the Hero Complex we need to deprogram it together with the Complex of Evil, which is a compendium of all the slandered parts of Nature, including human nature. It consists of all the things regarded as evil that the hero sets out to fight. The existence of the Hero Complex is not only what makes the Complex of Evil necessary, it is what creates evil and keeps it alive.

To deprogram the Complex of Evil and the Hero Complex we need to make a list of all the things we personally regard as evil, whether it be in Nature or human nature. This list, and the dragon of the hero, which rules both complexes, need to be deprogrammed as one unit.

The False Dependency Complex. This is one of the most important ego complexes because it, more than any other, turns us away from recognizing our true source of help, healing, nourishment, and protection. It is based on the following three spe*lls:*
- "You can't trust your feelings"
- "You can only rely on what you see and what is palpable"
- "We depend on the institutions of society for our needs"

The phrase "you can't trust your feelings" dismisses the relevance of our feelings and thereby disables the majority of our bodily Helpers, which are feeling consciousnesses. It additionally creates the demonic element in the psyche we have called the "dragon of essentials." This dragon stipulates that there is an accepted, exclusive list of means or sources to which a person must turn when in need.

For our general needs the dragon says:
- "It is essential to have money"
- "It is essential to have a good lawyer, doctor, accountant"
- "It is essential in business to have clients, or customers"
- "For our security it is essential to have a fall-back position" (savings, inheritance, insurance, particular people, family)

For deprogramming, we need to add here, as part of this complex, the things on which we believe we depend, and which we considers indispensable.

While it is correct that we need money, customers, doctors, and other such things, the *I Ching* makes us aware that our relationship with these things, as with all things in life, is dependent primarily upon the invisible Helpers that support our existence. It is the Helpers that, when asked, bring us the right clients, the money we need, or the dentist or doctor through whom the Cosmos can help, when that kind of help is needed.

What is problematical and counter-intuitive is looking to the doctor or to the medical community as the true and only source for our healing, because this obscures and blocks the invisible Helpers, and the unlimited kinds of help they can give. We cannot even imagine the numbers of ways in which they can help. Furthermore, very little is required to obtain their help: we need only have the modesty to recognize their existence, and the sincerity to ask for their help. These simple requirements create the attraction that draws them into our lives.

While these requirements are simple, access to the Helpers entails deprogramming those beliefs that are inherently immodest and that lead to the suspicion and distrust that keep the Helpers away.

The False Dependency Complex consists of immodest and distrustful phrases and views that block our recognizing the Helpers' existence. These immodest ideas have their root in the prevailing view that the universe revolves around humans; when we possess those views we also tend to see anything that helps us as "at our service."

In order to correct our relationship with the Helpers we need to deprogram the False Dependency Complex, and apologize to the Cosmos if we have adopted the mistaken belief that humans are at the center of the universe.

The Self-Doubt Complex or *Oppression Complex.* This complex is based on the poison arrows:
- "Human nature is divided into good and evil"
- "You do not know what is good and what is evil"

Sometimes the following poison arrow is also part of this complex: "You have to be good to avoid evil." ("Good" in the sense of this statement, is meant as an absolute, consequently

233

the goal of being good is never attainable.)

The first poison arrow mentioned above divides our heart and instills a fundamental self-doubt in the goodness of our nature and in our being in possession of the Cosmic truth that is imprinted into every body cell. Once we have denied the total goodness of our nature and our possession of Cosmic truth, other doubts are easily instilled in us such as the doubt that our life is only authorized when validated by the collective ego. Phrases in this context are heard in the psyche as:

- "You can't trust your feelings"
- "What you say has not been authorized"
- "Who are you to say this" (when what we are saying comes from our true feelings)
- "You need to be able to substantiate yourself" (meaning in such a way that others will agree)
- "How do you know that the Cosmos will come to your aid when you follow your inner truth"
- "How do you know that the Cosmos will come to your aid in time?"

An imp and demon of forgetfulness accompany this complex; they draw a veil of forgetfulness over our stored memories of when Cosmic help came just when we needed it. The *I Ching* refers to this help in Hexagram 29, *The Abysmal,* Line 4: "A jug of wine, a bowl of rice with it; earthen vessels simply handed in through the window."[7]

Self-images that accompany the Self-Doubt Complex are those of "the decision maker" (meaning the one who is obligated to make the decisions) and the image of the "unsure person." If we have these self-images we find ourselves preparing in our mind what we are going to answer when asked, although often the situation for which we are preparing never occurs. Busying our mind in this manner uses a lot of energy, which only benefits the ego.

When the Self-Doubt Complex is deprogrammed, the connection between our feelings and our mind is freed up so that

---

[7] Ibid, p. 336, Hexagram 29, *The Abyss.*

our mind is able to make decisions based on what feels right and appropriate at the moment. Then, what we say or do is not taken from a pre-written script.

The self-image of the decision maker is often accompanied by the spell, "I have to be in control of the situation, otherwise there will be chaos. I am responsible for what happens. Everything depends on me."

The Self-Sabotage or Self-Deprecation Complex consists of one or more deprecating self-images and the projection that "things will never get better." It may also consist of a negative phrase that contains the word "always."

The Emotional Blackmail Complex

The underlying pattern here is one in which we are falsely accused of being guilty for something over which we had no control. Our acceptance of guilt enables the ego to blackmail us by holding the event and the conclusions we drew about it over our head as a constant source of reproach and inner conflict. Our efforts to hide from the guilt (since guilt is unbearable to the psyche) provide the ego with a constant source of energy, and a perfect hiding place in our psyche from which it is able to control us by constantly making us put blame on others.

A person with this ego complex needs to identify the event that gave rise to feelings of guilt and recognize that the rationales that create those feelings are nothing but a myth.

We have come across the following version of an Emotional Blackmail Complex, in which the ego in our client blackmailed him by speaking to his conscious mind using the following rationales:

"It's your own fault what is happening to XYZ (the case in point was a pet). Now you have to fix it. You can't do anything to fix it, anyway. You are trapped. Don't try to blame it on others. You shouldn't have had XYZ to start with."

When the client remembered that it was his father's idea to buy the pet in the first place, the changeling element called the "excuser" shifted the blame onto his father. A habit of blaming others can have its source in this complex.

Conclusion

Dismantling the ego program of a long-standing or chronic illness is something that requires time and perseverance. However, when we consider the wonderful facts we learn about our true nature as we walk through the sections above, and take advantage of the opportunity to liberate ourselves from the ego's oppression, our time could not be better spent. Deprogramming what we discover along the way does more than free us from the illness, it removes the dross accumulated over time that has prevented us from fully enjoying our life.

This does not mean that we need to be ambitious in our efforts. In fact, ambition is counter-productive because it indicates that the ego has taken charge of the corrective process. Under these circumstances, it will manage to escape, and the healing will not take place. We notice the difference when we are working under the leadership of the ego and that of the Helpers. In the former case, the work feels hard and difficult. By engaging the Helpers, we feel supported and carried along from one insight to another as we are being lifted out of our difficulties.

Whether we are ill or not, learning how to get free of the ego, which is laid bare in the program of a long-standing illness, holds great rewards.

Appendices

Appendix 1.

Kinds of Sick-Making Thoughts

The *I Ching* led us to distinguish thus far among three basic kinds of *false thought forms*: spells, poison arrows, and projections. When all three combine and lodge in the body, they can form a "microchip." We are often asked why it is important to make these distinctions. The answer becomes clear when we understand their different natures.

Spells
A spell is a harmful thought form that has the effect *of fixing a person or thing in an unnatural behavior*. This includes objects such as cars and computers, and foods and substances. Even the earth and the weather, as well as water, air, and fire, can be influenced by spells. As we have learned, the consciousness in all things is influenced by the conscious thoughts we have about them. This is important to realize in the case of allergies, where there is a negative interaction between us and foods, or between us and Nature in general.

Applied to humans, spells consist of phrases that fix us as having a certain nature. They generally employ the word "is," or "has," or can include the words "always" or "never," as in, "He *has* a weak constitution," or "She will *never* recover." Because such phrases are absolute statements put not simply on our actions, but on our nature, they lock our psyche and body into the pattern described by the phrase, unless we have said a firm inner No to those phrases. An example occurs when someone calls a child a "bad kid." The emphasis here is on labeling the child's nature as bad, rather than viewing his deed as a mistake. The spell creates a fix in a particular psychic function of the child. Many compulsive behaviors indicate the presence of a spell. Judgment spells that categorize us as "being that way" can cause injury to the combinations of our genes, thereby creating health problems.

239

When someone puts a spell on us that ascribes a negative quality to our nature, it has a rigidifying effect on all kinds of body cells that decreases their healthy functioning; this includes whole bodily systems, organs, and glands. The rigidification of body cells causes misunderstandings in the communication between the cells, causing healthy cells to die, and the affected body part to gradually decrease in size. The cells affected can be brain cells (in particular cells of the brain stem), nerve cells, bone cells, white blood cells, lymph cells, and skin cells.

Spells can also create blocks between synapses in the brain that obstruct parts of our ability to think, and create blind spots in our perception. In most cases, because of the interconnected-ness of all parts of the body, the negative effect of a spell goes far beyond the body part on which it is put. In illness, spells can cause a condition to become chronic when the phrase contains the word "never," as in the statement, "she will never recover."

Spells that are put on our animal nature affect our whole body, including the mind that pronounces the spell. This is because our whole being is part of the animal kingdom. An example for such a spell is the mistaken idea that all things are achieved, or moved through the use of power. Acting on this idea requires that the mind put constant *pressure* on our will; under healthy circumstances, our will would be *supported* and *invigorated* by energy coming from our inner truth.

Spells can even be as broad as to influence our entire life, for instance, when they are sweeping conclusions about the way our life "is," or "will work out." The spell thus consists of a general-ized attitude that influences the way our life, and the lives of those dependent on us, unfolds. In sum, our thoughts are not passive in their effects; they are particularly harmful when they contain spells.

Here is a list of commonly encountered types of spells:
• *Spells that ascribe false characteristics to the nature of a thing,* thus fixing it as "being that way"

Examples: "Life is suffering." "The Cosmos punishes us for our sins." "We are born into this life without help from the Cosmos."

• *Spells that are created by fixing someone as "being that type of person"*

Examples: "He is a melancholic type," or "she is a Leo" (astrological type). Both statements cast a predefined image on the person. It acts as a prison for that person by leaving little room for his or her uniqueness and for self-development.

• *Spells created by self-images*

In illness we are concerned with certain self-images, such as that of the person "who can endure more than others," the one "with the mysterious illness," the one "who deserves the pity of others," or the one "who fights a heroic fight against the illness," to name but a few. All these self-images cause a resistance in the sick person to getting well, which in most cases is unconscious. In one way or another these self-images cause him to see illness as bringing him special attention and a recognition he thinks he would not get otherwise, and so he unconsciously welcomes the illness. (See the broader discussion of this subject in Part IV, Section 1.)

• *Spells created by phrases that contain the words "always" or "never"*

Examples: "She will never get well," "He will always have a problem with his liver," "He will never change." Such spells fix the person in the condition described.

• *Spells created by deeply ingrained beliefs that give rise to hopes or fears*

Hopes and fears are mentioned together because every phrase that expresses a hope is actually based on a fear. Behind the phrase "I hope I won't get sick," is the fear, "I may get sick," and an image of the sickness as looming and probable. The latter gives power to the illness feared and can actually draw it to the person with this fear. Both spells need to be deprogrammed together.

• *Spells created by the wish either to become like someone, or not to become like someone else*

Example: "I hope I will become as successful as A." This spell creates an identification with A that not only extends to A's successes, but also to the possible fates A creates by achieving successes at the expense of his body. Another example is the spell: "I hope I will never get cancer like my mother." This spell is based on a fear, which, as mentioned above, creates the opening to the illness. All spells that are based on comparing oneself with another person disrespect the fact that every person is unique.

Poison arrows

Poison arrows are a particular form of spells projected onto our own psyche and body or onto another; the danger they pose lies in the fact that they put poison into the body cells. We feel them immediately, either as a sharp pain, a crick in the back, a headache, or a sting in the heart, to give but a few examples. Some poison arrows even date back from the time *in utero*. When not removed, they always cause unhealthy physical conditions.

Poison arrows have no relation to geographical distance, as we can receive them from someone on the opposite side of the earth with whom we have some connection. They are transmitted to us the moment they enter the mind of the person sending them.

A poison arrow can also be lodged in our body from childhood or youth and be the source of repeated discomfort. In that case, it has become embedded in the body as a microchip. (See below for an explanation of microchips.)

As their name indicates, poison arrows contain a particular poison that affects the consciousness of the cells they enter; the word "arrow" describes both the degrading thought of their originator and their aggressive nature. Poison arrows have all the effects of a spell, but in addition to rigidifying the body cells, they inject them with their poison. The poison causes the normally good-natured body cells to become partially demonized and aggressive. When the demonized parts turn their aggression against the other parts of the same cell and other cells, we feel it as an ache. Certain poison arrows also have a direct effect on certain genes in the nuclear DNA. When these genes no longer function healthily, our whole organism is negatively affected.

Poison arrows are caused by different kinds of thoughts and ego emotions; the following are the most common:

• *Guilt*

Example: "I ought not to be sick," when that phrase implies "because others are having to take care of me and I am a bother to them." The concept of guilt, which has no Cosmic basis, creates the ego emotion of guilt whenever we go against our conditioned training. These poison arrows injure our DNA by blocking the gene that is responsible for the self-healing abilities of the body. (See Glossary: Guilt.)

• *Comparisons with sick people*

Example: "Because I am over 50, there is a 30% chance I'll get breast cancer." This kind of poison arrow creates a fear in the body that weakens its natural protection.

• *Commonly held presumptions about what is "typical"*

Example: "Once you reach the 50 year mark, it's all downhill." This poison arrow creates an image of the body that shows it in a constant decline of its abilities. If not deprogrammed, the body will comply with the image.

• *So-called inherited diseases, when they contain a comparison*

Example: "You have inherited your father's heart problem." Such a poison arrow actually alters the ability of a person's chromosomes to pair harmoniously. When "defective" genes are found in a child while still *in utero*, they can be the effect of a poison arrow put on the unborn child, such as a mother's fear that she may have injured her unborn child due to drinking or smoking habits.

• *Misnaming parts of the body and their functions*

Example: viewing the body as a system of mechanical functions and calling the heart a "pump." Such a mechanical view blocks the Helper of the Heart from fulfilling its function, which is to draw *chi* energy from the Cosmos. Another poison arrow is created by seeing the heart as the *source* of the love given to another. This poison arrow allows the ego to dominate the feelings that come through the heart, causing the heart to harden.

• *Speaking of an illness, or disability as if it were part of our nature*

Example: saying "my" arthritis, or "my" hearing loss. The disability is not part of our nature; it is caused by a *foreign* element

243

that has been introduced into our body and psyche through language.

• *Being angry at one's body*

Example: blaming the body when it aches, or has become ill. This poison arrow may not contain a phrase, but it *always* contains the image of the body as an enemy. It aggravates the pain, because it adds more poison to the original poison that has made the body sick.

• *Blaming the illness or the body*

Example of blaming the illness: "It's because of the illness that I am suffering." Another example is of blaming the body: "It's my body's fault that I am sick." Such poison arrows also aggravate the condition. The mistake lies in seeing the illness or the body as the cause of suffering, instead of recognizing that the illness is caused by sick-making thoughts.

• *Feelings of guilt, self-disgust, and fears of having something negative happen*

Examples: Feeling guilty for being fat; condemning parts of our body as ugly, repulsive, or weak. (The parts condemned receive the poison in the image of a demonic head forming the tip of the arrow.) The fearful thought, "I might contract the flu," is a typical poison arrow. We put poison arrows on others when we indulge in negative emotions about them such as envy, vindictiveness, hatred, spite, or condemnation, but also when we fear for them.

• *Curses*

Example: The phrases, "Damn you!" and "Let them be damned!" are typical poison arrows put on an individual, or on a whole group of people.

• *Poison arrows created by traumatic experiences*

An example is a woman who as a child was punished by being switched on the legs with a slender apple shoot, and admonished, "to never ever do that again!" The whole experience was stored as a "microchip" in her legs, causing her legs to twitch involuntarily when she was nervous, or felt she might be criticized for something. When a microchip like this is formed, the terror freezes into the memory of the cells of the punished body parts, preventing the *chi* energy from flowing abundantly through them; also, the body part wants to defend itself, which results in the uncontrolled twitching. In addition, those parts can draw inflammations because they expect to be punished. Such traumatic experiences may create a memory chip in the psyche as well as a microchip. A highly traumatic experience for the body occurs when as children we are first told (or it is implied by punishment) that our feelings do not count. (The consequences of this poison arrow are described in detail in Part IV, Section 6, "Fears Connected with the Illness.")

A poison arrow affects that part of the body at which it is pointed: for example, when we are called "a pain in the neck" we feel the pain in our neck; when we are described as "a burden that must be shouldered" we feel the poison arrow in our shoulder.

Poison arrows, like other spells, can also be put on our pets, objects, the weather, etc. When a poison arrow is put on food, it affects both the consciousness of the food and the consciousness of our digestive system as we ingest it, as is demonstrated in the two cases described in Chapter 11, *A Healing Language.*

Projections

We speak of these false thought forms as "projections" because they are mainly statements made as firm convictions that predict what will likely happen or not happen in the future. They include medical diagnoses and prognoses.

Although projections are not the actual cause of illness, they can play a role in opening a person to harm, or in influencing the course of an illness. Projections occur automatically when we think in terms of expectations, whether they are conscious or unconscious. Projections influence the *neurons* in those parts of the body onto which the expectation has been projected. Neurons are nerve cells that transmit information throughout the body. Their normal function is to carry our true feelings. Under the influence of a projection, however, the neurons become confused by those mental expectations that contradict what the feelings say.

245

The *I Ching* makes us aware of the hidden danger that lies in projections when it speaks of the need to keep our mind innocent by "not projecting/not expecting." (See Hexagram 25.) Both hopes and fears contain expectations, which are both projections and poison arrows.

The following kinds of projections can be distinguished:

• Expectations that keep an illness or condition alive through prognosis, and that exclude the possibility of Cosmic help

Example: "This will always hurt some." "Nobody has a cure for this."

• Expectations in the form of hopes or fears

Examples: "All you need to do is keep your hopes up." This projection creates resignation in the person's psyche that is communicated to the injured part of the body, which joins in the resignation. "We have to fear the worst." This projection brings on the worst.

• Expectations that create an opening for illness to occur

Example: "You will catch a cold!" This phrase projects an image of sickness, creating the potential for it to become a reality by injuring the person's natural protective system.

• Expectations (fears) that cause the condition to deteriorate

Example: "Given the seriousness of your condition, you have about three months to live." This projection gives a clear message to the body that it is useless to mobilize its self-healing abilities, because the condition is "too serious."

• Projecting by positive thinking

While these projections do not cause harm, they require constant effort because the underlying fear or doubt is not removed.

Example: A person with a back injury projects the positive thought: "There is nothing wrong with my back. It is strong and healthy." The problem with this is that a positive phrase, by itself, cannot overcome a problem. It can succeed for awhile, but the pressure of the underlying doubt that has not been rooted out, requires constant effort to counteract it.

Microchips

A microchip is a traumatic memory stored in the body, as in muscle tissues, or the gut, or heart. Microchips manifest as lumps, obstructions, arterial plaque, tics, twitches, and the like.

Microchips are created by a combination of a projection, spell and poison arrow. When they contain the spell, "there is nothing one can do about the situation," the body cells in the affected area die, and in their place a lump of unhealthy cells is formed that contains the projection, spell, and poison arrow. The word "contain" is to be taken literally, since the lump contains the damage that would otherwise spread to the body.

Example: A person is under the spell, "I am a sinner." When someone then projects the threat, "If you don't repent your sins, you will go to hell," it forms a microchip in that part of the body that is considered to make him a sinner. (Most often the threat is aimed at the lower body, in particular at the person's sexuality.) The microchip contains the combination of a spell, a projection, and a poison arrow. Their combined effect on that person's sexuality is devastating because certain neurons are not only confused, they become frozen in fear. Such a microchip is the primary cause of cancer of the sexual organs. Its outer manifestation may take years, occurring when another projection is taken in, perhaps by hearing or reading a cancer statistic that could pertain to this person. When the latter projection gives rise to the fear of getting cancer, the body cells comply.

Appendix 2.

Demonic Elements in the Psyche that Cause Illness

This section shows the demonic elements in spells and poison arrows that can cause illness.

Whenever a *false judgment* or a *conclusion* is pronounced regarding life, or the Cosmos, or regarding our own nature, the words and images that accompany them take on a life. This happens because we start believing in them, and believing is another way of saying that we invest them with *energy*. Whenever we give energy to false words and images, they manifest in our psyche and/or body as demonic elements that color many of our other thoughts. These can appear in dreams and meditations. They have been made the subject of literature, movies, and, more recently, of books on psychology.[1]

Unfortunately, these demonic elements in our psyche have not always been understood. They have been falsely assumed to be part of our nature, particularly of our animal nature. The *I Ching* has shown us that they are by no means part of us, nor are they natural; they are intruders in our psyche/body that need to be thrown out by identifying and deprogramming the words, phrases, and/or images to which they owe their existence. They can sometimes pose as harmless, while speaking in phrases such as, "it's just a thought," or by giving seemingly harmless excuses such as "you need to sin at least 10% of the time, otherwise you are too rigid." They may otherwise be heard as flattering, degrading, self-pitying, blaming, or fear-inspiring voices, or as authoritative and powerful, as if they know it all. They can show up in human or animal form, or in the mythical forms we know from folklore and literature.

The Sage made us aware that while we need to know about

---

[1]Baer, Lee, *The Imp of the Mind, Exploring the Silent Epidemic of Obsessive Bad Thoughts*. Dutton, NY, 2001. Lee Baer is associate professor of Psychology at Harvard Medical School and the director of research of the Obsessive-Compulsive Disorder unit at the Massachusetts General and McLean Hospitals.

demonic elements, we also need to keep them in their place. This is done by realizing that they owe their existence entirely to a wrong use of language. We also need to realize that "killing them" means we delete from our minds and psyche the fearful images created by this false use of language. Without this awareness on our part, the danger exists that they can take on an extra reality through being feared as "real." Indeed, they gain reality by being feared as possibly able to take over our consciousness, once and for all. On this account they like to be talked about either as powerful and dangerous, or as harmless and funny. Metaphorically speaking, as in the *Wizard of Oz*, they need to have a bit of water splashed on them.

The *I Ching* distinguishes between three main categories of demonic elements: imps, demons, and dragons. Imps have the function of acting as guardians over the main mistaken ideas that bind the individual to the collective ego. Therefore, they are heard to speak in the psyche in phrases that intend to make us conform in what we "should" or "must" think, feel, and do. As the most basic form of demonic element, imps can grow into dragons. Once dragons are formed, they take on a controlling function in the psyche. Demons are created by imps for the purpose of stealing our energy; they do so by hounding us with fears, self-doubts, guilt, and with wanting, worrying, and wondering, thus keeping the whole demonic theatre energized.

Examples

An imp, a demon, and a dragon

A single spell, such as the one created by the fatalistic statement, "there is no help from the Cosmos" can lay the foundation for a demonic reality in our psyche that is dominated by monumental fears. The spell itself seems harmless considering that it "only" contains an imp that says, "there is no help from the Cosmos." Note: the words here have created the imp. Then, when this spell is projected onto a person at a young age, it gradually grows from an imp into a dragon. It becomes a dragon when the person actively pronounces phrases that defend using

249

power to achieve goals. This dragon can be called "the dragon of dependency on the collective ego." The whole experience then gives rise to a "demon of fear of the unknown." This demon drives the person to "wanting to be in control," an urge that gives rise to yet another dragon—"the dragon of control through the mind." Once this dragon installs itself on the throne of the mind, it declares the body's wisdom to be untrustworthy. The stage is set for the conflict between the thinking mind under the dragon's control, and the body's feeling consciousness.

The relationship between projections/poison arrows and demonic elements

When a projection and poison arrow combine, they create an imp that can also metamorphose into a dragon and/or a demon. Projections by themselves do not create any demonic elements, although they can create an opening for illness, or influence the course of an illness.

Example 1: The spell, "You are prone to heart attacks" creates an imp, which is the fear of a heart attack. When another spell is added, as for example, " because your father died of a heart attack," that imp creates a "dragon of comparison." Like all demonic elements, the imp and the dragon need energy to stay alive. It is easy to see that the energy that keeps them alive comes from the fear of getting a heart attack. To keep this fear alive, the imp also creates a demon that has the sole function of triggering that fear. All three demonic elements take their residence in the heart, and live off any *chi* energy that is stored there.

Example 2: The spell, "I deserve to be punished," can have its base in a specific thought such as "because I have done something terrible." It can also occur for no apparent reason when something traumatic has happened in the person's life that has created feelings of guilt for simply existing. It can be that the individual has taken on guilt from a parent who originally did not want the child, or the parent's guilt for the sexual act in which the child was conceived. The resulting guilt-spell is what keeps the spell, "I deserve to be punished" active. That spell creates the opening for illness, which fulfills the function of punishment. Many inflammatory illnesses belong in this category because they attack the body in those places that are connected with the feelings of guilt. For example, when arthritis attacks the finger joints, it is the expected punishment for actually having done something one feels guilty about. When a person feels guilty for his mere existence, the expected punishment may come to any part of his body, but particularly to his heart, possibly in the form of a heart attack.

When we look at this situation in terms of demonic elements, we find an imp of guilt that starts the program of the illness. This imp gradually grows into a dragon of guilt when the person adopts the mistaken belief that he deserves to be punished for being guilty. This guilt and the personal belief in deserving punishment create a whole inner "court of justice" made up of demonic elements: a supreme judge (a dragon of justice), an inner prosecutor (a dragon of rationalizing that iterates the reasons why the individual is guilty), a defense attorney (a demon of hope, or of lame excuses that one knows are a poor defense), and a torturer demon, which carries out a continuous punishment. We can easily picture this inner court, and occasionally get a glimpse of its presence in dreams. (Also see "The Punishment Complex" in Part IV, Section 10.)

Unfortunately, the number of demonic elements does not stop there. Everyone who has experienced hope, or has uttered the words, "At least I can hope" is familiar with the dragon of hope. We also know that hope is inevitably followed by hopelessness (another dragon). These dragons are fed by demons of doubt, which are in their service. To illustrate this dynamic, we can picture the person's hopes being pumped up. When this energy has reached a certain level, it starts decreasing when doubts set in. At the bottom of the cycle of hopelessness, the dragon of hopes returns to start the process over again. These demons and dragons flash their subliminal images onto the screen of the mind, creating the whirlpool of ego emotions in which the person is caught.

This example illustrates how imps first give rise to dragons and demons, which then cooperate with each other like a gang of thieves to steal the person's *chi* energy and live on it. They are parasites that will feed off their host until there is nothing left to feed on. Thus, they have an interest in creating illness and keeping it alive. We see this interest at work in cases of long-standing or chronic illnesses. (See Part IV.)

Another important point is demonstrated here. Whenever guilt is the primary cause of an illness, the person cannot get well until this guilt is uncovered and deprogrammed. The *I Ching* makes it clear that we cannot become free of guilt through enduring our punishment. Guilt is a concept concocted by the ego to keep itself in power. There is no limit to the punishment the ego would put on us, while making us believe that guilt cannot be extinguished. (See Chapter 21, subsection, "Freeing Yourself from the Concept of Guilt.")

The Demonizing of Foods and Drinks

When we categorize foods and drinks into those that are good for us, and those that are bad, those that are labeled bad become demonized. The real distinction we need to make is between what "suits" the individual person's digestive abilities and what does not. (Also see Chapter 13, *Examples of Long-standing or Chronic Illnesses*, "A Case of Food Allergy.")

Example 1: When we categorize sugar as "bad for our health," we create several demons. One is created in the sugar when we buy it. This happens because sugar has consciousness and responds to our thoughts. Another is the demon of guilt that makes us feel guilty for eating it. Still another is the demon that causes us to crave sugar. Whenever we have categorized something our body needs as "bad" and are trying to withhold it from our body, a negative attraction is created to that particular food or drink, and is felt as a craving. This negative attraction is behind addictions.

Example 2: When we demonize wine as "bad for our health," we create the same demons of guilt and craving. It is quite possible that drinking wine does not suit a person's digestive abilities; such a person will normally not feel drawn to wine. Our body knows, on a feeling level, what is suitable for it and what is not. However, when we accept mental judgments about foods and drinks, the body's feeling knowledge becomes blocked.

The Demonizing of Substances

What we mean here by substances are natural products, such as tobacco, hemp, and mushrooms that have been used since ancient times for ritualistic purposes or for enhancing a state of trance. When used in controlled doses, these products do not have an addictive quality. However, these substances can be seized by the ego for purposes of controlling the user. It is then that they take on an addictive quality. Often an addiction is created by a person who takes the substance in the ego bravado that he can control it. This attitude gives the consciousness in the substance power over him by turning it into a demon.

Ego Complexes

The Sage made us aware that the fully developed ego in a person's psyche consists of a limited number of *complexes*. We have described some of these in Part IV, Section 10. In psychology, they are called "*neurotic complexes*"; however, the word *neurotic*, being related to *neuron* (a nerve cell) falsely suggests that they are a natural part of our makeup. Since they are instead products of the ego, we call them "ego complexes."

The ego is a program of mistaken ideas and beliefs that have been installed in our psyche through childhood conditioning. It consists of a number of basic notions and phrases that express fundamental untruths about the nature of the Cosmos, of Nature in general, and of human nature in particular. It also comprises fundamental untruths about the nature of our relationships in each of these areas. Because these untruths slander the Cosmic Order, they create fates. Fate has the purpose of showing us the harmful consequences of accepting these slanderous assumptions that lead to pain and suffering. However, the ego, which owes its existence to these slanders, has also invented rationales that point back to the Cosmos and to Nature, including human animal nature, as the cause of Fate. These *false explanations for fates* lead us into ever greater conflict with the Cosmos. The ego could ultimately be extinguished if humans realized that their *conflict with the Cosmos* is the main means through which the ego is kept alive.

When a person consciously or unconsciously accepts certain basic false phrases, over time these phrases give rise to a morass of ego complexes. Some of these complexes become autonomous in his psyche, at which time they exhibit as compulsive and addictive behaviors.

Other Types of Demonic Elements in the Psyche

The Changeling

Our awareness of the changeling came from several meditations. Various dictionaries give the following explanations and synonyms for the word "changeling": "a child secretly exchanged for another in infancy; substitute; alternative; shift; apology; alternate; representative; deputy."

In this book we use the general term "changeling," and in a few places we also give the names of specific aspects of the changeling that are connected with health issues, such as "the identifier," "the excuser," "the blamer," and "the projector of fearful images." (See Part IV.)

The name "changeling" points to the way the ego replaces Cosmic language with ego language by making subtle changes in the meanings of words, in the syntax of phrases, and by substituting or omitting words. The changeling creates *ego complexes* by twisting the meanings of words and phrases to support the ego.[2] Once ego complexes become institutionalized in our psyche, they determine the way we perceive our everyday reality by creating a framework through which all experience must pass and be framed to fit ego concepts. They can make us look at life through dark glasses, to make us forget any good experiences we have had. Or, they can cause us to fall into blind

---

[2]See a description of the genesis of the Guilt-Toward-God Complex in Chapter 9. Other ego complexes are listed in Part IV, Section 10, as the root causes of illness.

enthusiasm for clever schemes.

All ego complexes are accompanied by the changeling that has created them, a fact that is mentioned in the instructions given for deprogramming ego complexes. In addition, all mistaken beliefs and certain self-images are also accompanied by a changeling.

A Free-Floating Changeling

When we have overlooked deprogramming a changeling that is connected with a mistaken belief, self-image, or ego complex that we have deprogrammed, the changeling then floats freely in our psyche and/or body, in the manner of a free radical, looking for something to attach itself to. Its presence is characterized by the mischief it creates as when it causes a headache, or seemingly unrelated pains in other parts of our body. The pains, so to speak, randomly wander around in our body.

A Doubter

A doubter is a demonic element caused by a poison arrow that dissolves the natural attraction between psyche and body and lodges in the heart. An example of such a poison arrow is the phrase: "You can never trust anything unless it has been proven." When we have experienced the truth of a Cosmic Principle, the doubter introduces the words "maybe" or "perhaps," thus giving rise to a doubt, which is the poisonous head of the arrow. When the doubter is active, one doubt is followed by another, even though we try to disperse them. The doubter invariably calls into question anything that cannot be seen with the outer eyes, because it is based on the belief that you can only believe what you can see.

A Grabber

A grabber is a specific demonic element that shines a light on a worry, fear, or feeling of guilt, to put it into the forefront of our attention. A grabber is most noticeable at night when, after we awake for some reason, it keeps us awake by bringing to mind a situation that arouses fears, worry, or guilt. It keeps us examining this matter until we realize there is nothing we can do about it. Then it drops that issue and introduces another, hassling us with it until we realize that it, too, is something we can do nothing about. Just as we let go of that issue, it introduces yet another of the same kind, continuing in this way *ad infinitum.* Grabbers are the chief cause of insomnia. Grabbers are also the cause of hot flashes and nightly sweats, which they cause by inserting subliminal worries, fears, and feelings of hopelessness. The entire purpose of the grabber is to keep us from remembering that the best thing we can do is to ask the Cosmic Helpers to resolve the worries, and then turn the matter over to them. To this end it also makes us forget our unity with the Cosmos, and that we have the ability to activate Cosmic help for all seemingly hopeless situations. When we forget that we can deprogram the respective mistaken beliefs and ask the Cosmos for help, the grabber can feed off our energy endlessly.

Typical things that the grabber brings to mind are: untenable situations that are damaging the environment, wars abroad, disasters, social deterioration, and other negative news.

Typical fears introduced by the grabber are: that we will not get the help we need, and fears of the unknown, as in, "You don't know what will happen."

The grabber also grabs feelings of guilt and keeps us consumed with them, thus preventing us from becoming aware that guilt is an ego-made concept that needs to be deprogrammed altogether. The Cosmic view is that a part of our learning process is to make mistakes, and that we can correct them by finding and deprogramming the mistaken ideas behind them. (Also see Glossary: Guilt.)

The grabber uses the energy it gains from our feelings of hopelessness, helplessness, or guilt to keep the ego alive.

Appendix 3.

Glossary of Definitions Used in this Book
(Note: References to other glossary items are marked with >)

Animal Nature: In the Cosmic sense, humans are part of the animal kingdom. It is our animal nature that gives us our Cosmic dignity and our true place in the Cosmic whole. It is also our animal nature that holds us, through our feelings and our DNA, in a symbiotic relationship with the >*Cosmos*. The human desire to be special because we have language has led to the mistaken idea that our "self" is divided into a "higher" and a "lower" nature, the latter referring to our animal nature. Many mistaken ideas about the why and how of suffering and of >*death* have led to the assumption that it is lower. In this book, the term animal nature is often used as a synonym for our bodily nature, particularly when speaking of our sexuality. The slanders that have been put on our animal nature as a whole have made humans susceptible to illness, because they have separated humans from the Cosmic unity.

Chi **Energy:** In the context of health, we need to distinguish different kinds of *chi* energy:
- The life force that animates existence.
- *Heart chi* is Cosmic love received directly by our heart. It differs from other kinds of *chi*, which we receive through other parts of our body, in that it invigorates the body and enables us to fulfill our destiny.
- *Chi* energy received from Nature through our feeling relationship with it gives us stamina and emotional energy.
- *Chi* energy received from sunlight is necessary for a healthy metabolism.
- *Chi* energy produced directly in our body as a result of being in a feeling relationship with the Cosmos comes from our inner truth (our DNA). When we are in touch with it, this *chi* nourishes both body and mind. It is referred to in the *I Ching* as "a clear, cold spring, from which we can drink. The more

we drink from it, the more it flows." [1] It is the one dependable source of truth on which our mind needs to rely.

The different kinds of *chi* energy mentioned above—and others not mentioned here—are all part of the Cosmic Consciousness and of Nature.

Collective Ego: The collective ego is the parent of the individual ego. "Collective ego" is the name given to the totality of mistaken ideas and beliefs about the <*Cosmos*, Nature, human nature, and about the human place in the whole. These ideas and beliefs have separated humans and their cultures from the Cosmos and its way of harmony. The visible side of the collective ego is found in those aspects of social structures and institutions that support the human-centered view of the universe, which therefore operate in contradiction to the Cosmic Principles of Harmony. Since the collective ego in its totality is a false construct that has no Cosmic reality, it depends totally on the life energy it steals from people's true nature. For this purpose it encourages the individual, through early childhood conditioning, to develop an individual ego—a mental program which contains a replica of its values and beliefs. The conditioning is introduced, phrase by phrase and image by image into the psyche of the young child, where it takes on a life of its own. (For a more detailed description, see *How the Collective Ego was Formed* in Chapter 5.)

Commonsense: This is the name for the consensus of all our *inner* and *outer* senses of perception and our *metaphorical* senses. In humans, commonsense is the "inner judge" that discerns what is in harmony with our inner truth (and therefore also in harmony with the Cosmos) and what is not. Its judgment is in the form of a feeling of Yes or No felt on the inner plane. Our inner senses of perception tell us about the inner truth of situations. Examples include the inner sense of smell that tells us when something "smells foul," the inner sense of taste that

---

[1] Anthony/Moog, p. 526-528, Hexagram 48, *The Well*, lines 5 and 6.

makes us aware when something is "unsavory," the inner sense of hearing that warns us that something does not "ring true," the inner sense of seeing that shows us a situation's inner truth in meditation and insights, the inner sense of touch that makes us aware that something does not "feel right." Among our "metaphorical senses" are our senses of caution and circumspection, and our sensitivity toward everything around us.

Another function of our commonsense is to carry out transformations. It needs to be noted that our commonsense, our inner senses of perception, and our metaphorical senses are all part of our animal nature; they become dysfunctional when our animal nature is slandered as lowly or as being the source of evil, and when our feelings are disregarded, or slandered as unreliable. (Also see below: Senses.)

Cosmos: (from the Greek) means "the whole universe in its harmonious order." The *I Ching* shows us that the Cosmos is a system of Harmonic Principles. The Cosmos as a whole consists of two parts: the invisible Cosmic Consciousness and its expression in form, which is the visible world of Nature. Although the Cosmic Consciousness is composed of several kinds of consciousness, it is mainly a *feeling* consciousness. The discordant consciousness that is generated through the false use of language is a fluke that has put humans outside the Cosmic whole because that consciousness is not part of the Cosmos. The discordant consciousness has created its own sphere outside the Cosmic whole. This sphere of discordant consciousness has set itself up to compete with the Cosmos and to replace it with its hierarchically structured human-centered order in which humans see themselves as occupying the top position. From its place of isolation from the Cosmic whole, the negative energy of this sphere operates destructively on humans and on Nature like a "black hole." The visible side of the sphere of disharmonious consciousness is the "parallel reality" created by the collective ego. The more immersed in the parallel reality we are, the more susceptible we become to illness.

The Cosmos is not identical with what scientists have called "the universe." The idea of a universe is a creation of the human-centered view that eliminates, with the exception of the notion of "dark matter," consideration of what is invisible to the eye.

Death: When applied to processes in Nature, death marks the *>transformation* of a person, animal, or plant from its visible form into an invisible form of existence within the Cosmic whole. Applied to humans, it means that when the individual's uniqueness is fulfilled, his aggregate consciousness is transformed back into the invisible realm, where it continues to live in its unique identity and takes on new tasks. Those who have not developed their uniqueness or fulfilled their destinies are given another opportunity to do so by being returned once more to human form. They return into human form free and clear, innocent, and able to make an entirely new start. The Sage has made it clear that no such thing as *karma* exists.

It may happen that before the transformation has become completed, the deceased may contact a spouse or child to inform that person of something that is standing in the way of his transformation. An example is an attachment that person has to the deceased, or feelings of guilt. Holding onto the dead prevents both the living and the dead person from making progress, the living in fulfilling his uniqueness, the dead from the tasks he is to fulfill in the invisible dimension. When we say the inner No to such guilt, or any other ego emotion or attachment that ties us to the dead, and ask the Helper that Frees People from Guilt to do so, the transformation can be completed.

What we experience as the fear of death most often comes from the ego. Indeed, the ego is the only thing that dies when our life *in the body* ends. Because the ego is not part of the Cosmic whole, it sees death as loss, an end to its existence, and as a final punishment. To deceive itself about its own death, it has created the idea of an immortal soul, which it hopes to inhabit without the disadvantage of having a body after death. It urges the person to develop an existence in a spirit world it imagines to exist.

When we have fulfilled our uniqueness, we will feel that our time has come to die. We need no help in this process and it invariably occurs peacefully when we are not ill. However, a person who is dying from an illness can usually be helped by calling upon a team of >*Helpers* to help him make that step in harmony with Nature. These Helpers are: the Helper of Transformation, the Helper to Make Death Swift and Easy (to overcome the effects of the platitude that death is difficult and hard), the Helper of the Acceptance of Death, and the Helper of Seeing One's Inner Truth. The person who wants to help another in this way *always* needs to ask the Sage whether it is correct to do so. If one goes ahead without asking, the ego has taken charge of the action, which creates blame. Doing this would not harm the dying person, because the Helpers do not associate with the ego. (Also see Chapter 10, *The Origin of the Fear of Death.*)

Ego: The individual ego is a composite of self-images and their supporting rationales that a person develops in the course of childhood conditioning. This conditioning is carried out through the false use of language. The seeds for the development of the individual ego are put into the psyche at an early age, even before we have the ability to speak. In childhood we are told not only verbally, but by the inner urging of our parents, that we need to "become" something, implying that we are not good enough in and of ourselves, and that there is no help for us other than what we can get from the institutions of the collective ego. Thus as children we are made dependent on the collective ego for all our needs. We are also indoctrinated to believe that we need the authorization of those around us for our very existence. This generally means we must learn all the rules which make us acceptable to the collective ego and its institutions. To this end we are told that we need to "develop our character," i.e., step into the roles that will define us as acceptable.

Since these self-images, roles, pretenses, mistaken beliefs and ego emotions conflict with our true nature, they are the main causes of illness and injuries. Because the ego has no life force in and of itself, it must steal all its energy from the life force we are born with. This is achieved through making us feel inferior and faulty if we fail to strive to become something. Through this striving we suppress our true self, while investing our life energy into the buildup of the ego.

Guilt: The Sage has made it clear that the word guilt, together with all ideas related to it do not have a Cosmic basis. This includes the concept of original guilt or sin, as well as the idea that we can become guilty for whatever we do or fail to do. The idea of guilt, associated with the image of an inextinguishable stain, has only one purpose: to keep the individual under the control of the >*collective ego.*

When we are investigating an illness it is important to realize that the ego has a vested interest in making us fear that the cause may be due to something for which we are guilty. Since guilt has no Cosmic validity, the fact that this is a tactic of the ego is evident.

Throughout its text, the *I Ching* gives evidence that the >*Cosmos* does not hold things against us. Moreover, making mistakes is considered to be an essential part of our learning process. The exception is when we knowingly turn away from the Cosmic Way to follow the way of the ego. These decisions create Cosmic blame. However, we can free ourselves from this blame by regretting our mistake and extinguishing the mistaken ideas that caused us to make the mistake. If we continue to leave our path over and over, we create a fate. Even a fate only runs for a period of time; the end of the fate extinguishes the Cosmic blame. Like blame, we can end a fate at any given moment if we correct what has caused it and regret the harm it has caused to the Cosmos.

Because guilt is attached to all the mistaken beliefs we are taught by the collective ego, it is one of the main causes of illness. Another cause of illness is guilt for not fulfilling the duties we take on as part of the roles the collective ego gives us to play in life. Guilt furthermore is one of the factors that keeps us ill; the ego encourages guilt so that it can benefit from the negative energy that guilt produces. In illness, we encounter guilt in several guises: (1) as the false concept of guilt, (2) as the idea of "original guilt/sin", (3) as guilt for wanting to get well. (Also see Chapter 9 and Chapter 21.)

Helpers: The Helpers mentioned in this book are individualized aspects of the Cosmic Consciousness and of Nature. As such, they are mostly invisible. However, as the photo shown on page 54 indicates, the Helpers will sometimes show themselves when asked. Every Helper fulfills a specific function within the harmonious flow of the whole. The Helpers are not human beings, but they can give their help *through* humans, such as a doctor, nurse, therapist, etc. A lot of the help is given in the realm of the atom, through >*transformations*. Because the Helpers can help in ways that humans cannot, it is important to abstain from trying to imagine how they accomplish their tasks, how much or how little time they need to complete them, and in what form the result will manifest. (Also see Chapter 8.)

Poison Arrows, Spells, Projections: these names refer to different kinds of false thought forms, all of which are not in harmony with the >*Cosmos*. Because of this fact, they create a negative energy that harms the psyche and/or body of the human being, animal, plant, or other thing in Nature to which they are directed. False thought forms are the main causes of illness; they can also form a whole "program of an illness" in the psyche of a person who has become sick. We can project false thought forms onto ourselves (our body or psyche) or onto other people. Their harmful effects can be ended when we identify the words, phrases and/or images they contain, and thoroughly reject them by deprogramming them with Cosmic help. Once the >*Helpers* transform them, the healing process is initiated.

Psyche: What we refer to as "psyche" is the invisible aspect of our whole being. The psyche is the *complement* of our body as its invisible aspect. Together psyche and body form an inseparable harmonious whole. The psyche comprises the *aggregate consciousnesses that make up our invisible existence.* Central among these consciousnesses are our feeling consciousness, our thinking consciousness that forms language, our reflective consciousness that attracts mind-flashes, and our intuitive consciousness that forms images.

Under healthy circumstances our body functions on the basis of our feeling consciousness. Many of these functions occur without our thinking consciousness being aware of their functioning. This is why they are often referred to as "unconscious." In psychology, the word "unconscious" is often used to refer to our feeling consciousness without stating that it is a feeling consciousness. The word "unconscious" diminishes our feeling consciousness and inadvertently makes our thinking consciousness into the only consciousness we possess. Throughout this book we show the overall importance of our feeling consciousness. We also show how our thinking consciousness can cause illness by putting false thought forms (>*poison arrows, projections and spells*) on the feeling consciousness of our body. Healing ourselves the Cosmic Way means freeing our psyche from such sick-making thought forms. In this regard, the findings presented in this book confirm the theory that illness is *psychosomatic*, i.e., it comes from psychic influences on the body.

Senses: The senses include our five outer senses of perception (seeing, hearing, smell, taste, touch), our five corresponding inner senses of perception that produce insight, inner hearing, and inner smelling, taste, and touch. They also include a number of "metaphorical" senses that are revealed by everyday speech, as when we speak of a sense of appropriateness, a sense of danger, a sense of caution, to name a few. The function of our inner senses of perception is to tell us the *inner* truth of a matter. Thus our inner sense of smell can, for example, smell the intimidating quality of authority (since authority is not part of the Cosmic Order, but belongs to the demonic sphere of consciousness). (Also see the examples under >*Commonsense*.) Even though a suspicious odor or taste is not noticeable to the outer senses, they register in our consciousness unless our inner senses have been turned off by devaluing them at one time or another. Renewing our respect for them enables us to detect sick-making thoughts and ego emotions that can lead to illness. Listening to our inner senses requires practice in paying attention to our inner sense of hearing. Its function is to bring what has been smelled or tasted into our conscious mind. When the sense of inner hearing gives the message that something does not "sound" right, the figurative sense of touch comes into play; its function is to compare the perception with our sense of inner truth. The Sage informs us that every person is born with a memory of what Cosmic harmony *feels* like. This memory is our inner truth. When the figurative sense of touch compares a perception that does not sound right with this memory, the result is perceived as dissonance, an inner feeling that something does not "feel" right.

The function of our *metaphorical senses* is to automatically trigger the correct reaction to disharmonious situations. In addition to the ones mentioned above, the metaphorical senses include our sense of loyalty to our inner truth, our sense of fairness or neutrality, our sense of integrity, or wholeness, our sense of inner quiet, our sense of innocence, our sense of blame for going against our true self, our sense of the dignity of all things, and our general sensitivity toward everything around us. Any form of egotism shuts down these senses. One of the general characteristics of the metaphorical senses is their *simplicity*. They guide us from within to conduct ourselves appropriately in every circumstance. They keep us *centered and complete within ourselves*. We enjoy their full abilities when we consciously validate their importance by paying them our full respect. The result is self-respect in its true meaning.

Although our metaphorical senses may be under various spells, they continue to work on behalf of the whole personality as best they can. Those parts not directly under the spells try to make up for the functions of those that are.

Many of the metaphorical senses are located in the muscle tissues throughout the body. They bring about involuntary reactions such as blushing, retreating, fleeing, and also advancing along the line of no resistance; the latter is another term for saying they work through >*transformation*. However, this can only happen when they are not under a spell. One of the functions of our metaphorical senses is to protect us from harm coming from outside that threatens our wholeness.

Transformation: Transformation is the word for the way the >*Cosmos* brings everything about. It is another name for the Cosmic Way. Transformations are brought about through the attraction between the complementary aspects of the Cosmos. The most basic attraction occurs between the forces of the dark in Nature and the light of the Cosmic Consciousness. All processes of growth and death in Nature require transformations—growth being the result of transformations from non-form into form, and death being the transformation from form into non-form. The forces of the light and the dark need to be seen as inseparable because they are two primary aspects of the Cosmos.

The Chinese ideogram for "I" in *I Ching* means transformation, not "changes" as it has been falsely translated. Transformation is indicated by the fact that the Chinese ideogram is based on the image of a chameleon. This misunderstanding has had enormous consequences because people have assumed that the Cosmos and Nature work through changes. This incorrect assumption is part of the human-centered view of the universe, in which the forces of the light and the dark are seen as not only complementing each other as equals, but also as competing with each other for dominance.

When we see the light and the dark as opposite and competing forces, we prevent the possibility of transformations both within our body cells and in our relationship with Nature. Transformations are necessary to constantly renew our life force, and to enable a healing that endures.

The "world of changes," which is often taken to be the only reality that exists, is thus a creation of the rational mind. When we accept this view we separate from the Cosmic Whole. *I Ching, The Oracle of the Cosmic Way* shows how transformation, not change, is the true way of the Cosmos.

The belief that all life is subject to changes becomes a trap when we continue to only look at the appearance of things and listen to "what people say."

Humans cannot achieve transformation by any conscious effort. It is the function of a particular >*Helper* that operates on the plane of feelings, which is the realm of the atom. It is in this realm that true healing occurs.

Deprogramming a mistaken idea or belief with Cosmic help brings about transformations by erasing the disharmonious words or images from our psyche, along with their effects. Saying an inner No to these ideas and beliefs engages the Helper of Transformation and enables the Cosmos to correct matters. Saying a conscious Yes to what feels harmonious engages the Helper of Transformation and enables the Cosmos to manifest it in form.

Index

A

abstraction, levels of, 85

acceptance, attitude of, 1

aches and pains caused by spells on the weather, 95

Achilles Heel Complex, 229

addiction, 150-154; nature of, 150; relation to guilt,150; as hole in self-esteem, 150; related to feeling inferior, 152; freeing oneself from, 153; related to a "ball of conflict," 154

aging, 105-108

ailment, investigating an, 173-180

allergy, caused by microchip and memory chip, 99-100; food allergy, 117-120; Nature allergy, 239; hay fever, 104-105

ancestor, illness coming from, 91

animal nature, slanders on, 12; definition, 257

Aristotle, dualistic thinking of, 82; originator of names of illnesses 82

arterial plaque, a microchip, 98

arthritis, 95, defined as "attack on the joints", 82; a case of, 102-104

auto-immune system, diseases, 31

B

back, stiff, 95; crick in, 115, 242; injury, 208

bacteria and fungi as part of Nature, 145

bacteria, fear of, 146; demonized bacteria become part of Nature's immune system, 148

ball of conflict, 154

basal cell, a microchip, 99, 154

behavioral disorder, a memory chip, 98

bipolar disorder, 138

blamer, an aspect of the changeling, 202; deprogramming, 205

blaming, as a poison arrow, 29-30

blinders, 17

bodily functions, damaged ones being replaced by Helpers,

unity of psyche and body, 7
uterus, 122-125; heavy bleeding, 143

V

Victim Complex, 228
virus, 147, 215
vitamins, as Helpers of Nature, 57

W

weather related aches and pains, 98
Wild-Nature Complex, 231
Wilhelm, Richard, 1, 4; 89, reported how I Ching oracle developed from yes-no questions, 161
Wilhelm, Salome, 4
words and images, as devices of power, 27

Other books from Anthony Publishing Company

I Ching, The Oracle of the Cosmic Way
By Carol K. Anthony and Hanna Moog
1st ed. 2002. ISBN 1-890764-00-0. Cloth, 768 pp.

This new version of the *I Ching* is the result of the authors' having asked the question, why, since an oracle can speak, have humans not allowed it to define itself? To make this possible they used the ancient yes/no method from which the *I Ching* originated.

In their daily consultations on everyday issues, the Sage that speaks through the *I Ching* stripped away many of the overlays that were added to the *I Ching* text over the centuries. These overlays had obscured the Cosmic Principles of Harmony embedded in each hexagram. They also obscured the multitude of helping energies available to us from the Cosmos when we are in harmony with our true nature. Repeatedly, the Sage pointed to the human pretense of being special over all the other things that exist, as the number one source of human conflict with the Cosmos. That main idea shut us humans off from the constant stream of Cosmic energies that exist to support, nourish, and heal us. The Sage explained how our beliefs and attitudes alone determine whether our lives progress toward success or misfortune.

The new *I Ching*, therefore, is non-hierarchical, and non-feudal. It shows the conflicts we create when we use power, and forget our true place in the Cosmos. It helps us understand why, when we exceed our natural limits, we run into the wall of Fate that ensures the duration of Cosmic Harmony. This book shows us how we can return to harmony with the Cosmos by deprogramming the mistaken beliefs that have separated us from its help and blessings. It also details the many mistaken beliefs that are the cause of misfortune.

This book provides an invaluable background to the authors' companion book, *Healing Yourself the Cosmic Way*, and in particular, to healing long-standing and chronic illnesses.

A Guide to the I Ching

By Carol K. Anthony
3rd revised ed. 1988, ISBN 1-9603832-4-7

This book, which first appeared in 1980, was based on Ms. Anthony's experiences in using the Wilhelm translation over a period of years. It builds on Carl Jung's view of the *I Ching* as a mirror of the unconscious, showing the oracle to be a prognosticator of the consequences of being, or not being, in harmony with one's true nature. It remains highly popular today and has been translated into a number of languages.

The Philosophy of the I Ching

By Carol K. Anthony
3rd revised ed. 2004. ISBN 1-890764-02-7, paperback, 220 pp.

The great difference between the philosophy explained here of the *I Ching,* and that of all the other philosophies of the world, is that the *I Ching* presents, in every hexagram, the individual's relationship to the invisible Consciousness of the Cosmos. This relationship is dynamic and alive, not theoretical, because it concerns every thought we think. The *I Ching* makes us aware that every thought has the potential to create joy or to create suffering. The oracle shows us that by freeing ourselves from the harmful thoughts, we return to unity with the Cosmos.

Love, An Inner Connection,

Based on Principles Drawn from the I Ching
By Carol K. Anthony
2nd revised ed. 2003. ISBN 1-890764-01-9, paperback, 176 pp.

This book is about love as a Cosmic gift given to two people to awaken, strengthen and nourish their true selves. It is also about the Cosmic principles laid out in the *I Ching* that govern the love relationship. It shows, in a clear language, that by bringing ourselves into harmony with these principles, we can make our deepest and most meaningful relationships endure.

The Other Way
Meditation Experiences Based on the I Ching
By Carol K. Anthony
1st ed. 1990. ISBN 0-9603832-5-5, paperback, 264 pp.

Here, Carol Anthony describes the meditation method taught by the *I Ching* that leads to the inner realm where the poet finds his muse, the performer his ability to perform "beyond himself," and where the seeker after truth meets the Cosmic Teacher who speaks through the *I Ching*.

The I Ching Institute

The I Ching Institute was founded in 2000 by Carol K. Anthony and Hanna Moog to share what they had learned from the oracle about the psyche, about healing, and about the nature of the Cosmos and its Way, while working on *I Ching, The Oracle of the Cosmic Way*. Their research into new fields of application is ongoing.

The Institute offers a regular course of seminars and online courses based on *I Ching, The Oracle of the Cosmic Way*. and *Healing Yourself the Cosmic Way*.

www.ichinginstitute.org
www.ichingoracle.com

About the Authors

Carol K. Anthony, b. 1930, studied creative writing at Ward-Belmont College and at the State Univ. of Iowa. Throughout the 1960's she wrote newspaper articles and editorials, but after encountering the *I Ching* in 1971, her interest turned totally to understanding this ancient Chinese oracle. In the meantime she formed *I Ching* study groups, and gave lectures on it to interested local groups. After several years of collecting notes on her experiences with the hexagrams, she published them in 1980 under the title, *A Guide to the I Ching*. This was followed by three other books, *The Philosophy of the I Ching, The Other Way*, and *Love, An Inner Connection*. After her books were published in other languages, she gave seminars abroad, particularly in the U.S., England, and Germany. Since 1998 she collaborated with Hanna Moog in writing *I Ching, The Oracle of the Cosmic Way*, and this present book. Together, they founded The I Ching Institute in 2000.

Hanna Moog, b. 1946, studied languages and national economics in her native country, Germany. A major crisis in 1981 brought her to the *I Ching*, which from then on became her constant companion. Over the years, it helped her find an entirely new direction in her life. She became a free lance editor and translator of books on the *I Ching*, and authored two books on the subject in the German language. Since 1990 she has greatly enjoyed passing on what she has learned from the *I Ching* in lectures and classes. She moved to the U.S. in 1998 to join forces with Carol Anthony to research new applications of the *I Ching* in the fields of self-knowledge and healing, to write books together, give seminars and online courses, and also to provide individual *I Ching* counseling. Both women are presently preparing their third joint book, which will focus on understanding the psyche from the perspective of the Cosmos, as clarified through the *I Ching*.